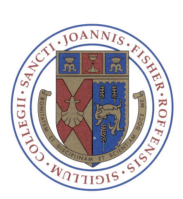

HIGH RISE LOW DOWN

*Who's Who and What's What
in New York's Most
Coveted Apartment Houses*

DENISE LEFRAK CALICCHIO
AND EUNICE DAVID
WITH KATHRYN LIVINGSTON

Photographs by Trevor Augustus Brown

BARRICADE BOOKS
FORT LEE, NEW JERSEY

Published by Barricade Books Inc.
185 Bridge Plaza North
Suite 308-A
Fort Lee, NJ 07024

www.barricadebooks.com

Library of Congress Cataloging-in-Publication Data

Calicchio, Denise LeFrak.
   High rise low down: who's who and what's what in New York's most coveted apartment houses / by Denise LeFrak Calicchio, Eunice David; with Kathryn Livingston.
      p. cm.
   Includes bibliographical references.
   ISBN 1-56980-316-1 (alk. paper)
      1. Apartment houses—New York (State)—New York—History.
2. Apartment houses, Cooperative—New York (State)—New York—History.
I. David Eunice. II. Livingston, Kathryn. III. Title.

HD7287.6.U52N724 2007
974.7'10440922—dc22

ISBN 13: 978-1-56980-316-5
ISBN 1-56980-316-1

First Printing

Manufactured in the United States of America

Contents

FOREWORD

I WAS THE zoning director for a land development company when the "new city" of Valencia, California, was developed. I was in on the ground floor when the entire city was planned and built on 44,000 acres of what had once been farmland. I was privileged to watch the architects at work designing a totally integrated and innovative new city with a wide variety of buildings, which all worked beautifully together yet were individual in style and design. The experience instilled in me an everlasting love of buildings and their architecture, and an understanding and appreciation of how an inanimate object such as a building can fit into and enhance our lives.

When I retired from land development, I studied interior design and opened my own design firm, which brought together my love for both the architecture of a building and the space within a building, which I firmly believe defines those who live and work in those environments—another element that fed my fascination with the subject of this book. There is no doubt that the buildings in which we live and work affect our life and daily well-being. Think of all the time we spend in those buildings—how many times a day we go in or out of those buildings.

I am from Los Angeles; it's in my bones. But I've traveled to New York all of my life, and finally, about eighteen years ago, I started to live in New York part time with my husband, the Academy Award–winning songwriter Hal David.

For years I've had a love affair with New York buildings. I would walk around craning my neck to gape at the wondrous spires, globes, triangles, and other unique shapes that can be found on buildings nowhere else on this earth. The fact that I constantly bumped into strangers never deterred me. Now that I am living on the forty-first-floor of a midtown Manhattan apartment building, I no longer have to strain to see some of the wondrous rooftops: I am surrounded by them. From my views looking east and south, I can see the endlessly intriguing Chrysler Building and many other world-renowned architectural wonders.

When the idea for this book first started to perk, we thought it would be interesting to write about the totally incredible tops of some of those special buildings at which I used to gawk. We thought we would research the architects of those buildings and tell you about the bricks and stones that went into constructing them. But we started to wonder: Why did certain buildings seem so special—what was their unique cachet? What caused someone to want to live in one building, as opposed to another? And what did it take to get into some of those "A-plus" buildings? Was it the building itself that was the draw, or the people who already lived in the building? That was the genesis of the book, which prompted the title "High Rise Low Down." We were not only fascinated with the buildings themselves but also with the people who lived in the buildings—buildings that we thought were some of the most beautiful in the city and, could they only speak, would tell some of the most incredible stories to match their beautiful facades.

We felt that if we were so interested in the buildings and their illustrious tenants, others might be also. So we began our quest to find which buildings to photograph, which to write about, and which might have people living in them who would be as fascinating and incredibly interesting as the buildings themselves.

Here is the result.

—Eunice David

INTRODUCTION

$\mathcal{M}$ARK TWAIN SAID, "Buy land. They're not making it anymore." When I was a girl, I played with dolls and toys as little girls do, but even then I realized my father had other plans for me. He would show me floor plans, and on Sundays, his day off, we went to see his job sites. Real estate was not only in my blood, but in my future.

My father wanted his family involved in his every project, dream, and vision. After I married and had children, I decided a career in real estate would be my next move. I began studying, earned my license, and started working. Since I had been schooled in real estate my whole life, it came naturally to me.

I worked in residential real estate for fifteen years—mostly buying and selling on the Upper East Side. When I had a property to sell, I was hell-bent on getting the best price for my seller. When I had clients who were buying properties, it was all important to me to put them in the "right" buildings, knowing how important it was to place people where they would feel at home. And I negotiated nonstop to get my clients the best possible price. Every deal was equally important to me.

I spent the majority of my working career at Sotheby's, considered by many to have the best properties and the most dedicated brokers. I listened to what was going on at the office, to other brokers sharing their thoughts. I learned the buildings and their various interesting stories, as well as who lived in them. Looking at these buildings, I became fascinated not only by the architecture, but also the history and the lives of the people who inhabit these grand buildings. If I was this intrigued, I suspected that other people might feel the same. Thus the idea of this book was conceived. These are our selections of some of the most interesting and coveted buildings in New York. Our picks may surprise some readers, and some may disagree. But we are satisfied with those that are included in the book.

Like my father, real estate has become an important and inextricable part of my life. I dedicate this book to him, an extraordinary man and visionary who helped change the skyline of New York. As he did in his lifetime, he has continued to guide me through the writing of this book. I would also like to thank all the wonderful people who have helped to make this a reality. Some of them are not acknowledged, because that was their wish. I so hope that you find these stories as interesting as I have!

—Denise LeFrak Calicchio

HIGH RISE
LOW DOWN

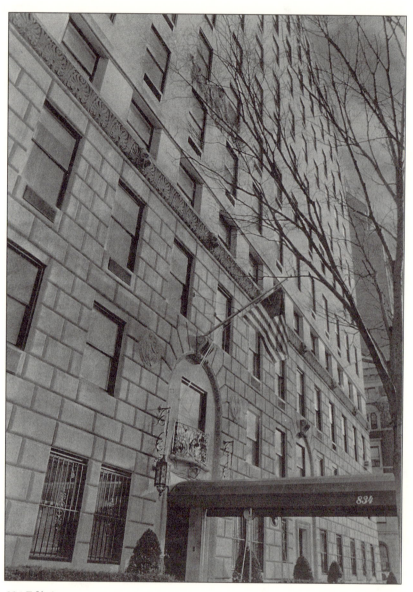

834 Fifth Avenue

· 1 ·

834 Fifth Avenue

BIG DEAL

*I*T WAS DUBBED a "battle of billionaires," and New York's excited newspaper columnists, who love ego-pitting conflicts between men of globe-girding ambition, were salivating over who would emerge the winner.

Would it be fashion emperor Ralph Lauren? Clearly he was in the running, having returned three times after an initial visit. Would it be Australian-born media mogul Rupert Murdoch? In the middle of the 1970s, during the terrifying summer of a serial killer named Son of Sam and a crippling citywide blackout, Murdoch had recognized New York as the bargain of the century, bought the *New York Post, New York* magazine, and the *Village Voice*, then embarked on a fearless expansion, adding Fox TV, 20th Century Fox films, HarperCollins Publishers, and the satellite British Sky Broadcasting, all of which made his News Corporation second only to Time Warner as a U.S. media giant.

Another contender was guessed to be financier-philanthropist George Soros, guardian angel of emerging democracies, "open society" universities, and patients seeking medicinal marijuana, who made his $7 billion-plus fortune in currency speculation and high-risk funds. He was already a Fifth

Avenue resident but had been recently divorced from his second wife and was seen on occasion in the company of a comely Korean concert violinist. Then again, it could be one of the city's billion-dollar litigators, someone like David Boies, who may have been on the losing side of the Gore-Bush contested election but had won the $512-million price-fixing suit against Christie's and Sotheby's, among several other triumphs. But most likely, the bet was that the contest would fall among the latest big-money boys in town: one of the new hedge-fund heavyweights from Connecticut. Someone like Steve Cohen of SAC Capital, who had just emerged as the most aggressive collector of Impressionist and contemporary art.

The 2006 *Forbes* list names fifty billionaires in New York State, more than in any other state in the Union. There is no question, on a per-square-foot basis, New York City contains a higher concentration of wealth and puissance than any other place on earth. And most of these successful people want to live on Fifth Avenue. To be precise, at one of the especially prestigious addresses along a mile-and-a-half stretch of the avenue facing Central Park, between 59th and 96th Streets. Of these hyper-exclusive, ultra-glamorous "blue-chip buildings" or "A-plus apartment houses," three palatial, doormen-guarded urban fortresses are hallowed. They are 820, 834, and 960 Fifth Avenue.

The billionaires' prize that all avid acquisitors were supposedly chasing in the fall of 2004 was one of the rarest, most beautiful, and exclusive "trophy" apartments to come up for sale in New York City in years. It was the terraced three-story penthouse on top of 834 Fifth Avenue, on the southeast corner of 64th Street, where Laurance S. Rockefeller, the passionate conservationist and trailblazing venture capitalist, had lived for fifty years.

For the majority of Americans, purchasing a place to live is the most significant investment of a lifetime; between the mid-1990s and the first decade of the twenty-first century, New York City real estate had become much more than just a matter of shelter. Suddenly, a couple of dozen sterling, old co-op buildings, and a few shining new condominium complexes had become superstars. They were sizzling hot. They were coveted like never before, not only by New Yorkers, but also by millionaires, movie stars, corporate heads, and second-home shoppers from all over the world.

Timeless in elegance, luxurious in comfort, splendid in style, and oozing with status, the hallmark of these preeminent urban dwellings was that their availability was very limited. Though they were outrageously expensive and their headline-making prices kept soaring, the frenzied intrigues that went on to gain entry into them were a constant source of gossip—sometimes hilarious, sometimes heartbreaking, sometimes downright ugly.

The anecdotes were revealing glimpses into the life-styles of people at the top of today's international money pyramid. Watching these brash, confident, powerful men and women—who've been to the mountaintop, know every angle, and usually get their way—literally hit a stone wall as they tried to buy one of these exquisite high rise homes was quite a spectacle. What went on inside these grand high-rise homes was titillating social history in the making.

The heated-up Manhattan real estate climate and the wildly blatant social climbing that whirled around it were peopled with all sorts of buzz-worthy characters, a veritable roster of the kind of names that appeared in the pages of *Fortune* and *Forbes, People* and *Us Weekly* magazines.

Building by building, behind the brick and mortar, these most wanted apartments held human stories that elicited empathy and glee. Each of the scrupulously protected, doorman-posted enclaves had their special brand of elan, their scandalous, sometimes even murderous, histories, and their quirky mix of illustrious and intriguing personalities. As apartments changed hands, there were occasionally dramatic clashes. These involved elements of class, race, religion, politics, architecture, social ambition, fall from grace, love and divorce, bullies and underdogs, infighting among prominent American families, the spending patterns and style preferences of Arab princes, Italian industrialists, Hong Kong bankers, Turkish heiresses, Latin American media kings, and beautiful Russian playgirls.

Each of these Manhattan signature buildings also overflowed with ruthless professional rivalries, secret personal agendas, colorful games of one-upmanship, and wrenching dramas of individuals facing financial ups and downs. It was all a reflection of the turbo-charged real estate market and twenty-first-century life on a vibrant, limited landmass that everyone, it seems, wanted a piece of—Manhattan Island.

Money alone couldn't guarantee you entrée into these multimillion-dollar dream dwellings because, like private clubs, their gates were guarded by formidable watchdogs—the often tyrannical co-op boards. For many of these select apartment houses are exclusionary and legally so. They want the people who live with them under one roof to be kindred souls.

As if constituting a secret code, these pluperfect, mostly prewar buildings simply go by their prestigious numbers: 960, 834, 820, 720, 740, 770, 778—their instantly recognizable addresses on Fifth Avenue and Park Avenue. Others have names: River House, Beresford, Time Warner Center. Some say in only a few words that they are the absolute tops of their high-end neighborhoods: One Beekman Place, One Sutton Place South. And still others go by a somewhat reticent, reverse-snob insistence on their side street addresses. For example, 4 East 66th Street is actually located on Fifth Avenue and faces Central Park, and 450 East 52nd Street rises from the water's edge, like Sutton and Beekman Place buildings, and glories in great East River views.

The stakes kept getting higher for securing a suite in one of these pedigreed and architecturally superior buildings. Since more and more people had the financial means and wanted to get in, Manhattan co-op boards were feeling more powerful than ever about rejecting even the most famous and successful, often people with as much as $60 or $70 million to their names.

By the turn of the millennium, price tags on a precious few available old co-op apartments had become stratospheric and were still climbing, because there were enough people willing to pay for them. With a bevy of high-profile personalities buying and selling splashy apartments in Manhattan, the city's media had taken to spicing up its property coverage. But when some of the celebrities picking new homes were media moguls as well, the coverage got a bit tricky.

When it came to Laurance Rockefeller's penthouse triplex atop 834 Fifth Avenue, considered one of the finest apartments in the entire city at one of the most desirable locations, Gabriel Sherman in the *New York Observer* reported that "brokers are waiting with bated breath for what they think will be Manhattan's next record-breaking sale." Sources familiar with the property called it "the best of the best" and "something that comes on the market once in a blue moon."

They cited another distinctive Rockefeller property, the John D. Rockefeller Jr. penthouse at 740 Park Avenue, for which Wall Streeter Stephen Schwarzman had paid $37 million in 2000, a sum that had set the previous co-op price record in Manhattan. News items in the *Times,* the *Post,* and the *Wall Street Journal* predicted Laurance's penthouse would fetch something around $40 million. But they speculated: Who would pay that kind of money? Would the person willing to come up with that kind of cash be able to pass the scrutiny of one of the most onerous co-op boards in the city?

Of course, both the seller's fame and the potential buyers' names made good copy.

Laurance S. Rockefeller was the middle and most mysterious of the five prominent and philanthropic grandsons of John D. Rockefeller. He was more reserved and private than his political brothers, second son Nelson, the four-term governor of New York and vice president under Gerald R. Ford, and fourth son Winthrop, who was governor of Arkansas. A philosophy major at Princeton, Laurance was considered more introspective than his oldest brother, John D. Rockefeller III, who founded the Population Council and played a major role in the creation of the Lincoln Center for the Performing Arts, and his youngest brother, David, who headed the Chase Bank and was vastly influential in international finance. Laurance, whose name was spelled the way it was because it derived from his mother's "Laura," long pondered how he might most efficiently and rewardingly use the great wealth into which he had been born. Although he hardly figured in the more than two hundred books written about the Rockefeller family, it was he who probably devoted himself to projects that had longest-range effects—the preservation of America's natural heritage and historic landscapes. His particular energies, considerable amounts of money, connections, and negotiating skills were turned to ecological concerns, wilderness conservation, and the growth of what has since become known as ecotourism. He was an unabashed believer in the restorative powers of nature in an age of anxiety. As a young man of sixteen, he had spent time in the national parks of the West and was profoundly influenced by two men: the park superintendent of Yellowstone, Howard M. Albright, a cofounder of the National Park Service; and Fairfield Osborn, also Princeton educated, who retired from Wall Street to head the New York Zoological Society in 1940 and was one of the first to sound the alarm of environmental threat in a 1948 book called *Our Plundered Planet*. While Laurance Rockefeller, following in the footsteps of his father, John D. Jr., was instrumental in establishing and enlarging national parks in Wyoming, California, Vermont, Maine, Hawaii, and the U.S. Virgin Islands— plus giving generously to preserve land as a public parkland and urban open space—his preservation activities extended also into commercial enterprises such as his Rock Resorts, where he built exceptional hotels in dramatic natural settings, with an emphasis on close access to nature.

Yet he was anything but sanctimonious. He loved fine food and frequented New York's top restaurants. Besides his favorite home, the Fifth

Avenue penthouse, he owned several large houses, paintings by Cezanne, Bonnard, and Gainsborough, a Bentley (among other cars), a private plane, and a sixty-five-foot speedboat. And from the time he first took his seat on the New York Stock Exchange, until his last days at age ninety-four, when he still went to work, putting in half days at his Rockefeller Center office, he had compounded his inherited wealth many times over. He was proud of his native instinct to identify "the next big thing." He invested in 221 start-ups, initially providing most of the capital to help the World War I fighter pilot Eddie Rickenbacker start Eastern Airlines. He later branched out into computer companies, Intel and Apple, and still later into biotechnology, particularly research related to the treatment of cancer, a cause to which he also gave generously.

It is ironic—maybe a mischievous exercise in moxie—that the one time that Laurance Rockefeller put pen to paper publicly, it was a 1976 article for *Reader's Digest*, "The Case for a Simpler Life," in which he advocated "chopping and splitting firewood" for relaxation and spiritual uplift, instead of the relentless pursuit of materialism.

The Fifth Avenue penthouse was, of course, something else. So was the building and its inhabitants. And so would be the two famous billionaire competitors who fought for it to the finish line.

The twenty-room, three-floor unit atop 834 Fifth Avenue, which had hidden cameras everywhere, would become the most expensive co-op apartment ever in the history of New York. Occupying the fourteenth through sixteenth floors, with three glorious terraces facing out over the Central Park Zoo entrance, it had seven bedrooms, twelve bathrooms, a huge library with at least ten shelves of books on the Rockefeller family alone, a solarium where Mrs. Rockefeller, the former Mary French, liked to paint, an enormous dining room with a painting by Maurice Prendergast of the same Children's Zoo the room overlooked, a spacious living room with a wood-burning fireplace and a conservatory, a massive reception gallery that displayed Rockefeller's favorite Toulouse-Lautrecs, plus extensive quarters for the Laurance Rockefellers' full-time staff of eight, including a butler, a chauffeur, a Norwegian woman who was the major domo, several maids and secretaries, and a twenty-four hour bodyguard.

"It is in my opinion, one of the five best apartments in New York," commented Edward Lee Cave, real estate broker to New York's elite, in the *New York Times*. "It's everybody's wish list complete, because the first thing people say is 'I want a terrace,' then they say they want high ceilings. It's a triplex with great entertaining space and great bedroom space." Kirk Henckels, the director of Stribling Private Brokerage, a high-end real estate agency, said apartments of this size on Fifth Avenue rarely came on the market. It encompassed around 8,000 square feet and 4,000 square feet of terraces spread over three floors. Its monthly maintenance at the time of the sale in 2004 was $21,469.07. "It's extremely significant," Henckels added. "Nothing like this has been on the market in years."

The whole building was bought by Laurance Rockefeller in 1946, and when he turned it into a co-op, he picked the best apartment for himself.

Originally, several members of the Rockefeller family lived in the discreetly elegant limestone building, which has a high preponderance of duplexes. There are three to a floor. Bing Crosby moved into one of them shortly after the building was completed in 1931, and in 1997 Bing Crosby's son Harry bought one of the two lovely duplex maisonnettes. One of the most spectacular residences has enormous arched windows, strikingly visible at night from Fifth Avenue, causing people to wonder who might live in such a luxurious tower. Actually the glass-enclosed light shaft of a dramatic stairway, spanning three floors of the suite, it is part of the apartment owned by Johnson & Johnson heir and New York Jets football team owner Robert Wood Johnson IV, who was very much in the spotlight in 2005 for wanting to build—along with his friend Mayor Bloomberg—a new sports stadium on the West Side of Manhattan overlooking the Hudson. Amazingly, Woody Johnson, who is head of the co-op board at 834 Fifth, has not lived there in years. Since his divorce from socialite Sale Johnson, he has kept another lavish apartment across the park at the Trump International Hotel, One Central Park West.

The apartment complex at 834 Fifth Avenue was designed by Rosario Candela, the great masterbuilder of supreme addresses in pre-Depression Manhattan. The exquisite sequence of rooms articulated the highest standards of New York living for a succession of people with grand American fortunes. Among them were Cornelius Vanderbilt Whitney and his exuberant wife Marylou, who in 2004 won the Belmont Stakes with her horse Birdstone, upsetting Smarty Jones's hopes of winning the coveted Triple Crown. Other owners were dime store multimillionaires Jessie Woolworth Donahue; Hearst Corporation head Richard Berlin and his wife Honey; Canadian tycoon and Derby-winning, horse-breeding giant Frank McMahon; New

York financier Thomas Millbank; the first Mrs. Henry Ford, Anne, with her second husband, lawyer Deane Johnson; one of the richest African Americans and the first black man to pass muster with an A-plus Fifth Avenue co-op board—the late Reginald F. Lewis, who was an international financier and the head of Beatrice Foods; George and Lita Livanos of the legendary Greek shipping clan whose sisters were the wives of Stavros Niarchos and Aristotle Onassis; another Greek shipping heiress, the former Eugenie Carras (now married to John Radziwill, the son of Prince Stanislas Radziwill, who was the husband of Jackie Kennedy's sister Lee); the Broadway producer Hal Prince; Charles Schwab, founder of the eponymous brokerage firm; and much married philanthropist socialite Carroll Petrie.

A. Laurance Kaiser IV, one of the premiere brokers for high-end Manhattan real estate, has sold more apartments in the building than anyone else. He was the broker on the first New York apartment to sell for more than a million dollars and that headline-making deal happened to be apartment 8-B at 834 Fifth Avenue. It had belonged to Jean Flagler Matthews, an heiress to *Reader's Digest,* whose husband was a grandson of the railroad magnate who developed Florida and established Palm Beach as a princely resort community. The buyer of 8-B was the famous Bolivian tin king, Antenor Patiño. Kaiser, who is a walking encyclopedia when it comes to Fifth Avenue's signature buildings, recalls that 834 was from the beginning a home of legendary characters. Among them were cosmetics queen Elizabeth Arden; Eduardo Sarmiento of the vast Colombian coffee fortune; dashing New York society figure Horace Schmidlap; and the ninety-five-year-old sister of Nubar Gulbenkian, the eccentric British industrialist, Middle East oil heir, diplomat, art dealer, philanthropist, and attaché to the Iranian embassy, who for decades was considered the wealthiest man in the world.

Over the years, few couples knew how to enjoy their luxurious quarters at 834 Fifth Avenue more than Marylou and Sonny Whitney, though it was but one of a half-dozen exceedingly marvelous places they called home, depending on their whims or social schedules. There was their white-columned Kentucky mansion set on 500 acres of Blue Grass country, where they grew everything from asparagus to champion horses and entertained in their Roman atrium of palm trees and pillars, which surrounded an Olympic-sized pool filled with flowers and (sometimes) guests. There was their wilderness preserve manor in the Adirondacks, with a nine-mile driveway, and in Majorca a wonderfully rustic former olive mill transformed into an escapist villa. They owned a palatial habitat in Palm Beach, Florida, and a resplendent 120-acre, twenty-one-room estate in Saratoga Springs, New York. During the Saratoga social season, they reigned as king and queen, with Marylou usually showcasing a different set of jewels every night. She wore the emeralds to her annual dinner dance at the Canfield Casino, which launched the resort's August racing month. She wore her rubies for the Museum of Dance benefit, and the diamonds and pearls to the Racing Museum Ball. Perhaps their most famous of the Saratoga soirées was her *Gone with the Wind* party in 1986, for which she wore her huge emerald pendant and earrings, to match the frilly, green, off-shoulder gown Scarlett O'Hara wears when she first meets Rhett Butler in the film.

That night, sitting at the same table was another flamboyant character of the horsey set, the late Liz Whitney Tippett. By that time she was going to parties in a wheelchair, but always with a bottle of chilled champagne tucked under her voluminous ball gown. She liked to name her horses after musicians—a favorite was Cab Calloway. The two women were making plans to go to the Whitneys' private log cabin chapel for services the following morning. Meanwhile, others at the table told the story of how the women both independently went to Hollywood to be considered for the Scarlett O'Hara role that went to Vivian Leigh. Each lost the part but ended up marrying two handsome, glamorous, East Coast millionaire cousins, who, along with David O. Selznick, were the original investors in the film. Beautiful and spontaneous Liz reportedly failed the screen test because her voice was too abrasive, but she landed Jock Whitney, on whose aristocratic charms Cary Grant supposedly modeled his screen image and who, among his many accomplishments, started the *International Herald Tribune*. Marylou, a green-eyed, ash blond dynamo from Kansas City, who was already the mother of four, had entered a worldwide contest for the role and met Sonny during the preliminaries. It was love at first sight for both.

Cornelius Vanderbilt Whitney—"Sonny" to those who knew him—was the grandson of robber baron Commodore Vanderbilt, whose frock-coated statue on the south side of Grand Central Station looks down on Park Avenue South, and William C. Whitney, who built New York's early streetcar system. He grew up in a Fifth Avenue mansion with fifteen live-in servants. His mother was Gertrude Vanderbilt Whitney, founder of the Whitney Museum. His father was Harry Payne Whitney, owner of America's richest racing stable. Sonny went to Groton and Yale, and upon his father's death, when he was only thirty-one, he inherited $30 million. Sonny, tall, dark and handsome, with a cultured voice that contained both power and poetry, and his equally dashing cousin Jock Whitney combined a life of privilege with lucrative cutting-edge pursuits. Sonny's entrepreneurial acumen led to a clever deal in Mexico and to getting him in on the ground floor of the infant airline industry, cofounding what was later to become Pan American Airways. Besides *Gone with the Wind,* he invested millions in such classic films as *Rebecca, A Star Is Born,* and *The Searchers.* He started the Hudson Bay Mining and Smelting Company and the first ocean aquarium in the world—Florida's Marineland. He bred an astonishing 141 stakes winners and led his polo team to two U.S. championships. His life was punctuated by associations with people of fame. He flew with Charles Lindbergh and Eddie Rickenbacker, served with General Douglas McArthur, and socialized with John Wayne, Fred Astaire, and Clark Gable. Yet he was unlucky in love for much of his life until he married his fourth wife, Marylou Schroeder Hosford. He took over as father of her four children and they had a daughter of their own.

Irrepressibly vivacious, Marylou Whitney has been called "one grande babe" and "the last of the great social hostesses." Much of her energy and sense of self were wrapped up in creating extravagant and wondrous occasions: legendary Derby dazzlers in Kentucky, a giant silver snowflake and icicle ball during the Lake Placid Olympics, and another gauzy, stylized Olympic bash for 400 in Sarajevo in 1984, attended by kings, presidents, movie icons, and star athletes. At their vast and incomparable Fifth Avenue duplex, filled with signed French furniture, plumply upholstered chintz sofas, and pillow-strewn chairs, and sporting a partially glassed-in terrace with a scintillating view, they gave one of the most exquisite private parties of the 1980s for Queen Sirikit of Thailand. One London social columnist called the Whitneys' guest list "the magi of New York's whipped *crème de la crème*" and *New York Post* columnist James Brady described the invitation as "the toughest ticket in town." Among the elegant, elite, and superachieving were the Laurance Rockefellers; the Walter Cronkites; CBS chairman Bill Paley; Doris Duke; Charlotte Ford; Kentucky governor John Y. Brown and his pretty Miss America bride Phyllis George; Florence van der Kemp, whose husband was the curator of Versailles; and of course Sonny's Vanderbilt and Whitney cousins, Whitney Tower, Flora Biddle, Pamela Tower le Boutillier, and Mrs. Harold Payne Whitmore, the Listerine heiress from Palm Beach.

But the building also had its whiff of scandals. Gregg Dodge, a platinum-blonde beauty and the sexy young widow of Horace Dodge, had tongues wagging when she fell madly in love and married a handsome New York policeman named Danny Moran. Although she inherited her husband's huge Dodge fortune, the young couple quickly went though the money. Destitute, living on diet pills and red wine, and unable to pay the maintenance fees, they would have to sneak in and out of the building through the side entrance. Then one night, Danny shot an intruder in their Palm Beach house, soon after which he himself died under mysterious circumstances, generally believed to be suicide. There was John H. Gutfreund, once known as the "King of Wall Street" and celebrated for his "trophy wife" Susan who was savaged back in the 1980s by *Vanity Fair* for her Marie Antoinette–style entertaining in the apartment's trellised garden room, which was adorned with exotic birdcages and a phenomenal French chateaux-worthy staircase. The Gutfreunds' duplex, all 12,000 square feet of it done by the legendary Parisian decorator Henri Samuels and boasting four gigantic reception rooms overlooking Fifth Avenue, is considered the finest apartment in the building. In 1991, Gutfreund was forced to resign as the Chairman of Salomon Brothers because of his part in some Treasury bond shenanigans. Then there was John DeLorean, the handsome, highly publicized inventor of the gull-wing-door DeLorean car, married to stunning supermodel-turned-movie actress Christina Ferrare; he was asked to leave the building because of his drug money laundering. Most recently, Sotheby's chairman Alfred Taubman served seven months in a federal penitentiary for his auction house's price-fixing deal with Christie's.

High-profile scandal is handled differently by different buildings. During and after one of the most fascinating big-business trials of the new century, the proceedings growing out of the price-fixing collusion that rocked the auction world and put one of the richest men in America behind bars, Taubman was generally treated with warmth and sympathy by his 834 Fifth neighbors.

Much of New York society was riveted by the conspiracy case involving millions of dollars, an inside look into a secretive and glamorous industry. What was revealing is how the two former gold-plated aristocratic British businesses—Sotheby's and Christie's—became slick, clandestine, highly profitable international corporations sometimes engaged in illegal activities. That is, until the perpetrators were caught by federal prosecutors. The cast of characters who played key roles in the case included the most powerful woman in the art world, chic, bright, superambitious Dede Brooks, who was chief executive of Sotheby's; wily British Christie's executive Christopher Davidge; a dramatic-looking Indian woman named Amrita Jhaveri, who was Davidge's third wife; Sir Anthony Tennant, the Eton-and-Cambridge-educated former chairman of Christie's; Lord Hindlip, Christie's famously charming auctioneer and chairman, a friend of Diana, Princess of Wales; Lord Westmorland, Sotheby's director and a master of the hounds (a close friend of Queen Elizabeth); Christopher Burge, Christie's respected star auctioneer in New York; and rival French conglomateurs Bernard Arnault, chairman of LVMH Moët-Hennesy-Louis Vuitton, who tried to buy Taubman's controlling interest in Sotheby's in 1999, and François Pinault, the French luxury-goods billionaire who acquired Christie's in 1998.

Not the least of the interest generated by the trial was focused on Al Taubman's smashing second wife, Judy, a former Miss Israel named Yehudit Mazor. She had been on the cover of *Town & Country* magazine and graced a twelve-page beauty portfolio by famous British photographer Norman Parkinson in 1984, shot around the swimming pool of her streamlined, all-white, Richard Meier contemporary house in Palm Beach. This was only one of several homes the couple maintained. They had a residence in Michigan, an apartment in the Swiss ski resort of Gstaad, a summer house in Southampton, and a flat in the fashionable Mayfair section of London.

The Taubman apartment at 834 Fifth Avenue, in the words of one of Judy Taubman's friends, was "a duplex of perfection, full of world-class paintings: subdued, elegant neutral colors, the best Modiglianis, Renoirs and Monets."

Much was made in the press about Judy Taubman not being present during the court hearings in downtown Manhattan, though New Yorkers made snide comments that it was multilingual Judy's inexhaustible desire to mingle with titled Europeans that had propelled the Michigan shopping-mall magnate to buy Sotheby's in the first place. No question, the social standing of well-dressed Judy Taubman and her tycoon husband from Pontiac—who had been a good friend of Henry Ford II, chairman of Ford Motor Company, and a protégé of prominent Detroit businessman and political fund-raiser Max Fisher—had risen dramatically after his purchase of Sotheby's. The couple was suddenly swept up into a dizzying round of parties with a steady stream of dukes, princesses, and sundry foreign potentates. "Every prominent citizen in Paris, London, New York, Southampton and

Palm Beach suddenly seemed eager to befriend the all-American 'Big Al,' whose plain talk and refusal to put on airs won him plenty of fans," according to Christopher Mason, a frequent contributor to the *New York Times* and *New York* magazine on art, society, and fashion who wrote a book about the auction house scandal in 2004, titled *The Art of the Steal.*

Most likely, these same qualities endeared "Big Al" to fellow residents at 834 Fifth Avenue, and in 2006 he was still on *Forbes's* list of New York's billionaires. A tall, corpulent man—imposing in his charcoal-gray double-breasted, pin-striped suits—Taubman was respected for the exceptional visual intelligence that had accounted for his huge success as a developer of luxury shopping centers throughout the Midwest, which he had also applied to marketing rarified art objects.

Some residents would steadily defend Judy's absence from the trial of the seventy-eight-year-old tycoon, whose lawyers tried to convince the federal judge not to send a man of such advanced age to jail. One said, "She stayed away on the advice of the lawyers. Because she looked too young, too pretty, too elegant, the lawyers felt that she would hurt Al's case." The same neighbor added: "But Judy was totally devoted to him during his seven months' lock-up. She kept flying back and forth with all the children. She put a lot of thought into organizing the best books to take to him to keep him up-to-date. Even found a doctor to help him keep fit and lose weight in prison."

As it turned out, a new, younger wife was also part of the incentive for both of the fiercely competitive, final, and highest bidders for the fabulous penthouse being sold by the estate of Laurance S. Rockefeller, after his death on July 11, 2004.

Though initial headlines on December 11, 2004, breathlessly reported that someone had agreed to pay $44 million for the coveted triplex, the buyer was identified only as "a prominent New Yorker."

Douglas Elliman's star realtor, Dolly Lenz, whom Donald Trump once flatteringly introduced to an audience of real estate brokers as "one of the great killers of all time," in what he proudly described as "the only business where the people we deal with are worse than in Hollywood," was quoted in the *Post* about the 834 Fifth Avenue penthouse: "Anyone who was anyone went through there. They had billionaires going in at half-hour intervals."

The next day another newspaper scoop reported that "the new champ"—the buyer of the $44 million apartment—was "none other than Wilbur Ross, who has many reasons for upgrading his lifestyle." Ross, who was sixty-six at the time, had recently been the subject of a *Business Week* cover story and the focus of a *Fortune* magazine feature. He had just made a killing snapping up previously moribund U.S. steel companies and making a $291.3 million profit off these undervalued assets. Alternately tagged with the sobriquet "Man of Steel" and "King of Bankruptcy," Wilbur Ross almost overnight had become the best-known turnaround financier in the United States, having been involved in the restructuring of over $200 billion of defaulted companies' assets around the world.

After twenty-six years as the executive managing director of Rothschild Inc., the U.S. affiliate of the Rothschild family's merchant banking group, he had purchased the firm's distressed investment activities in 2000 and formed his own company, WL Ross & Co., opening offices in New York City, Tokyo, and Seoul. Since then, WL Ross has created private investment and hedge funds totaling more than $2 billion. Earlier, he had been awarded an honorary medal by President Kim Dale Yung for his help in Korea's 1998 financial crisis, President Clinton had appointed him to the Board of the U.S.-Russian Investment Fund, and he had served as privatization advisor to former New York City mayor Rudolph Giuliani.

Ross, the ex-husband of former Lieutenant Governor Betsey McCaughey, under New York's Governor George Pataki, had recently married a leggy, blond, socially prominent columnist for *Quest* magazine, Hilary Geary, whose mother, Pat Wood, is part of Southampton's Murray-McDonnell clan. Pat's sister Catherine is the Marchesa Alessandro di Montezemolo, and her other sister, Jeanne, was married to Alfred G. Vanderbilt. It is often said the attractive family had a lot to do with putting that Long Island seaside resort on the international Jet Set map.

But alas, the trophy apartment at 834 Fifth Avenue did not go to Wilbur Ross after all. The man who shattered all previous prices for a Manhattan co-op a few days before Christmas 2004, and plunked down $44 million in cold cash, was not Ross but former Australian, now U.S. citizen, Rupert Murdoch. Like Ross, however, the seventy-three-year-old media billionaire had also just embarked on a new phase of his life with his vibrant, gumptiony, young Chinese wife, Wendi Deng.

The rules for sale were exacting, as laid down by Laurance Rockefeller himself. They required that the prospective buyer exhibit cash assets well in excess of the asking price and be able to pay the amount in cash, with no loans affixed. In buildings like 834, 820, or 960 Fifth, each building has in addition to the price of the apartment something real estate brokers refer to as a "number." This number is the multiplier for the amount that the buyer must show in liquid assets in addition to the cost of the apartment. These numbers retain their power to overwhelm. Certainly they limit the playing field of would-be contenders. Then there remains the question of who among the billionaires would be approved by the clublike co-op board.

The chairman and CEO of News Corporation, whose personal worth in the 2006 *Forbes* magazine's list of the world's richest people was an estimated $7.8 billion, is not only in the news business but also an ongoing newsmaker himself. He is forever adding to and innovating the vast global media empire he built upon a single newspaper he had inherited from his father in Adelaide, Australia. When, in 1981, he bought the *London Times*, he had faced down powerful British unions, angry competitors, and daily maligning by the BBC (which hated him) to build his television-film-newspaper-book publishing-satellite conglomerate. To all the above, in 2006 he added the Internet community MySpace.com, purchasing it for $580 million. According to *Slate* magazine's David Plotz, "Almost single-handedly, Murdoch has modernized the world's media, forcing competition on stagnant businesses, cracking open monopolies and oligopolies, vanquishing 'traditions' that were often an excuse for laziness, unleashing the creative destruction of capitalism on an industry that thought itself exempt from it." Despite Murdoch's right-leaning politics, former governor Mario Cuomo admired Murdoch in a *New Yorker* article: "He's feisty, he's resilient, he's self-made, he stands up for what he believes in, and he can even, on occasion, be charming." Interviewed by Charlie Rose on television: Murdoch described himself as "intuitive, innovative and an outsider. Not a club joiner."

Then there is the public's fascination with Rupert Murdoch's private life. They called him "Rupert the Ruthless," when, after thirty-one years of marriage to his second wife, Anna, the mother of three grown children who had been pressing him to ease up on his workload and enjoy the fruits of his labor, he asked for a divorce instead of retiring. He was not ready to give up the stressful challenges of the far-flung empire that rested pretty much on his shoulders. "As long as my brain and my body are ticking over, I just love it," he commented.

The Czech-born Anna, a devout Catholic who is said to attend mass daily, has been described as a "formidable" personality. She was a pretty, eighteen-year-old junior journalist for one of Murdoch's Australian newspapers when they met. Soon Murdoch divorced his first wife, the mother of one daughter, and married Anna. At first, when Rupert proposed divorce as an alternative to retirement, things seemed amicable enough. So much so, that Anna Murdoch initially remained on News Corporation's board. Later, however, in tears, Anna Murdoch said she wanted "at all cost" to save the marriage, but suspected that he had a girlfriend.

Rupert Murdoch met Wendi Deng, a tall, good-looking, witty executive fresh out of Yale School of Management on the business-development team of Star TV, Murdoch's Hong-Kong–based satellite business in Shanghai, China—a country that might prove to be the biggest media frontier of the future. Her father, an engineer, had managed a factory of 20,000 workers for the Communist government in Guangdong, a province in southern China.

In 1999, seventeen days after Rupert and Anna Murdoch's divorce came through, Murdoch married Wendi Deng aboard his boat, *Morning Glory,* which he later sold to Silvio Berlusconi. While Anna wanted him to stay at home, Wendi loved traveling with him to the far corners of the earth. He told friends he felt revitalized, never more physically fit. He called her "a very loving, supportive wife." By the time he bought the Rockefeller penthouse, she had given him two little daughters, Gracie and Chloé, whom he adored. Before 834 Fifth, the couple were living in a SoHo penthouse—also a triplex—atop what was once a candy factory. It was expensively designed, with a huge media room and dramatic wraparound terrace by Christian Liagre, the French decorator responsible for the interior of the chic Mercer Hotel, one block from the Murdochs' SoHo apartment. They sometimes invited Rupert's fellow Australians, movie stars Russell Crowe and Hugh Jackman, for relaxed rooftop barbecues. They had commissioned Liagre to design the interior of the Fifth Avenue penthouse.

Since marrying Rupert Murdoch, Wendi Deng's role in her husband's empire has been an incessant subject of speculation. But she has steadfastly kept quiet. But while his third set of children regularly played with his grandchildren from his second marriage, and during weddings and baptisms the family regularly got together and had a seemingly cordial relationship, soon after Rupert and Wendi were approved by the Fifth Avenue apartment co-op board, and the sale was finalized in May 2005, an underlying tension over control of News Corporation suddenly erupted.

Anna Murdoch, who had meanwhile married a popular Palm Beach society figure named William Mann, had at the time of the divorce agreed to a relatively smaller settlement (if $200 million can be called small) in exchange for securing control for her children of a trust that holds 28.5 percent of News Corporation voting stock. The trust represents most of the family wealth, but more importantly is key to the control of News Corporation. In other words, the divorce agreement controls the appointment of trustees to the trust (Rupert's daughter, Prudence, from his first marriage, was included in the trust). According to the agreement Rupert Murdoch has four votes and each of the four children have one vote. When Rupert dies, his votes disappear. Then the kids control the empire. When Murdoch wanted to add his two infant daughters' names to the trust, which may or may not have precipitated the resignation of Murdoch's oldest son, Lachlan, from the News Corporation, the media mogul was again in the headlines.

There was a lot of gossip among Manhattan's top-tier real estate brokers that the reason Murdoch beat out other billionaires like Ralph Lauren and Wilbur Ross is because the Rockefeller estate was certain that he would be green-lighted by the co-op board. This was because, decades earlier, he and Anna had already gone through the process and were happily admitted to live among the residents of this exclusive Fifth Avenue bastion of privilege. It was from an earlier duplex in the building for which they had paid $350,000 that their three children went off every morning to three of New York City's top private schools. Elisabeth, who attended the Brearley School, now lives in London, runs her own independent film company, and is married to a grandson of Sigmund Freud. Lachlan, who went to the Allen-Stevenson School, ran the Australian newspapers for six years before he took charge of Murdoch's worldwide newspaper and a television division outside the Fox TV network, is married to a former Australian supermodel. Murdoch's younger son, James, who was enrolled at New York's Horace Mann School, is chief executive of British Sky Broadcasting. While raising their brood, Rupert and Anna were very much part of their children's school activities. No doubt, when moving from downtown, this was a consideration. Always a doting father, Rupert was looking forward to little Gracie and Chloé gaining the educational advantage provided by these excellent Manhattan institutions of learning, most of which are located uptown. One headmistress said, "After you attend a New York school like Spence or Brearley or Buckley or Collegiate, college is only a frosting on the cake."

Wendi Deng, whom friends describe as "the opposite of the trophy wife" because she's casual, outgoing, mischievous "and anything but a spendthrift," had mixed feelings about leaving the hip vibes of SoHo for a more staid atmosphere on doorman-guarded Fifth Avenue. But Rupert Murdoch admitted, in an October 13, 2005, interview with Mokoto Rich in the *New York Times,* that he had had his eye on the Rockefeller penthouse for three decades. Back in the 1970s and 1980s, when he first lived in the building, Laurance Rockefeller was the chairman of the co-op board. Murdoch had attended a few shareholder meetings in the penthouse. "I said if I could ever afford this, I would love it." At which point Wendi Deng spiritedly added, "It was your American dream."

· 2 ·

THE TIME WARNER CENTER

EPICENTER OF THE GLOBAL CITY

*T*HROUGHOUT HISTORY CERTAIN cities and certain buildings in those cities seem to define all that is novel, modern, energetic—what may be the birth of an era—something that symbolizes the seemingly unlimited possibility of the place, to which people from all over are drawn by a drive for power, prestige, and pleasure.

Such a building is the Time Warner Center in New York.

A soaring, glamorous affirmation of millennial ambition, and solid proof of the city's reach and power, the Time Warner Center has, within a short time of its unveiling in February 2004, become a privileged perch for an intriguing global group of super-rich individuals.

Its south tower—official address One Central Park—boasts New York's most expensive apartment ever: an opulent megacondo of two full floors near the very top, with a mind-spinning price tag of $54,762,982. And that's for the raw space alone. It does not count the cost of the lavish inner architecture—millions of dollars more—for the spectacular duplex penthouse, which boasts a glass-walled, two-story living room that centers on an indoor reflecting pool with a fountain in the middle, has a fanciful fireplace of

The Time Warner Center

transforming presence, and, as the *pièce de résistance*, offers a jaw-dropping seventy-sixth floor wraparound terrace with a lordly 360-degree view of the pulsating city. Its designer is Peter Marino, famous for the Milan apartment he created for Giorgio Armani and for the luxurious interiors he created for Valentino's sleek black yacht. The purchaser of this matchless Time Warner Center pleasure dome is a forty-seven-year-old Mexican-born, London-based hedge-fund manager named David Martinez. He initially paid an (until then) unheard of $42.5 million in August 2003 for all of the seventy-sixth floor and about half of the seventy-seventh floor. In July 2005, he acquired the rest of the upper floor for an additional $12.5 million. Martinez thus eclipsed the history-making $44 million paid by media mogul Rupert Murdoch for the Fifth Avenue triplex that had belonged to the late Laurance Rockefeller.

While newspapers around the world reported the $42.5 million record payment by the Mexican bachelor financier, who wanted a capacious aerie for his prized collection of Calders, Picassos, Lichtensteins, and art deco furniture by Jacques-Emile Ruhlman, a similarly priced floor-through penthouse on the eightieth story of the north tower—official address, 80 Columbus Circle—was a more closely guarded transaction. The condo was bought quietly by an American woman with homes in Utah and Hawaii. Its layout, however, was designed for a very different high-altitude high-life. The apartment had six bedrooms and as many white-marble bathrooms, each with a view to write home about. It was intended to put up the owner's children and grandchildren whenever the family fancied a trip to New York. Who was she and where did the money come from? Well, her name is Sandie Tillotson, and she's one of those low-profile high-achievers you don't read about in *W* magazine or gossip columns, though she is a willowy blonde and a generous donor of $6 million to Thailand's tsunami victims. She is a self-made entrepreneurial phenomenon, cofounder of Nu Skin Enterprises, the global empire of personal health care products that began with a plant-based acne medication and now operates in thirty countries. The original skin-healing formula was expanded into a variety of antiaging and face-protecting products, and in no time, Nu Skin concoctions gained the official endorsement of the U.S. Olympic team. So, in little more than a decade, Sandie Tillotson went from being a struggling working mother of four in Salt Lake City to the head of an international company with $1 billion in annual sales. Clearly, here's a woman who can afford to invest in a luxurious third home in the skies. And she made her commitment to live in New York's newest twin towers, in the fall of 2001, undaunted by the horrific events in the city just weeks before.

An instant, twenty-first-century icon of astonishing and unexpected beauty, the immense 2.7-million-square-foot Time Warner structure with its two 750-foot glass spires jutting out from a massive, curving base, set where Columbus Circle meets Broadway, was designed by one of today's hottest architects, David Childs of Skidmore, Owings and Merrill. It is a brilliant statement of urban contemporaneity and is everything a great New York skyscraper should be.

Its glittering, perfectly calibrated facades, sharp-edged precision, and elegant symmetry redefine the look of mid-town Manhattan. Its 198 condominiums in the clouds are angled so that their floor-to-ceiling windows embrace both the surreal density of Manhattan and its almost mythic verve and sweep. The views are stupendous, even humbling. You can see both rivers, all of Central Park, and most of the legendary landmarks: the Chrysler and Empire State buildings, the George Washington Bridge, even the Statue of Liberty. In these apartments you feel like you are on top of the world.

From these towering residences, the building morphs streetward into its dynamic, sprawling, mixed-use enormity. It boasts four 4-star restaurants, two state-of-the-art health clubs, a dozen or more hip boutiques, and America's most dazzling organic food supermarket. The north tower becomes the top-rated Mandarin Oriental Hotel, offering twenty-four-hour hotel amenities to the private apartments within its wings. The south tower houses CNN's New York television studios and the office headquarters of one of the world's largest media entities, Time Warner.

Jazz at Lincoln Center, sixteen years in the making and costing $128 million, under the stewardship of star trumpet player, Pulitzer Prize winner and artistic director Wynton Marsalis, and partly supported by the city, is housed in the dramatic central glass prow of the building. The structure's distinguishing architectural feature, the virtually transparent cable-net glass wall, forms a breathtaking stage backdrop of Central Park skyscrapers for sunset jazz concerts. It has three major performance components: Rose Hall, the Allen Room, and Dizzy's Coca Cola, an intimate jazz club named after Dizzy Gillespie.

In these semipublic areas there's an incessant movement of people, artistic ideas, and creative influences. This is best reflected in the ecstatically reviewed new restaurants created by four of the world's most acclaimed chefs. These are Per Se, from Napa Valley's renowned culinary innovator, Thomas Keller; Michael Lomonaco's Porter House Restaurant, next to Randy Gerber's Stonerose Lounge; Café Gray, from New York's cutting-edge master of French-Asian fusion, Gray Kunz; and the tiny, satiny, hinoki-wood, twenty-six-seat sushi bar Masa, from Masa Takayama, who made his reputation in Tokyo and Beverly Hills. At Masa, a prix fixe meal costs $450 per person.

The dazzling thirty-sixth-floor health club, for residents' use only, sports an Olympic-size swimming pool enclosed by picture windows and gives the illusion of spilling into the Hudson River on the horizon.

The great food halls of London and Milan served as a model for Time Warner's Whole Foods market, to date the largest supermarket in Manhattan. But it has a brisk, all-American atmosphere of its own, capitalizing on the willingness of affluent, health-conscious consumers to pay more for goods free of additives, preservatives, hydrogenated oils, and artificial flavorings while finessing a global array of taste treats. In a peculiarly American way, as the *New York Times* put it, Whole Foods subscribes to "a religion that might be called moralistic hedonism." While the food is guaranteed to be good for you, the display is both theatrical and educating. Much care is lavished on the produce section, where greens and herbs are stacked four feet high, their immaculate leaves bedewed with droplets from a misting system in near-constant operation. A photo identifies each fruit and vegetable and provides nutritional information. Tags explain the differences between jalapeno, Scotch bonnet, and poblano peppers, along with suggested uses. There are fancy add-ons like a self-service soup stand with chowders, bisques, and bouillabaisse. The meat center emphasizes free-range products and a remarkable array of sausages from many countries. A dizzying variety of gustatory globalism comes out of pizza ovens, sushi bars, cold antipasto stands, Asian steam tables, a spicy Latino spread, an Indian table, a Jamba Juice post, and a sybaritic desserts counter.

A thousand and one trappings of luxury make an epic coming-together for the diverse internationals that live under one roof here. But one thing's for sure: From its celestial private heights to its earthly breakneck-paced commercial ground, the Time Warner Center importantly takes advantage of that old real estate maxim: "location, location, location." It stands at the exact epicenter of New York. Fittingly, Columbus Circle has always been the designated point from which the distance of everything else in New York is officially measured. So for those for whom New York is the center of the universe, living at the Time Warner Center means having a home at the throbbing heart of the capital of capitals.

Little wonder that savvy condominium seekers of exceeding wealth from around the world, wanting a foothold in Manhattan and wishing to buy into what's "cool," have thronged to the Time Warner Center's lofty dwellings. Within a year, 85 percent of the costly apartments were sold.

And already, three years later, some are being resold at a handsome profit. Several of the original tenants have already cashed in on their investments. Brian M. Stolar, a New Jersey real estate developer, paid $4.46 million in April 2004 for a sixty-second-floor apartment and within a year sold it for a million and a half more to John L. Stryker, an heir to a medical equipment fortune from Kalamazoo, Michigan, listed at 185 on *Forbes's* 2005 list of the richest people in the world. Stryker's grandfather invented the mobile hospital bed and started a company that last year alone reported $4.3 billion.

Stryker epitomizes the kind of people pouring into these wondrous New York towers from all over the United States But because this is an apartment building, the crisscrossing and interacting of worlds that take place in the lobby or on elevator rides is truly mind-boggling. There are celebrities, of course. Television star Kelly Ripa and her family live in a three-bedroom unit on the seventy-third floor. Latin pop singer Ricky Martin signed a contract for a three-bedroom condo for $6.7 and quickly found himself in court with another Time Warner tenant. The dispute had nothing to do with the typical conflicts between neighbors in New York apartments. Turns out that a week after Ricky took possession of his sixty-fifth-floor digs, his lawyers filed a $2.5 million lawsuit against Martin's longtime manager Angelo Medina, who had, unbeknownst to Martin, become his Time Warner Center neighbor, having himself slapped down $3.7 million for another sixty-fifth-floor apartment. Luckily Medina's two-bedroom unit was in the north tower facing north, while Ricky Martin's was in the south tower facing south. Medina, who also owns a professional sports channel and basketball team in Puerto Rico, eventually settled with the recording star. Peace was restored, and these days when the two multimillionaires from San Juan bump into each other, they exchange cordial nods and "hellos." Another young film actress, Christina Applegate, was a Time Warner resident during her Tony-nominated run in her first Broadway show *Sweet Charity*. She famously injured her foot, but went on dancing every night and always flashed a broad smile in the lobby. She was beloved by all the doormen.

Though not show biz luminaries, many Time Warner condo buyers have names that had celebrity moments. There is the son of billionaire John W. Kluge of MetroMedia fame, whose Iraqi-born, former belly dancer spouse, Patricia, was one of the most photographed of the younger second wives of the phenomenal moneymakers of the 1980s. In those days, Kluge, who made his fortune selling television stations and wireless licenses, was the richest man in America. For this two-bedroom pied-à-terre on Columbus Circle, the younger Kluge had put down $2.1 million.

A much larger sum of $8.4 million for a three-bedroom apartment in the Time Warner Center was spent by the widow of Dr. Robert C. Atkins, developer of the controversial Atkins Diet. Atkins was reported by the *Boston Globe* to have left a $600 million estate after he slipped on a snowy New York street and unexpectedly died in 2003. To his widow's great dismay, word got out that Dr. Atkins at the time of his fall weighed way more than an exemplary diet guru should.

Credited with coming up with the Pepsi slogan "It's the real thing," adman Keith L. Reinhard, chairman of DDB Worldwide, one of the world's largest advertising agencies, spent $9.1 million on a four-bedroom tower apartment on the seventeenth floor, where on a clear day you can see forever—or at least as far south as the Verrazano Bridge and as far north as the Tappan Zee.

And remember the sixty-year-old New Jersey techno-tycoon who made news when he paid $20 million in October 2005 for an eight-day trip in a Russian Soyuz Space Capsule, to reach the International Space Station? His name was Gregory Olsen and he recently spent almost half as much, $9.1 million to be exact, for his sky-high apartment in the Time Warner Center. The Brooklyn-born scientist-engineer, who was the third private citizen to go into space, made his fortune in fiber optic research. His Princeton-based company, Sensors Unlimited, makes infrared sensors used by both the military and private industry. He sold his company at the height of the technology boom in 2000, then two years later, when the high-tech balloon burst, he bought it all back for a mere $7 million. What, above all, besides the views, appealed to Olsen about living in the Time Warner Center was the futuristic, space-age wiring in the towers. Each condominium comes pre-wired with sixteen different types of telecommunications lines, phone, and cable lines, making each apartment capable of live television transmission, the teleconferencing of business meetings, or, if you're in the entertainment world, "broadcast-ready." All this extraordinary wiring and high-tech, of course, also applies to security. Closed-circuit cameras, computer screens, surveillance alarms, electronically coded cards instead of keys—they are all monitored around the clock at a hidden command center deep in the bowels of the building.

Speaking of Soyuz, emigré social celebrity Anna Anisimova was, at age nineteen, one of the youngest condo owners at the Time Warner Center. She acquired a three-bedroom, 3,800 square foot suite in the summer of 2004 for $10 million. New York's first Russian-American "princess," she is sometimes called Moscow's answer to Paris Hilton, because she's colossally rich, tall and pretty, skilled socially, and uninhibitedly fun. The lissome brunette with cornflower blue eyes and an elegant carriage is a New York University student. She modeled for a while, mainly tossing her long, shiny tresses back and forth in shampoo commercials. Her Time Warner apartment—plus a $500,000 summer rental of a Southampton house owned by Denise Rich, the ex-wife of fugitive wheeler-dealer Marc Rich, whose pardoning by President Clinton on his last day in office caused such a sensation in 2000—was, however, not paid for by Anna's modeling earnings.

Anna is part of the new generation of Russian heiresses, who are coming to New York to browse for designer dresses, hire their own tennis pros, and chatter freely with the likes of football team owner Woody Johnson, without a burly bodyguard standing nearby. For Anna Anisimova's daddy is one of the Russian "oligarchs" who managed to enrich themselves during Boris Yelsin's reign. Anna's father, a reclusive aluminum tycoon, was number sixty-seven on *Forbes's* list of the "Richest Russians." His estimated worth is $350 million. Many "oligarchs," though they work in Moscow, dispatch their families to live abroad. For more than a decade, the wives and daughters of these new Russian capitalists have lived in costly town houses in London's Eaton Square, or on fancy estates in Surrey and West Sussex. But Vassily Anasimova chose to stow his family in New York, at a multi–time-zones remove from the wild aluminum business in Russia, where his eldest daughter was brutally murdered. Now Anna's parents are getting divorced, but another sister also lives nearby in the Trump International Tower.

Russians have been quietly buying up property in Manhattan, upstate New York, Connecticut, and in New Jersey towns like Fairlawn, Marlboro, and Old Bridge. "They spend a lot of money on real estate because they have a lot of cash," says one Russian. "In Russia, there is no such thing as a mortgage, and nobody trusts anybody, so people are paid up front." Anna's family has been playing Monopoly with New York and Florida real estate for years.

Anna Anisimova is not the only deep-pocketed Time Warner Center condo buyer to hail from the former Soviet Union. On the seventy-fifth floor of the north tower, a heavenly three-bedroom suite with a truly out-of-this-world panorama of New York and its surroundings was acquired for $8.5 million by Nurzhan Subkhanberdin, the chairman of Kazkommertsbank, the biggest private bank in Kazakhstan, which has assets of $4 billion.

Maybe not to the world at large, but in art circles the name Tobias Meyer has a certain resonance. The handsome young director of Sotheby's Contemporary Art Worldwide presided over several of the most successful twenty-first century sales of contemporary works, at auctions that in recent years have brought in hundreds of millions of dollars. For his Time Warner personal loft with "a totally addictive view," Tobias Meyer plunked down $5.3 million.

Meyer and his art-consultant flatmate, Mark Fletcher, spearheaded the phalanx of art aficionados who have decided that the air and light high above Columbus Circle would be ideal for their prized collections. A three-bedroom $15.3-million home on one of the top floors houses the wondrous sun-catching collection of colorful glass sculptures by the much praised Dale Chihuly, as well as the works of several other modern artists. The luxurious gallery-like apartment belongs to Gerard L. Cafesjian, who made $3.4 billion when West Publishing was sold to the Thompson Media Group in 1996. Cafesjian has also endowed a modern art museum to be built in Armenia, the land of his forebears, with $50 million.

Yet another envied collection moved into the Time Warner complex with Pamela and Richard Kramlich. She is the director of the San Francisco Museum of Modern Art, and he's a venture capitalist who finesses high-tech companies. The couple's noteworthy stash of avant-garde video art is sure to be fought over in coming years by leading museums across the United States.

Floridians Susan A. Hancock, who serves on the acquisition committee of the Whitney Museum of American Art, and Raymond W. Otis sold their computer marketing firm and decided to invest in a $8.2 million seventy-first-floor apartment. Enfolded all around by the beiges and grays of the skyscrapers outside their windows, they hired a designer to make the cityscape work as the perfect foil for their contemporary Japanese art, specifically several important works by Takashi Murakami.

While this towering real estate triumph contains many of Manhattan's highest priced homes, an amazing two-thirds of the apartment units were purchased in cash. And this cash flowed in from the farthest corners of the planet, from people whose backstories might not necessarily meld comfortably while they rub shoulders in a crowded elevator. Still, this is New York, and people respect each other's differences.

Take Ali R. Bozkurt, chairman of BMB, a Turkish company specializing in the construction of roads, airports, tunnels, and power plants, who has a two-bedroom residence on the sixty-sixth floor in the south tower. When the Iraqi army invaded Kuwait, where he was working on a project, he was briefly taken hostage by Saddam Hussein. He could easily ride the lift one day with Prince Turkin bin Khalid, a Saudi royal and sports buff who is an official of the Saudi national football team. Prince Turkin was one of the earliest buyers of two adjoining apartments in the summer of 2001, before the building was even finished. The prince might also be fascinated by the story of a Pacific-American import-export firm's managing director named George F. Meng, who was trapped in his company's forty-seventh-floor, World Trade Center, north tower offices, during the September 11, 2001, terrorist attack. After the first plane hit, Meng tried to seal his office doors with paper towels and tape to keep out the smoke. But when he saw the south tower collapse, he rushed down the stairs. He made it out of the building just minutes before it, too, started coming down.

Another high-ranking Asian businessman in the south tower is David Kwok Po Li, chief executive of Bank of East Asia in Hong Kong, which has $24.9 billion in assets. Mr. Li, who is also a director of Dow Jones, Campbell Soup, and China Gas, owns a $9.5 million condominium apartment at Time Warner Center.

The advanced high-tech security systems at the Time Warner Center, one of the building's special features that has a profound meaning for foreign investors, is what sealed the deal for Pablo Ardila, member of a well-known Colombian newspaper dynasty. Like the Turkish Mr. Bozkurt, the Ardilas had experienced what it's like being taken hostage. Pablo Ardila, the governor of Cundinamarca, the province that includes Colombia's capital, Bogota, is heir to Bogota's newspaper *El Espacio,* as well as to some Florida real estate and various ranch holdings in South America. He bought the Time Warner pied-à-terre for his eighty-five-year-old father, Jaime Ardila, founder of the popular tabloid, who in 1993 was kidnapped by guerrillas and held for a terrifying month before finally being released. "My father always wanted to have an apartment in New York," Pablo Ardila mused. So the son granted that wish.

On the floor below Jaime and Hellen Ardila, a Turkish industrialist named Sakip Sabanci, who with his estimated family fortune of $2.8 billion was the richest man in his country, purchased two separate apartments at a total price of $8.6 million, just before he died at age seventy-one. The apartments belong to his two daughters, Sevil Sabanci Sabanci and Dilek Sabanci, who have spent a lifetime avoiding publicity. Five floors above the sisters, one of the wealthiest men in Britain, a London bond trader, Michael A. Spencer, at $8.7 million spent a little more for a single apartment with three bedrooms, each bedroom angled so as to wield an amazing, nearly 300-degree view.

But the Time Warner Center, where "five star living" means that on a stormy day condo owners can find just about anything their hearts desire under one voluminous roof, without having to brave the elements, is far from being an outpost for fabulously rich foreigners. According to Louise M. Sunshine, former head of the Sunshine Group, who marketed and sold the building's 198 apartments, Americans make up 75 percent of the buyers. They range from smart-looking baby-boomer couples, rolling baby carriages through the lobby, to older, retired couples, often former suburbanites with grown children, longing to be back in the midst of the city's excitement. For example, more than ten doctors, several dentists, and pharmaceutical tycoons have bought large pads in both towers. Perhaps the most lavish of these is the seventy-fifth-floor, six-bedroom spread of Dr. and Mrs. Joseph H. Levine, the renowned cardiologist who directs the far-famed Arrhythmia and Pacemaker Center at St. Francis Hospital in Roslyn, New York.

Time Warner Center's high-in-the-sky home away from home is a natural for Hal Wendel Jr., the retired chairman of Polaris Industries. A sporting Minnesotan, whose company made snowmobiles, he clearly likes high places, since he's scaled all seven of the world's highest mountain peaks.

Chester P. Davenport, of Bethesda, Maryland, considered one of the richest black entrepreneurs in America, who heads the private investment firm

Georgetown Partner has a handsome $4.2 million duplex on the fifty-sixth floor of the south building.

Another enthusiastic, super-rich Time Warner condo buyer is bandwidth and telecommunications service provider Michael Hirtenstein, chief executive of WestCom—80 percent of which was recently bought by J. P. Morgan Chase. Hirtenstein spent a cool $15.7 million to have access to the seventy-sixth-floor terrace and to be able to enjoy "the perks of living over a hotel and thirty-two seconds from a swimming pool."

Living above the Mandarin Oriental Hotel and being able to order up a meal via room service was the biggest allure of the north tower for Jack Silver, president of SIAR Capital. He splurged $24 million on what is one of the largest duplexes in either building. Only the full-floor penthouses are bigger. The 6,511-square-foot duplex has a real "master of the universe" view extending all the way to New Jersey, out to Long Island Sound, and far up the Hudson. Silver is a self-made man who, by the way, hails from Brooklyn.

The razzmatazz view of New York's highlighted skyscrapers seems irresistibly seductive to producers. There are almost as many of them living in the building as there are doctors. One of them is elated to be living in what she calls "eighty floors of great global glitz." Her name is Verna R. Harrah and she is glamorously ensconced in an $8.8 million, five-bedroom nest high-in-the-sky. Nice going, she observes, for a girl who started out as a Las Vegas cocktail waitress. It was there she met and married Mr. Harrah, the Nevada casino magnate, in 1973. After his death, she decided to produce films. It was a fortuitous move. With her very first film, she made a killing. That was the thriller *Anaconda*, which earned $136 million worldwide. The movie financed her apartment in a great glowing spire, which makes a megawatt statement among the many glittering lights that make the resplendence of the New York night.

Husband-and-wife Broadway producers Fran and Barry Weissler, whose hit musicals have included *Chicago* and *Annie Get Your Gun*, moved simply across the street from an apartment at Trump International. Joining them, also from the Trump International building, in a two-unit, high-floor apartment with an $8.45 million price tag were husband-and-wife Hollywood producing team Anne and Arnold Kopelson. The Kopelsons—who produced such hit movies as *Platoon*, *The Fugitive*, and *Seven*—love to put up actor friends in their Time Warner digs while they're filming in New York. "It helps them get totally immersed in the city through the building's magical views."

After enjoying a halcyon season as coproducer of Tony Award–winner *Monty Python's Spamalot, Dirty Rotten Scoundrels,* and the brilliant, gut-numbing shocker *Pillowman,* Roy L. Furman is the latest convert to the building. The Broadway producer, philanthropist, and vice chairman of Lincoln Center traded life in one of the city's most pedigreed prewar co-ops at 770 Park Avenue for a complete change: a riveting $9.7 million, seventy-first-floor surrounding of twenty-first-century modernity.

The grand opening of the Time Warner Center was generally greeted as a great day for the city. This prime Manhattan location at the bustling southwest corner of Central Park, where once stood Robert Moses's New York Coliseum, had been lying fallow for too many years.

On the evening of February 4, 2004, Mayor Bloomberg was literally beaming as he greeted the black-tie gala crowd, including celebrity New Yorkers Kevin Bacon, Cindy Crawford, Salman Rushdie, Isabella Rosselini, Calvin Klein, and I. M. Pei. Four thousand guests were expected, but 6,500 showed up, including Larry King. "It's a great part of New York," the mayor proclaimed. "It tells you what's really happening here."

Governor Pataki also attended the christening of the $1.7 billion building. "It's just very impressive," he exclaimed. "It's worthy of the world headquarters of a great global New York corporation."

Finally! A real winner of a building where Midtown and the Upper West Side meet gracefully under sleek, spectacular towers! At last! A truly pedestrian-friendly skyscraper with dazzling dining, shopping, big-screen broadcasts of sporting events in the lobby, courtesy of the major multimedia entity whose headquarters this is. Hurrah! A tip-top new international hotel! And bravo! A spectacular new cultural facility for the city—evenings of jazz! The effulgent new structure was overwhelmingly hailed as the triumph of reason over chaos. For it represented the victory of determined enterprise over nearly two decades of quibbling, indecision, and paralysis as to what to do with this vital Manhattan site. The obstacles included economic downturns and fierce efforts to block anything from being built. For years almost all enthusiasm for the project was killed by an earlier plan for a building that would have cast a huge shadow on Central Park. As if New York isn't a city of tall buildings and the shadows they cast!

Anyway, the final product is a resounding success and has an instant pedigree. But there definitely were some heroes behind the horrendous challenges this large-scale project presented.

First of all, despite all the sniping by antidevelopment forces, both Governor Cuomo and Governor Pataki saw through two separate sales to two different developers of this precious plot of land, owned by the bureaucratic MTA (New York's Metropolitan Transit Authority). As it turned out, the first, Boston Properties, led by Mort Zuckerman, was unable to go ahead and build. By sticking with the project through years of controversy and obstructionism, however, Zuckerman helped set a precedent for the site's eventual developers, Related, led by Stephen M. Ross and Apollo Real Estate Advisors under the aegis of Bill Mack. Related and Apollo had the courage to go forward, and the good luck of much better timing. Time Warner chief Richard Parsons was bold enough to recommend moving his company to an interesting new location. Because this was city-owned land, Mayor Rudolph Giuliani insisted on the new building having some performing arts component. Giuliani was thinking opera, his own favorite cultural diversion, but then Lincoln Center's jazz impresario, Wynton Marsalis, provided one worthy of the location. Also indispensable to the project was architect David Childs. Long before anyone knew there would one day be a "Freedom Tower" at Ground Zero, Childs designed an optimistic two-towered skyscraper for Columbus Circle that is practical, beautiful, and sensitive to a score of what would appear to be conflicting needs.

Putting all these elements together was no small feat.

It takes a certain kind of person to make a mark on the physical layout of the world's greatest city. For the most part, they're tough guys like Stanford White, Robert Moses, and Donald Trump, made up of equal parts vision and congenital ruthlessness to suffer fools or willing adversaries gladly. Then there is Bruce Warwick. He's a developer, yet he doesn't fit the mold. In the early 1990s, he was helping "the Donald" put together Trump International Hotel and Tower, the distinctive, bronze, needle-nosed edifice that hovered above the lifeless site once occupied by the Coliseum. He would look down at the demolition and think, "What a wonderful thing it would be to work on that challenge!"

Warwick, a tall, calm, imposing man, who was a football player in college, has been in the development business for more than forty years, a career of steady achievements for which the Time Warner Center is a fat and fitting capstone.

Philip Pitruzzello, vice president for real estate at Time Warner, and the media conglomerate's chief overseer of its Columbus Circle project, calls

Warwick "a huge asset. A project of this magnitude requires tremendous experience, and he has that."

Stephen M. Ross, the Detroit-born CEO of Related who was the leader of the AOL-Time Warner Center development team, also believes Warwick's participation was critical. As Ross and project partner Kenneth A. Himmel drew up plans for the new building and sought someone to run the day-to-day operations on-site, they knew it had to be "someone with gray hair."

It was Irving Fisher, yet another consultant to the project, who suggested Warwick, with whom he had built apartment complexes in Puerto Rico back in the 1960s.

"Related is a multifaceted organization, but no one had the experience to build a job of this magnitude and complexity," Fischer recalls. "It's a very, very diverse-type job, to bring all these uses under one roof. Normally, when you build an office building, it's just an office building. Same thing with a shopping center. Or a performing center. Not to mention a 251-room hotel like the Mandarin Oriental, which was the other anchor tenant. Then you had CNN's broadcast studios, where news personalities like Lou Dobbs and Paula Zahn could make use of eye-popping sight lines as backdrops for their globally watched programs. You had all those components together. And more. Bruce had to coordinate all the pieces."

"Bruce Warwick was the axle of the wheel," remembers David Childs of Skidmore, Owings & Merrill, the principal architect. Childs designed the overall look and function of the gigantic structure. Ismael Leyva was the main architect of the residences. Six different architects were brought in, each given responsibility for a single piece, like the concert hall, the restaurants, or the food market. For example, the prestigious German firm of Brennan Beer Gorman was responsible for the design of the Mandarin Oriental Hotel, and Rafael Vinoly Architects created the four separate performance spaces for Jazz at Lincoln Center. Several of the shops facing Columbus Circle were done by the Boston-based architectural design team of Elkus/Manfredi Ltd. "It's not just coordination but creativity. Bruce was like the conductor of an orchestra. He's the one who had to get everyone to do their best."

It all took tremendous stamina and sanity. "There's a problem every day in integration, scheduling, cost containment, weather. All of these come into play while a skyscraper goes up on a daily basis," says Warwick. "There are so many interest groups pulling on you when you go through the zoning process, the building department process, the neighborhood process. Then you're dealing with the construction. It's probably the most costly market to build in. The skill of New York tradesmen is incomparable; but, of course, so are their wages. So efficiency is an issue. Timing is essential. Scheduling must not get out of control."

There was a very strict timetable. The concrete superstructure was completed at a rate of two floors a week. Months before its formal opening, 90 percent of the center's retail space was leased, and sales agreements for an amazing 40 percent of the condos were inked. Main credit for this goes to a propulsive redhead, Louise Sunshine, who for many years worked with Donald Trump on his ambitious real estate ventures. It was Louise Sunshine who trademarked the building's promotional motto of "Five-Star Living," and with the help of Marjorie Reed Gordon convinced *Architectural Digest* magazine to involve twenty-three of New York's best and brightest interior decorators, like Victoria Hagan, Juan Pablo Molyneux, Mario Buatta, Tom Britt, and Ellie Cullman, to create a benefit showhouse on the seventy-third floor. The charity event was brilliant public relations for all participating parties and resulted in a thirty-page photographic portfolio titled *Rooms with a View* about the then not-quite finished Time Warner Center. The project was executive directed by marketing specialist Alana Frumkes.

Developer Steve Ross, who was hell-bent on trying to bring the 2012 Olympics to New York and who has since been contracted by the City of Los Angeles to rebuild its whole downtown, calls the Time Warner Center the city's "most important building since the Depression. Most people still don't yet conceive what this will mean to the city of New York," he exclaims. And in an unguarded moment, he divulges that he himself has bought a home in it: an awesome, supersized penthouse with a magnificent 360-degree view, sprawling across the very top floor of the south tower. As he sinks back into his streamlined office chair, with a mischievous grin, he quips, "You see, I've always wanted to live above the store!"

"It's been a prize fight," admits Bill Mack. "We never had a round where we weren't slugging it out."

And Manhattan is no welterweight venue.

· 3 ·

RIVER HOUSE

ART DECO GEM

SOME OF THE most luxurious apartments ever built on the planet were created as New York was plummeting into the Great Depression in 1930. Foremost among these was River House at 435 East 52nd Street.

The contrast between the jobless, hungry, desperate people living in the surrounding tenements, discarded breweries, and slaughterhouses, and the well-off, well-dressed sophisticates who lived in a shining new apartment building looking very much like River House was memorably captured by the 1935 movie *Dead End* starring Humphrey Bogart and Sylvia Sidney. Originally a play of social protest by Sidney Kingsley, adapted for the screen by Lillian Hellman, the classic film is unforgettable for its scenes of spunky street kids making endless trouble for the building's doorman, swimming in the East River, and looking up with envy and wonderment at the apartment life so above the havoc and chaos of the streets.

To this day, of all the exclusive New York palaces of the rich and power-ful, none has a more forbidding aura of staunchly protected privilege than kingly River House. Rising twenty-seven stories above the East River, with its central tower topped by a crown, its two massive fifteen-story wings

River House

embellished with loggias, terraces, and balconies, its myriad windows glinting like platinum in the sun, this magnificent structure on a 40,000-square-foot property fronting the waterway is the quintessential symbol of a very particular kind of social status.

Indeed, behind the limestone walls of its rarified heights, a heavy concentration of leading figures from business, the arts, and world affairs have taken refuge from the prying eyes of lesser mortals. Today they include former Secretary of State Henry Kissinger; one of New York's most active and stylish grand dames, Ambassador Robin Duke—widow of another diplomat, Ambassador Angier Biddle Duke, whose Philadelphia grandfather Biddle was the subject of the Hollywood biopic *The Happiest Millionaire*, and whose Duke ancestors funneled their tobacco fortunes into the creation of Duke University; Sir Evelyn de Rothschild, who heads the British enterprises of the famous banking family, and his statuesque, blond American wife, Lady Lynn; best-selling novelist Barbara Taylor Bradford, and her movie and television producer husband Robert Bradford; financier and former ambassador Donald Blinken and his wife, Vera; former Lehman Brothers chairman and now Blackstone finance giant Peter G. Peterson and his wife, Joan Ganz Cooney; Academy-Award-winning film and theater producer Marty Richards; the grand niece of the Impressionist painter Mary Cassatt, Mimi Halsey; and real estate magnate Francesco Galesi and his wife, Princess Marina Wolkonsky, whose royal Russian title predates the Romanoff dynasty by two centuries.

Facing the imposing 52nd Street entrance, a visitor can easily be intimidated by this hallowed co-op, where rococo iron gates, whose ziggurated art deco stanchions, topped by two eagles bearing bronze plaques, needlessly inform visitors of what is already obvious: This remarkable hunk of real estate is PRIVATE. The cobblestone courtyard—the width of a city block—beyond the gate and beyond the windowed sentry box is off limits to the unwelcome. Other visual reminders of the eminently private domain within are numerous privately owned stretch limousines waiting inside the courtyard. Their drivers, however, are not visible. According to the many strictly upheld house rules, the chauffeurs of privately driven vehicles are not permitted to loiter at the front entrance door and must use the chauffeurs' room. The idea is this: at River House, even the chauffeurs have a private room.

Entering the lobby through the polished revolving door, one is struck by the high sheen of the equally polished terrazzo floors, and as the first lobby gives way to the richly carpeted, elegant main hall in the rear, there is the breathtaking view of the large formal garden, the enclosed lawn with its splendid circular fountain, and the river beyond.

Naturally, while one makes one's way through these various phases of entering the sacred realm, one is inspected at once by at least four pair of eyes, which seem to gaze into the soul of one's financial assets. One pair belong to the doorman; the next to the sous doorman; the next to the lobby deskman (presiding like the officer of a bank behind a marble-topped mahogany desk); the next to the hall captain, who indicates the way to the appropriate elevator with a white-gloved hand. And they are only a sampling of the over thirty staff members of River House, who spend their considerable skills and well-honed acumen to serving the needs of the building's prominent and refined residents, and successfully intimidate everyone else who enters, especially if he or she is a newcomer to the place.

From the moment it went up, River House had a private boat landing on the East River and its own social and recreational adjunct, the River Club. At the time, its builder, James Stewart, recognized that, while many New Yorkers had to battle just to put food on the table, others were financially insulated from the chilling effects of the country's economic crises. He saw the potential of the phenomenal forty-thousand-square-foot property facing the East River and retained William L. Bottomley, of the architectural firm Bottomley, Wagner & White, to develop a spectacular co-op between 52nd and 53rd Streets. A restrictive new building code—and the dead-end streets—were among the liabilities Bottomley turned into assets by creating the exceptional courtyard with its lush green shrubbery, fountains, and one of the grandest drive-in arrival sites in Manhattan. Cornelius Vanderbilt Whitney was among the first New York bluebloods to claim one of the palatial residences. The co-op's crowning glory was the seventeen-room tower triplex with multiple terraces, a cavernous drawing room that was forty-six-feet long and twenty-two-feet high. No apartment is less than nine rooms or short of magnificent. Every apartment has a river view.

Only the richest of the rich could afford to buy when River House opened. Among them were Marshall Field III, man-about-town William Rhinelander Steward Jr., social arbiters Harry Cushing and James A. Burden Jr., and the widow of the son of the founder of Standard Oil, Ruth Baker Pratt. Somewhat later, movie stars Dina Merrill and Cliff Robertson lived at River House, as did Clare Boothe Luce, IBM chairman Thomas Watson, Coca Cola's president Robert Woodruff, Georgia-Pacific founder Owen

Cheatham, first major female Wall Street broker Muriel Siebert, jazz pianist Joe Bushkin, real estate developer Daniel Mauck Galbreath, former Yale president Beno C. Schmidt, Texas oil heiress Carolyn Skelly, violinist Fritz Kreisler, Tiffany president Walter Hoving, and legendary Broadway director-writer-producer Joshua Logan.

The collective thinking process of the residents of River House has been called an enigma. The co-op board that runs this kingdom abhors the merest jot of publicity. Clearly the notorious need not apply. One real estate agent read the building's bylaws from the copy of the lease when a reporter asked her about an apartment that was for sale: "River House forbids any TV, radio or newspaper (coverage) including articles to be written or people to be in the apartment to use them for any such purpose."

Why did this building reject Richard Nixon as a tenant, and then roll out the red carpet for Henry Kissinger? Perhaps the most famous anecdotes involve Gloria Vanderbilt's rejection by the board because its members felt she would bring "unwelcome publicity" to the co-op building. Most cooperatives carefully screen potential purchasers, but this board is especially vigilant about maintaining standards. A name and a few million dollars are far from being enough to gain entry here. Actress Diane Keaton, at the peak of her Woody Allen movie period, was turned away.

Also a big name applicant was the much married Gloria Vanderbilt in 1980. Seeking to purchase the coveted tower duplex, she was rejected even before she could appear in front of the board members. Money wasn't the issue. Maybe it was the company she kept: She was often seen on the arm of the nightclub singer Bobby Short. Maybe it was the jeans she was promoting on TV. Maybe it was the fact that the tower duplex she wanted was the most desirable apartment in the place, with its 360-degree view of the city. When she sued the building for not accepting her, the publicity went on and on. But the spectacular aerie Gloria Vanderbilt wanted more than anything—which had originally been Marshall Field's—next time around brought even more unwanted attention to the building. The lusted-for tower duplex was next purchased by Salomon Brothers chairman John Gutfreund and his wife Susan.

The fireworks that followed when two mega-rich couples warred over the exclusive elevator to the coveted tower triplex has entered the annals of Bad Behavior in Good Buildings. At the height of the ostentatious 1980s, trophy wife Susan Gutfreund clashed several times with Joan Postel, wife of lawyer-financier Robert Postel, with whom the couple shared the original triplex tower suite's private elevator. The final straw was Susan's hoisting a twenty-two-foot high, 500-pound Douglas fir Christmas tree up through the window by using a rig anchored to the top of the building—part of the apartment belonging to the Postels. The Gutfreunds were taken to court over the incident by the Postels. When the lengthy legal battles finally ended, the Gutfreunds decided to move to a $6.5 million apartment on Fifth Avenue.

River House represented a bold confidence in the basic economic health of New York City, built as it was on the very heels of the 1929 stock market crash. Replacing a cigar factory and a furniture plant, it set the standard for the development of several later stylish residential complexes along the shores of the East River, on nearby Beekman Place, Sutton Place, and East End Avenue. Part of this shorefront developmental dream was not just to view the water but also to have access to it. Before River House went up, in 1925 the developer Joseph B. Thomas had planned a Venetian-style gondola station for his medieval fantasy of an apartment house at 455 East 51st Street. And the 1927 Campanile—which became the longtime home of Greta Garbo—now facing River House on 52nd Street but originally backing up to Thomas's Venetian structure, featured a broad open terrace in the late 1920s with a lively riverside restaurant.

One of the main draws of the sprawling River House on the banks of the East River was its glorious private yacht landing at water's edge, and the elegant, still very-top-caliber five-floor River Club, which has two tennis courts, three squash courts, a gym, and a swimming pool. When the *New York Times* commented in 1930 on the club and the co-op building, as it was not quite clear whether the apartments offered "to acceptable persons," as they were advertised, would automatically allow tenants to be members of the sporting club, the paper acknowledged the facilities "for the convenience of members addicted to their yachts and motor boats." The *Times* noted that "it will be possible to step out of a boat and be whisked immediately by fast elevator to the topmost floor of the building."

The president of the club was Kermit Roosevelt, a writer, steamship executive, and son of President Theodore Roosevelt. He may not have been particularly interested in boats, but many of the original River Club organizers certainly were. Club member Vincent Astor made headlines when he threw a party on his famed white yacht, the *Nourmahal*, to bring about a rapprochement between the estranged cousins, Kermit Roosevelt of the

Republican branch of the family, whose members had supported Herbert Hoover in the 1932 election, and the Democrat Franklin D. Roosevelt, who had just been elected president of the United States.

Among them was the leading yachtsman of the day, Harold S. Vanderbilt. He won the prestigious America's Cup in 1930 with his much admired, highly engineered boat the *Enterprise* defeating the English boat *Shamrock V* in four straight races. Another River Club member was the department store heir Marshall Field III, whose swift yacht *Corisande* represented "the acme of the ship-building art" at the time. It made the trip from his country house in Port Washington, Long Island, in thirty-five minutes, at fifty miles per hour. Yet another boat-loving River House resident was Representative Ruth Baker Pratt, a New York congresswoman who used to commute on her boat *Tuna* between the Pratt family's country estate at Glen Cove, Long Island, and her city apartment's private harbor. The block-long landing at River Club consisted of a wide quay with steps leading down to a large H-shaped floating dock with handsome striped railings. There, the tied-up yachts were tended to by crews in spit-and-polish sailor uniforms. The dramatic dichotomy between these sleek white luxury vessels and the coal-blackened chutes, industrial chimneys, and grimy warehouses on 53rd Street, one block from River House, surely illustrated the poignant proximity of the very poor and very rich in the changing neighborhood. According to a *Time* magazine study in the 1960s, it was this very thing—the side-by-side existence of rich and poor—that made great cities great throughout history. They all had this special dynamic in common, from ancient Babylon, through nineteenth-century Paris and London, to modern Hong Kong.

But the romantic style of patrician residents summoning their pleasure crafts to where the East River lapped gently at the building's ankles did not last long. It fell victim to the streamlined, reinforced concrete of Franklin D. Roosevelt Drive, built in the late 1930s. Today's F.D.R. Drive, originally known as the East River Drive, in the words of the *New York Times's* Streetscapes columnist Christopher Gray, "remains one of New York's most elegant public works. But it deprived many well-to-do East Side riparians of their river views and access. Among these, perhaps none sacrificed more than the members of the ultra-discreet River Club." Various buildings from Sutton Place to Gracie Square worked out widely different compromises with the city as construction began. As for River House, today the six-lane highway runs through exactly where the dockside landing had been.

The River Club, with its own entrance on 52nd Street, is still going strong, however. Its original mix of classicism and art deco, with a tropical twist of bamboo and wicker, and its ballroom of blue glass, silver leaf, and Chinese screens remains an elite seven hundred-member preserve. It is still a favorite party site for debutantes. The club's five floors contain a library, a living room, an excellent dining room and bar overlooking the river, and guest rooms with four-poster beds. The two tennis courts are very popular, so reservations are hard to come by. The athletic area is lined with portraits of handsome tennis greats in their spiffy tennis whites—the best-looking of them all is the late Frank Shields Jr., father of actress Brooke Shields. There are also photos on display of Katherine Hepburn and Spencer Tracy, who once used these tennis courts, as well as of Fred Astaire and his sister, Adele Astaire, who was a River House resident for years.

These days, however, there are clear lines drawn in the sand in the back of the building between the residents' garden and the terrace of the private club, where children in wet bathing suits and perspiring tennis players snack on sandwiches and sip iced tea. Unfortunately, nowadays, in neither pretty spot can one hear the water—only the hum of hundreds of automobile tires speeding by on the highway.

· 4 ·

THE DAKOTA

ENIGMATIC LEGEND, JOHN LENNON'S SHRINE

*N*O, MANHATTAN RESIDENTIAL enclave has attracted so many larger-than-life characters as the eccentric-looking structure known as the Dakota, on the corner where Central Park meets West 72nd Street. From haughty society snobs to lionized music makers, from dotty dowagers to a celluloid Frankenstein with a wicked sense of humor, each of these big-time personalities accepted the role of bit player in the ongoing drama of a buff-colored German-Gothic building with a legend even more enduring than their own. For no other New York apartment house has been wrapped in so many layers of magic, mystery, and myth as the Dakota.

Twenty-five years after he was gunned down at point-blank range in the Dakota's former carriage entrance, as he and his wife Yoko Ono were returning home, on December 8, 1980, ex-Beatle John Lennon continues "to captivate people in some mystical way," according to Ed Koch, who was New York's mayor at the time,

Lennon was an audacious millionaire rock star who once boasted that his band "was more popular than Jesus." But Yoko recalls that in the weeks leading up to his death "he was just a happy Dad," loving nothing more than

The Dakota

gamboling in the stretch of Central Park nearest their Dakota apartment with his little son Sean and enjoying every moment of living in New York City, "which he thought was the most happening town at the time." New York was a natural fit for Lennon in 1971, when he decided to move to the city. He was the king of rock 'n' roll, who had just divorced his bandmates and was now married to an affluent Japanese banker's daughter, an avant-garde artist in her own right. Where else to escape the stodgy conservatism of England—where Lennon had been set up for a drug bust, according to the *New York Post*, by an overzealous cop—than the culture capital of the world? Initially, he and Yoko lived at various Manhattan addresses before taking up residence at the Dakota—but not without some resistance from the other high-intensity, rich, high-profile residents of the storied apartment building on Central Park West.

His nine years in the Big Apple would test John Lennon's love for Ono, America, and his fellow Liverpool lads, the Beatles. During this time, the Nixon administration tried to have him deported, and the finishing touches were put on the Beatles' acrimonious breakup. Even he and Yoko Ono separated for a while in 1973, when he took off with their assistant, May Pang, for a year of partying in Los Angeles—a period Lennon liked to refer to as his "lost weekend." Returning to New York, Lennon reconciled with Yoko, thanks in part to the birth of their son Sean in 1975.

The couple, fond of dressing in fancy hats and sable capes over tattered jeans, and moving about the city in separate "his and her" silver Rolls Royces, were, in PBS talk-show host Dick Cavett's words, "like a magnet sucking fragments to itself. They were instantly surrounded" wherever they went. Yet, according to TV journalist Geraldo Rivera, "John was incredibly approachable." Lennon was very serious about recording, so he almost never allowed visitors at the studio. But one day Jackie Onassis dropped by with her two children, Caroline and John-John. Lennon did not know them at all. They had just called up and asked if they could see him record—and he said "sure." But there were times when noisome autograph-seekers and suffocating fans really got to Lennon and gave him a scare. Though in the early 1970s Lennon was mainly obsessed with not being deported, shortly after he moved in, Black Panther chairman Bobby Seale paid at least two visits to Lennon's Dakota apartment. On the day of the twenty-fifth anniversary of Lennon's murder, Seale was quoted in the *New York Post*: "My two bodyguards—who were armed—were with me. The guard on the street told us his partner was off that night and there was this white guy who'd been coming by hassling John. So I told my bodyguards to stay downstairs. I went upstairs alone. Turns out the guy came by a little while later. My bodyguards told him, 'If you keep hangin' 'round here, you will get hurt.' The guy didn't leave, so my bodyguards jacked him up. Later John said, 'Thanks, Bobby.' He thought it was great how we scared this guy off.'"

During their life at the Dakota, Yoko and John were involved in several New York fund-raising events, perhaps most famously volunteering to donate the initial $50,000 that allowed the mounting of a Madison Square Garden concert to benefit Willowbrook, an institution for the retarded. The event raised a quarter of a million dollars, huge at that time. Again in 1974, Lennon agreed to appear in the March of Dimes Walkathon. Then, after being mainly a "househusband" for five years, while Yoko managed their finances and pursued her own avant-garde visual projects, the recording artist whose outlandish looks, seismically different songs, and rebellious style had incited such mass fervor, youth quake, and cultural tumult in the 1960s, suddenly in 1980 released *Double Fantasy*. It would be both his comeback and final album. Documentary filmmaker Albert Maysles visited the couple in their Dakota apartment a few weeks before John was killed. "What struck me was how conscious they were of security. Why all this fear?" he recalled thinking. "It almost seemed inappropriate." But, in fact, it wasn't.

Lennon's killer was a young misfit named Mark David Chapman, and at the time of the murder, he had been reading a novel about another young misfit in New York: Holden Caulfield, the protagonist of J. D. Salinger's *The Catcher in the Rye*.

In the days and weeks that followed the murder, thousands of fans and curious people thronged the streets and sidewalks outside the Dakota. Floral tributes were strewn in front of the building's doorway, at the spot where John had fallen after Chapman had shot him four times with a .38 caliber pistol—on the same day the forty-year-old musician's new album had gone gold. Candlelight vigils were kept night after night. The mass media tried in every conceivable way to gain access to the building, and telescopes were set up in Central Park in attempts to glimpse into individual apartments. People who lived in the building, and had always believed theirs was "the most perfect apartment house in the world," could not enter or leave their homes without having microphones thrust in their faces. The police department put up barricades, but crowds managed to push them aside. Taking advantage of potential customers, street vendors put up concession stands near the site.

Meanwhile, the Dakota's other rich and famous tenants closed their shutters and pulled down their shades. Most of them were already somewhat used to having their building viewed as an oddball, ominous New York landmark, especially after it served as the setting for Roman Polanski's frightening film about devil worship, *Rosemary's Baby.* In the wake of the highly successful movie, starring Mia Farrow and John Cassavetes, the Dakota had increasingly become a tourist stop for visitors to New York. Now, of course, the building had gained notoriety around the world. And residents were troubled. Most of them assumed that Yoko Ono would want to put away her bad memories, sell her apartment, and move away. But Yoko Ono was not a conventional woman and didn't do the expected thing. Instead, she donated to Central Park—across the street from her seventh-floor east-facing windows—a Strawberry Fields Forever garden in memory of her husband. To this day, Yoko continues to live at the Dakota—as does her son Sean in a separate apartment. According to another widowed resident raising a young child by herself, "She is quite liked and respected. In fact, most people in the building feel very protective of her."

On the twenty-fifth anniversary of John Lennon's death, December 8, 2005, they came all day to Strawberry Fields—the fans, the fanatics, the curious, and the crazy, true believers and travelers from as far as Scotland and Japan. Some were middle-aged people who grew up worshiping the former Beatle, others looked more like punk rockers, with multiple piercings in their lips and noses, and hair dyed every color of the rainbow. Extraordinarily, most of these young people were not yet alive when all four Beatles shook up the world with songs like "Lucy in the Sky with Diamonds," "She's Leaving Home," "A Day in the Life," and "Sgt. Pepper." They had come by bus and plane, by car and train. They brought roses, candles, pictures, and love beads. They sat around from early morning on and were singing. At 3:45 in the afternoon, Yoko Ono, who never shows up at the many mass celebrations of Beatles milestones, suddenly appeared at the Dakota's gate. With brisk steps, wearing a black visored Scandinavian sailor's cap over her short black hair, John Lennon's widow walked silently over to the mosaic that graces the center of Strawberry Fields—inspired by the Beatles' song of the same name. Without a word, her eyes masked by huge sunglasses, she placed a bouquet of fluffy white flowers on the spot. Then she vanished. She disappeared back into her all-white Dakota apartment that still has her husband's famous Steinway & Sons white piano, which is supposedly haunted by the prematurely cut-down rock idol.

The passing years have been kind to John and Yoko. He was once viewed as a leftist firebrand. She was blamed for the Beatles' breakup. Their racy nude photographs and cheeky protests, which once scandalized millions, are now misted over by the memory of gentle songs about love and peace. They are both assured legend status now.

However, thorough originals that they were, John and Yoko are just two of the many one-of-a kind individuals whose comings and goings resonate in the corridors of the Dakota.

Not since the 1940s and 1950s heyday of the Garden of Allah, on the corner of Los Angeles's Sunset Boulevard and Crescent Heights, has a single address throbbed with so many entertaining, charismatic, and eccentric personalities as the Dakota. Actress Lauren Bacall knew both locations. She and Humphrey Bogart were regulars at the Garden of Allah until her husband's death and the hotel's closing in 1957. Three years later, Bogart's widow and children, Steven and Leslie, were occupying a stylishly decorated, park-facing fourth floor apartment at the Dakota.

Bacall, Boris Karloff, Judy Garland, Leonard Bernstein, Rudolf Nureyev, Roberta Flack, José Ferrer and Rosemary Clooney, Jack Palance, Judy Holliday, Theresa Wright, Zachary Scott and his wife Ruth Ford, playwright William Inge, director John Frankenheimer, feminist Betty Friedan, dancer Gwen Verdon, opera singer Cesare Siepi, fashion photographer Hiro, Warner Bros. heir and restauranteur Warner LeRoy, movie critic Rex Reed, TV stars Maury Povich and Connie Chung, plus such well-known society couples as Carter and Amanda Burden, Frederick and Solange Herter, Peter and Susan Nitze, Gil and Susan Stein Shiva, William and Jean Stein vanden Heuvel—they all endured the occasional madness and mayhem to call themselves residents of Manhattan's most cosmopolitan address.

Looking at its utilitarian car park, it's hard to imagine that a century earlier there stood a rose garden, which almost succeeded in countering the odor of stables inside the Dakota. From its drab foyer, you'd never know that it once was a fully staffed, starched-linen and fine-silverware dining room serving residents and their guests three meals a day.

The Dakota—with its sixty-five large and thoroughly unique suites of rooms, renowned for their fourteen-foot ceilings and richly detailed fireplaces—is perhaps the most famous of New York's "Western" apartments: luxury buildings that began going up in the late nineteenth century west of Central Park. The name derives from a joke that it was so far north and west of civilized life in Manhattan that it might as well be located in the Dakota Indian Territories. The gabled, sturdy, storybook structure, with its mansard windows and two-story entryway, is one of the city's architectural gems. Eclectically combining German-Gothic, French-Renaissance and English Victorian architectural elements, it was designed by Henry Janeway Hardenburgh—whose most famous creation is the Plaza Hotel in New York—and completed in 1884, at which time it was surrounded by squatter's shacks and farm animals.

To New Yorkers' great amusement, a newly minted millionaire named Edward Clark—a canny lawyer for the notorious womanizer Isaac Merrit Singer of Singer Sewing Machine fame—was building, of all things, a luxury apartment house at a location that wasn't even an address. According to Stephen Birmingham's 1979 book *Life at the Dakota,* public opinion was that his folly would never work. Still, New York in the 1880s had become a city of crazy entrepreneurial schemes, and into this mood of hectic speculation and wild risk-taking, Edward Clark's planned project fitted perfectly.

Besides, Edward Clark's achievement was already considerable. For although the sewing machine was Elias Howe's invention, it was through Clark's marketing genius that at one point practically every American housewife of every economic level wanted a sewing machine—or as she called it, "a Singer." This had been no easy task. Psychologically, wealthy women sewed for pleasure. They embroidered, crocheted, and needlepointed. Poorer women sewed and darned out of necessity. But the point of a woman and her sewing was that it was feminine, lovingly done by hand, prettily arrayed in her lap. The bulky, expensive sewing machines were impersonal, industrial looking, and, annoyingly, always breaking down.

What's more, Clark's business relationship with Singer was always tempestuous. Of the background of the man whose name is synonymous with home sewing, very little is certain. At the age of twelve, Isaac Merritt Singer ran away from home, and for the next forty years of his life he was an itinerant, unskilled laborer, who was often unemployed. At one point, he was married to five women, none of whom was aware of the existence of the other four, and was supporting as many as six mistresses on the side. He had twenty-six illegitimate children at the time of his death. By 1851 there existed many patented mechanical sewing devices when, by sheer accident, Isaac Singer happened to become involved with them. Working in a Boston machine shop, luck had him repairing a Lerow & Blodgett sewing machine. Suddenly, some long-buried talent inside Singer burst to the surface. Within twelve hours, he had made a sketch of a better machine, and eleven days later he had built one. But of course when he began to peddle his device, he found himself in patent law trouble. So Singer sought out Edward Clark. But why Clark, of a respectable middle-class family from the upstate New York village of Hudson, took on an unsavory character of Singer's reputation became clear only later. He accepted Singer's highly complicated case in return for a 50 percent share in I. M. Singer & Co. Edward Clark was possessed of both a promoter's instinct and a talent for making deals. Within a short time both Clark and Singer became immensely wealthy.

Edward Clark gallantly supported Singer's final wife, Isabella Boyer Singer, in her claim to be the legal widow. Isabella went on to live a glamorous life in Paris, where she married a duke and became Bartholdi's model for the Statue of Liberty. Princesse Edmond de Polignac, born Winnaretta Singer of Yonkers, the oldest daughter of the sewing machine magnate, occupied an important place in the cultural life of Paris for more than half a century. Educated in Europe, she was an accomplished painter, pianist, and organist and devoted her fortune and energy to an astonishing variety of artistic, scientific, and social concerns. She was a friend of Proust, Verlaine, and Marie Curie. She commissioned works by Fauré, Ravel, Stravinsky, de Falla, and Weill. *Chez* Winnie, Americans like Cole Porter and Gerald Murphy could meet the likes of Nadia Boulanger and Darius Milhaud. Another one of Singer's heirs, Paris Singer, became a famous Riviera playboy with a huge chateau in Cap Ferrat. He was also an early backer of Addison Mizner, the architect whose splendid villas in Palm Beach set the signature style of that world-class playground for America's super rich. It was in Paris Singer's speeding Bugatti that his mistress, dancer Isadora Duncan, famously was strangled when her long floating scarf caught in the wheel of the car on the coastal road to Monte Carlo. Eventually Edward Clark became the president of the Singer Company.

By the 1880s New York was on its way to becoming the largest and most important city in America. In less than ten years, the city's population had doubled, climbing to one and a half million. Not only was Clark's completed Dakota promoted as "the most perfect apartment house in the world," but it was a stately presence on the city skyline that afforded its tenants extraordinary views. The location Clark had chosen for his folly had the advantage of sitting on one of the highest points of land in Manhattan. From the Dakota's upper windows one could see the entire island and much of the surrounding countryside as well. The Dakota "guaranteed to the tenants comforts which would require unlimited wealth in a private residence." This accounted for the building's instant popularity. One could live like a king at the Dakota without paying a king's ransom to do so.

One of the delights of the Dakota from the beginning was that it appeared to be run more as a sociable, charitable, luxurious rest home than as a business. When things went wrong, tenants simply rang downstairs, and someone immediately appeared to fix it. No one seemed to realize that Clark had put up the building to make money. Despite its popularity, the Dakota didn't really show a profit. Many of the early tenants were prosperous New York businessmen and their wives, like the Schirmers of sheet music fame or the Steinway piano clan. They were solid folk who cared more about their pleasant, busy lives than about striving to be in Society. They tended also to be older people, either childless or couples whose children had grown and moved away, and this gave the Dakota somewhat of a reputation that children were unwelcome. The fact was that the Dakota at first was not convenient to the city's better private schools, though a number of excellent ones—Ethical Culture, Collegiate, and Trinity among them—would later appear on the burgeoning West Side.

Just one look from the Dakota's roof was all it took for celebrated Russian composer Peter Ilyich Tchaikovsky to convince himself—along with countless numbers of his countrymen who would read his diaries for nearly a century afterwards—of the wicked inequity of American society. While in New York in 1891 to conduct his own works at ceremonies celebrating the opening of Carnegie Hall, Tchaikovsky was invited to dinner at the apartment of music publisher and Dakota resident Gustav Schirmer. Handed a customary after-dinner brandy and cigar, the Russian was among a group taken to the roof by his host, who proudly pointed out the Park below and the city lights beyond.

Because Tchaikovsky spoke just a few English expressions and understood even less, the great man completely misunderstood his host's gesture and assumed the entire Dakota complex was Schirmer's property as far as the lowly workmen's shanties in Central Park. He presumed for the rest of his days that America supported a wealth disparity of czarist proportion.

In his diary, Tchaikovsky seethed at the U.S. publisher of his works: "No wonder we composers are so poor!" More than two decades before the Russian revolution, envy is apparent in the words of the staunch nationalist who, as a child, would kiss the map of Mother Russia on an atlas and spit on other lands.

Tchaikovsky's diary reads: "Schirmer took us on the roof of his house. The huge, nine-storied house has a roof so arranged that one can take a delightful walk on it and enjoy a splendid view from all sides. The sunset was incredibly beautiful.... We sat down to supper at nine o'clock ... and ... were presented with the most splendid roses, conveyed downstairs in the lift and sent home in Schirmer's carriage. One must do justice to American hospitality; there is nothing like it—except, perhaps, in our own country."

At around the same time, Herman Melville, by then well into his seventies, often walked with his little granddaughter in Central Park. He had been living quietly in New York for years, convinced that his literary career was over, working as a customs inspector on the Hudson River piers. The Schirmers "discovered" the almost forgotten author of *Moby Dick* and gave a dinner for Melville and his wife. The Schirmers apparently found Melville charming, but a little sad. He was working again on a final novel, to be called *Billy Budd*. But, he said, he was sure that his book would never be published unless he had it privately printed, because his popularity of more than thirty years earlier had all but vanished. Another American literary man of consequence the Schirmers befriended and liked to entertain was Stephen Crane. He was working on a second book with a Civil War setting, to be called *The Red Badge of Courage*.

The first celebrity of cinema to call the Dakota home was Boris Karloff, already typecast as Hollywood's best known monster by 1939, when he moved in without his fourth wife of eleven years, Dorothy Stine, whom he would divorce seven years later in 1946.

Perhaps in reaction to his relegation to B-movie star status—at the time, he was between shooting *The Invisible Menace* and *The Mystery of Mr. Wong*— or in retaliation against mutterings from certain Dakota residents that a thespian in the building simply wasn't *de rigeur*, this cultured scion of British diplomats, whose real name was William Henry Pratt, saved his most convincing performances for his neighbors. Even the Dakota's snootiest dowager, a certain Miss Adele Browning, would become damp-eyed at Karloff's oft-told admission of his annual Halloween heartbreak. He claimed profound sorrow that trick-or-treaters were too frightened by his gaunt, hollow-eyed appearance to even approach the bowl of candy he routinely set outside his door, only to have to bring back in, untouched.

Having toyed with their emotions for amusement, Karloff and his best buddy, British film actor Basil Rathbone, who lived down the street from the Dakota, purposely set tongues wagging at the apartment complex. Sashaying through the courtyard for their twice-weekly constitutional in the park, they would surreptitiously converse in what was taken to be a suspiciously foreign tongue. Only a few Dakota staffers were clued in to the fact that the duo—known as Frankenstein and Sherlock Holmes—were puckishly playing on domestic paranoia during those World War II days about Fifth Column Euro-spies infiltrating the fabric of America. This they did most effectively by speaking out of the corners of their mouths and behind their hands in fluent gibberish. At the park entrance, eyewitnesses at the time reported the actor chums chortling and slapping each other on the back, delighted as naughty boys that their little joke on Dakota residents had worked yet again.

Except for John Lennon's murder, nothing brought the international spotlight on the Dakota quite as powerfully as Roman Polanski's 1968 film of Ira Levin's best-selling novel, *Rosemary's Baby*. It recorded in cinematic perpetuity—though rather eerily—all the building's architectural quirkiness and individuality. The story was set in a Manhattan apartment that wasn't called the Dakota but, with its dark storage spaces, rooftop lofts, and labyrinthine hallways opening into cul-de-sacs, looked suspiciously like it. For several days the Dakota's carriage entrance—the same spot where John Lennon would later be gunned down—and its courtyard were commandeered by the diminutive Polish-born moviemaker, for the sum of $1,000 a day, to shoot a particularly gruesome scene. Early in the movie, Mia Farrow's character, Rosemary Woodhouse, meets a traumatized young woman in the building's laundry room, who warns the pretty newcomer of an inherent evil within, then promptly falls to her death from a window in an apparent suicide.

It says much about the studied aloofness of Dakota residents that for several days they made a point of ignoring a smashed and bloodied life-size mannequin that the moviemakers had hurled from the roof for cinematic effect. With the so-called "money shot" in the can, it was simply left on the cobblestones, where it had landed with a resounding splat. Why did residents see fit to act with such contrived nonchalance, as if a corpse routinely landed in their courtyard? In fact, they were in a communal snit at the time. Management had deemed it unnecessary to inform them of the deal with Polanski to shoot a movie in their backyard—or to mention compensation of $1,000 a day for the interruption of their lives.

Shortly after its release during the summer of 1968, *Rosemary's Baby* became the number one movie in the country. Mia Farrow, who was filming *Secret Ceremony* by that time in London with Elizabeth Taylor and Robert Mitchum, comments in her memoir, *What Falls Away*, "Its success, and my own too, were abstractions that translated into surprisingly little satisfaction."

Though *Rosemary's Baby* catapulted her to Hollywood's A-list of actresses, it also largely precipitated the end of her marriage to Frank Sinatra. Except for the Dakota scenes, plus a dangerous segment where Rosemary has to dodge the on-coming two-way traffic on Park Avenue, and a vignette with Ruth Gordon at Tiffany's, the movie was filmed in Hollywood. But the shooting went way over schedule because of almost daily confrontations between Polanski and the male lead, John Cassavetes. Polanski was a perfectionist, famous for his endless retakes, sometime as many as forty, and his expectation that actors utter every word precisely as written. In this case, he himself had adapted the script and was determined to be faithful to the best-selling novel. Cassavetes by this time was known not only as an actor but also as a highly respected independent film director whose specialty was spontaneity and naturalistic dialogue, often improvised by his team of actors. In Farrow's reminiscing, "[Polanski's] method of working drove John Cassavetes nuts." The marvelously sharp, witty character actress Ruth Gordon, who Mia thought, "saw to the heart of everything," usually served as peacemaker between the combatants, who several times came close to physical blows.

Meanwhile, Sinatra was fighting his own demons and was impatient with Mia's long absence. He had been in a nasty, drunken 4 A.M. brawl in Las Vegas, where, as Mia describes it, "all his caps had been punched clear off his teeth and some other guy had been hurt and headlines were sure to follow.... His speech was unclear ... and his dentist was on the way with new teeth. He sounded bewildered and upset as he said he loved and needed me, and with my whole being I loved and needed him, too." What with one thing and another, particularly the sudden death of the director Anthony Mann, Mia's previous film, *A Dandy in Aspic*—a spy thriller mostly filmed in London and Berlin—had already resulted in absences from her new husband "that were long and stressful." What's more Sinatra himself had planned to work with Mia in his next film, *The Detective*, costarring Lee Remick. The timing of *Rosemary's Baby* could not have been worse for the marriage. But Roman Polanski, at thirty-three, was a hot, new international movie figure, and the film would be Mia's "first opportunity to star in a feature film, but more important, to prove myself as an actress." It was an offer she couldn't refuse.

As the shooting of *Rosemary's Baby* dragged on during the hot New York summer, Sinatra gave her an ultimatum: him or the movie. Though she called him several times each day, the marriage did indeed collapse under the Dakota's haunted eaves. The day she was scheduled to start working on *The Detective* was drawing close. Sinatra pressed his ultimatum once more, but she could not walk out on her commitment and abandon *Rosemary's Baby* before it was completed. "To lose Frank was unthinkable, but I didn't believe he would leave me," she insists. "I applied myself to the remainder of the movie with a fervor usually reserved for prayer." But shortly thereafter Mia's role in *The Detective* was rewritten for Jacqueline Bisset, and there were rumors in the press of an affair between Frank Sinatra and Lee Remick.

"Then without warning, on an afternoon in November," Mia recalls, "Frank's lawyer, Mickey Rudin, appeared on our set carrying a brown envelope. He pulled out a document that I looked at just long enough to see [it was] made out in my name: [it was] an official application for a divorce from Frank Sinatra. I remember the unprofessional look of surprise as Mr. Rudin realized I had not expected his visit, nor did I know anything about the papers he carried. This was the first mention of divorce. I held myself together and signed all the papers without reading them. If Frank wanted a divorce, then the marriage was over."

The delicately built Farrow, who, as Rosemary, is tied to a bed and raped by members of a Satanic cult, lost enormous amounts of weight during filming. She looked wan and fragile, all of which enhanced the ultimate success of the movie. But she remembers "the days were long and difficult." It didn't help that Roman Polanski, whom she liked and admired, quipped one day to a journalist while publicizing the movie during the shoot, "There are 127 varieties of nuts. Mia's 116 of them."

Long before Polanski used the Dakota for *Rosemary's Baby,* the trace of an afterlife cult at the aging, Gothic castle was already flourishing. As more and more of the original families made their quiet exits out the Undertakers' Gate, it was perhaps not surprising that a building with such a long history, touched in addition by the sinister legacy of *Rosemary's Baby,* should have acquired a cast of spectral characters. Believers in independently supported ghost-sightings claim that John Lennon is far from being the only one to return and haunt his former abode. In many people's minds, a spooky place like the Dakota is capable of sheltering its fair share of restless souls.

"Some buildings garner a reputation that is based more on perception than reality. There are buildings across the world that are said to be haunted merely because they look as if they should or because of some tragic event once took place there," writes Susan Blackhall in *Ghosts of New York.* She reports that John Lennon, who met his violent senseless death just outside, "is just one among many that walk the corridors. Lennon himself told of seeing a female wraith weeping in the corridors. . . . More chilling, a small golden-haired girl bounces her ball along the hallways. Who she is no one knows, but despite her seeming innocence, her appearance always portends death in the building. . . . Apart from actual apparitions there have been many instances of lights going on and off by themselves and the building's elevators starting and stopping erratically. Objects such as bags of trash have been seen to levitate, and during one rather frightening period, several fires started at various points in the building, seemingly without human involvement."

Among the ghostly manifestations, such as reports by residents of seeing visions of old-fashioned furniture they don't own suddenly appear in their rooms, is said to be Edward Clark himself, who built the Dakota and keeps a watchful eye over his investment.

Among Clark's descendents still living in the building is Susan Nitze, wife of Peter Nitze, whose father, Paul Nitze, was the cofounder of The Johns Hopkins School of Advanced International Studies and who, along with his sister, Elizabeth Paepcke, and her husband, Walter Paepcke, a prominent Chicago industrialist, was one of the original catalysts and phenomenal fund-raisers for both the Aspen Institute and the original Aspen ski lifts. The Pentagon's former deputy defense secretary, Paul Wolfowitz, in a recent speech, called Nitze—in whose honor the U.S.S. *Paul Nitze* destroyer is named—"the best secretary of defense we've never had." Believed to be too outspoken to be given a cabinet post, Nitze for several decades was among the most powerful advisors to U.S. presidents, from the position of influence he held as head of the policy planning staff on weapons and warfare. Except perhaps for George Kennan, he was the most important strategist of U.S. security policy and military capability during the Cold War.

Susan Nitze's distant cousin, Dr. Frederick Herter, and his second wife, the vivacious French-born Solange de la Bruyere—said to have been Jackie Onassis closest confidante— also lived at the Dakota for a time during the 1980s. Now retired from his post as head of surgery at Columbia Presbyterian Hospital, the tall, imposing Dr. Herter also has an illustrious foreign policy heritage. He is the son of Christian Herter, President Eisenhower's secretary of state, and for several years, he was head of the American University in Beirut, Lebanon.

For a long period, the descendents of Edward Clark were said to have exercised considerable clout as to who was or who wasn't allowed to buy a co-op at the much-coveted, elegant Dakota.

Unfortunately, because of a couple of fires, wild parties involving a homosexual couple, and another unsavory incident involving two gay hustlers picked up by a Dakota resident in Central Park, there was a period in the 1970s when things were building to a head of steam. The board declared, "We don't want to show any more apartments to homosexuals." In charge of interviewing and screening prospective tenants in those days was a well-known woman lawyer. She used to annoy people by asking "rather nosy lifestyle questions," remembers one resident. "Are you married?" was one that anybody who wanted to buy an apartment had to pass acceptably.

When the mild-mannered, bookish-looking playwright Mart Crowley applied to the building he had just become a major celebrity, a result of his highly lauded off-Broadway play about gay men in the city, *The Boys in the Band*. Though he was enthusiastically sponsored for the Dakota by two popular Dakota apartment owners—the film critic Rex Reed and Zachary Scott's widow, Ruth Ford—Mart Crowley was flatly turned down by the board.

"I really felt terrible, afterwards, about sponsoring Mart," Rex Reed divulged in an interview with author Stephen Birmingham, "because it opened such an ugly vein."

Stephen Birmingham observed, "In taking a stand against homosexuals in the building, the Dakota board was touching an extremely sensitive nerve. It was not that the Dakota was the first or only New York apartment building to discriminate in this fashion. A number of buildings, particularly on the East Side, routinely denied applicants to partners of the same sex.... But that this should happen in the Dakota seemed particularly repugnant. the Dakota had long provided a safe harbor for the gifted, the brilliant misfits, the different."

In fact, some of New York's most distinguished homosexuals have lived at the Dakota over the years. Russian-born ballet legend Rudolf Nureyev used to have an extravagant, art-filled apartment on the second floor. His beautifully appointed bathroom with gold faucets, an enormous marble tub, and an adjoining sauna with an eight-foot-long bench was the talk of people in the building. Nureyev was said to have slept in his dining room, which faced the Dakota's courtyard and was quieter than the bedrooms facing the park and the traffic noise coming down Central Park West.

Leonard Bernstein lived next door to Nureyev, in fact, their back service entrances faced each other and the two legends were very close neighbors and intimate friends.

Stunningly handsome interior designer Jed Johnson, who died in the famous TWA flight that was on its way to Paris when the plane exploded just a few miles off the Long Island coast, had bought two apartments he had joined together on the fourth floor. One of them had belonged to the Italian socialite Priscilla Ratazzi and her husband Chris Whittle—publisher turned controversial education entrepreneur with former Yale University president Beno Schmidt. After Jed Johnson's death, the apartment was purchased by the television newscaster Connie Chung and her TV-investigative reporter husband Maury Povich. They promptly moved into the perfectly decorated quarters with their young son.

While the building was once considered "unfriendly" to children, according to one young mother, "today there are a lot of kids living at the Dakota and the atmosphere in the building is very neighborly. The pervasive feeling is: 'We're all in this together.' All the kids love recording legend Roberta Flack's wonderful dogs. Everyone looks forward to the courtyard party and Yoko Ono's high-end sashimi potluck contribution to the event. She always attends, is coolly friendly and dances by herself."

The once virulent homophobia seems to have evaporated. If anything, the gay faction exerts considerable power in the building on everything from the planting of trees and flowers to the rules governing bicycle storage. These days, it is said, the most powerful person to determine who gets in and who gets blackballed is Jane Rosenthal, film star Robert de Niro's right-hand production executive and head of New York's mushrooming Tribeca Film Festival. She is not uncontroversial. As one resident puts it, "She is sweet to celebrities. Not so sweet to people who are successful but have no fame." She and her husband, Craig Hatkoff, have been major supporters of both President Bill Clinton and Senator Hillary Clinton and reportedly slept in the Lincoln bedroom during the Clinton administration. The head of the board, Barrie Wigman, who is better known by her nickname "Dee Dee," is a veteran of the investment firm Goldman Sachs and owns an art gallery on Madison Avenue and 76th Street.

Actress Lauren Bacall has always exuded a cool, almost caustic insouciance on and off the screen,—especially in her early noir films with Humphrey Bogart—as if an appearance by even the president of the United States or the queen of England beside her might trigger no more than a quizzically raised eyebrow. But in December 1960, not long after she moved to the Dakota, residents caught a telltale earful of the star's celebrated toughness. At the time, Bacall's fourth-floor apartment, for which she paid in excess of $53,000—and which is now valued at around $8 million!—had at great expense and creative deliberation just been newly decorated by one of the city's top interior designers. Thus it was with bewilderment that she found the building's most upright tenants rapping urgently on neighbors' doors and sounding the alarm about an imminent catastrophe of biblical proportions. Word was that real estate czar William J. Zeckendorf, the august and feared Donald Trump of the times, famed reshaper of the Manhattan skyline, was about to buy the Dakota.

At a hastily convened tenants' meeting in the old dining room, Bacall was told that Zeckendorf had bid $4.5 million for the building, an offer the struggling Clark Foundation owners had little choice but to accept. A relative newcomer to the building, Bacall asked the obvious: How big a deal was it if ownership of the Dakota changed hands?

She was assured that Zeckendorf would tear down their beloved home to build afresh on it prime, parkside location. The distressing image of a wrecking-ball crashing through her walls caused Bacall to experience what old-timers in the building recall as a full-fledged emotional meltdown. Bacall is said to have climbed onto a huge oak table to unleash a tirade of vile curses against the edifice rex who would dare to threaten her newly decorated home. More revealing than the emotion of her growled invective was its graphically profane call for Zeckendorf's slow and agonizing demise.

Galvanized by Bacall, the mood among concerned tenants—typical reaction of most Manhattanites when their private, coveted piece of the island is threatened—quickly turned from fear to anger. They began a chant, which turned into a battle cry: "Hands off the Dakota!" Feelings ran so high that there were even whispers about buying shotguns to pepper Zeckendorf's demolition team.

The solution came not with a shot but with the scratch of a pen on a check for $4.6 million—just $100,000 more than Zeckendorf's rumored offer—written by wealthy New York realtor Louis Glickman. He counted many friends among the building's residents and readily agreed the Dakota was a landmark worthy of preservation.

Lauren Bacall was able to contain Dakota tittle-tattle about her short fuse and eloquent profanity by turning her cool, caustic insouciance on anyone alluding to it. But to this day she is quite involved in the building, arriving at meetings with a list of specifics, usually involving the aesthetics of the building or moving the bus stop from in front of the apartment house.

There was a big, celebratory party held in 1961, when the building became a cooperative. And after another fracas, when frazzled nerves from a construction explosion next door caused what became known as "the revolution," the October courtyard party became a neighborly, annual get-together, to which Bacall usually brought brownies, Roberta Flack contributed spoon bread, and the Lennons brought sushi.

John Lennon made an indelible impression on the Dakota long before his young life was snuffed out at the hands of deranged fan John Chapman. For it was Lennon at his irreverent best who effortlessly offended Dakotans with an offhand zinger about the building's architecture. Officially labeled "German Renaissance," the Dakota's style is eclectic enough that nearly a century after its completion in 1884, residents were still known to bicker over whether a wittier design description might be Victorian-Chateau, Victorian-Kremlin, Brewery-Brick, Pseudo-European or even Middle-European Post Office. Enter Lennon with the ultimate *bon mot*. Customarily uncommunicative with his neighbors, the reclusive musician and self-described "house husband" of the seventh floor nevertheless found himself cornered by several elderly Dakotans debating their favorite topic, that being the cleverest description of their home's unique architecture. Prodded for an opinion, the golden tongue behind such lyrics as "red and yellow custard, dripping from a dead dog's eye" peered through his Coke-bottle glasses at the Dakota's solid walls and high ceilings as if for the first time. Finally, he raved in Liverpool twang: "Polish fook'n rococo is what they should call this fook'n place!"

Until an inner gate was installed in the old carriage entrance (the one the Lennons' maid Rosa always claimed was haunted), Dakota doormen had their time cut out preventing kids from posing for sick photos spoofing the Beatle's violent death. Here's how it worked. After approaching a doorman with a bogus question, to get as far inside the entrance as possible, kids would suddenly lurch into a grimacing death pose, then hit the ground clutching imaginary chest wounds, as pals recorded their grotesque little parody on film or video.

Aside from the drama of the shooting, residents and staffers alike recall two little known facts about the unassuming celebrity, victim of the only known killing ever to take place at the Dakota. The first was the rapt, almost mesmerized attention with which Lennon spent days lacing butcher's string between the staircase balustrade at the elevator entrance. Some believed it was an exotic macramé craft project, its looped and knotted significance known only to its gifted creator. Others recognized it for what it was: a safety precaution to keep his and Yoko's toddler son, Sean, from toppling through the railings. The second was the tenants' acute discomfort at Lennon's and Yoko Ono's incongruous pairings of his 'n' hers silver limousines and sable coats with bare feet and the audible mastication of chewing gum. Yet such sins paled beside what was seen to be the ultimate crass act: discussing business matters within the hearing of others!

To Yoko Ono's enduring consternation, she remains most talked about among Dakota old-timers for an incident that happened in 1973, not long after she and John Lennon moved in. Their apartment had formerly belonged to the late actor Robert Ryan, who vacated the place after many years following the loss of his beloved wife, Jessie, to cancer. Because Jessie Ryan had, before succumbing, endured a lingering death in the master bedroom, the Lennons saw fit to hold a séance to ascertain what spirits inhabited their new living space and the spirits' intentions. To no one's surprise, their clairvoyant of choice claimed to have made contact on the other side with the spirit of Jessie Ryan. According to the medium, Jessie wanted to make it crystal-ball clear that she would consider the apartment her home for eternity, although the Lennons would be wholly unaware of her presence, as she had no intention of intruding on their lives. So far so good. Residents who remember the era still shake their heads at the well-intentioned naiveté of Yoko, who actually called the Ryans' daughter, Lisa, whom she had never met, to inform her that the mother she mourned was well, although admittedly not alive, and residing happily in spirit form at the Lennons' apartment.

An unamused Lisa Ryan reportedly snipped from her California home: "If my mother's ghost belongs anywhere, it's here with me—not with *them!*"

Yoko still makes occasional headlines as a performance artist. For several years, she regularly commuted between the Dakota and the Danube, with her close companion of almost twenty years, Hungarian artist and furniture designer, Sam Havadtoy, who in 2000 moved back to Budapest. In 2005, Yoko worked with Angela Lansbury's brother, the producer Edgar Lansbury, to stage a Broadway musical in which several different actors—both male and female—played John Lennon. As John was the subject of much whispered conjecture among Dakota residents, so in recent years has been Yoko, widely believed to be hoarding behind her apartment's twelve-inch thick walls a fab fortune in Beatles memorabilia. According to residents claiming to be in the know, the memorabilia is destined to be her son Sean's inheritance upon her death (like he needs the money!). This twenty-three-karat treasure-trove is said to comprise everything from John's never seen poetry and paintings, his eyeglasses, wardrobe, even intimate videos of him and Yoko—all accruing in value faster than any stocks or bonds ever could.

· 5 ·

960 FIFTH AVENUE

THE ABSOLUTE PINNACLE
OF NEW YORK LUXURY LIVING

*N*o TWO OF the magnificent, spacious apartments in the building are the same. No one residing in them nowadays has a net worth of less than $100 million. No similar elite edifice on Fifth Avenue has such lavish amenities: a glassed-in, rooftop, stainless steel exercise set-up, and on the ground floor, an elegant, Old World, private restaurant with a French chef. Significantly, few major apartments in the building have changed hands in years. So, in the midst of the millennial media frenzy about the almost obscenely skyrocketing prices of the city's choice real estate, this secretive bastion of privilege and pleasure has pretty much stayed out of the news. Yet in the eyes of cognoscenti, 960 Fifth Avenue is the grandest cooperative apartment house in New York.

"It's the premier building in Manhattan," Louise Beit, one of the top agents at Sotheby's International Real Estate, who's been selling multimillion-dollar apartments in New York for years, was quoted as saying in the *New York Times* magazine.

While "960," as it is simply referred to, as if the number were some secret code for a private club, represents the finest living accommodations

960 Fifth Avenue

in Manhattan—and probably the world—it remained a silent sanctum during a time when similar buildings—740 Park Avenue and 834 Fifth Avenue—made splashy headlines with their opulent triplex penthouses formerly belonging to the Rockefeller brothers. Each of those attracted staggering sums. But according to experts, if any of the dazzling, high-ceilinged, one-of-a-kind suites at 960 were to come on the market, surely they would command price tags in the same range as the $37 million that Wall Street whiz Stephen Schwarzman is supposed to have paid in 2000 for John D. Rockefeller Jr.'s three-tiered penthouse at 740 Park Avenue, or the $44 million that media mogul Rupert Murdoch plunked down in 2005 for Laurance Rockefeller's fifty-year residence atop 834 Fifth Avenue, or the $35 million that film and recording entrepreneur David Geffen closed on in March 2006 for the top two floors of what was part of the three-story penthouse once owned by Governor Nelson Rockefeller and his first wife, at 810 Fifth Avenue.

In July 2006, a three-bedroom, four-and-a-half bathroom apartment in the building that had belonged to Hugo Bich, chairman of the Bic Group and son of Baron Marcel Bich, founder of the company that makes Bic pens and lighters, sold for $18 million. It was bought by Roy J. Zuckerberg, a former vice-chairman of Goldman Sachs, who is the founder and chairman of Samson Capital Advisors.

The building called 960 unabashedly asserts its aura of solid wealth on the north corner of Fifth Avenue and East 77th Street. Distinguished by a Fifth Avenue entrance that has both a canopy and a marquee, and a façade garlanded by eleven mysterious hooded figures, it enfolds the incomparably fabulous New York anchorages of some of the deepest pocketed influence wielders of the Western World.

Take Venezuelan multibillionaire Gustavo Cisneros and his refined Cincinnati-born wife, Patty, internationally recognized as a vibrant power couple and supreme connoisseurs of art. Their magnificent 960 duplex is an awesome showcase for what is considered the finest collection of South American paintings. Gustavo Cisneros, who occasionally weekends in a private Caribbean villa with the first President George Bush, his wife, Barbara, and former Secretary of Commerce Robert Mosbacher, presides over a vast beer, baseball, and broadcasting empire that makes him one of the most powerful men in Latin America. His global conglomerate of seventy companies include Coca-Cola Bottling, controlling stakes in Spalding

Sports Worldwide and America Online Latin America. He is a shareholder in Univision, a Spanish-language network that has eighteen stations across the U.S.A. The Cisneros Group has the widest reach of any broadcaster in South America. Cisneros' Venevision produces 19,000 hours of programs in Spanish and Portuguese each year, to 40 million households on three continents.

All this allows him unfettered access to high-ranking political and economic officials in nearly forty countries. Who else could orchestrate a scene where Julio Iglesias smooths the jagged moments of a tense energy-investment meeting between President Jiang Zemin of China and President Hugo Chavez of Venezuela by getting everyone to sing a few verses of "When I Left Cuba"?

Or take Canadian-born liquor king, five-times married, ruggedly good-looking Edgar Bronfman Sr., who sold his penthouse at 740 Park Avenue in the late 1970s to move into the handsome, green-awninged, garden-ringed penthouse at 960 Fifth Avenue. He bought this topmost apartment after his divorce from the former Ann Loeb, the mother of his five sons, when he married his second wife, Lady Carolyn Townshend, a classic English blonde who, ten years before they met, had been London's "Debutante of the Year." The splendidly proportioned penthouse, partitioned off from the glass-enclosed rooftop gym via a parapeted bulwark that partially takes away the owner's Central Park view, features architectural grace notes such as walls with all sorts of surprise niches for displaying treasured *objets d'art.* As things turned out, Lady Carolyn never got to occupy the place. By the time the complex renovations were done, the marriage was finished. Shortly after its annulment, and a financial arrangement stipulating that Lady Carolyn may never use the Bronfman name, Bronfman met another young, blue-eyed, blond Englishwoman. Only a couple of years older than his firstborn son, Sam, Georgiana Webb, Edgar Bronfman's next wife, gave him the two daughters he had long wished for soon after they wed.

While he was chairman of Seagram's, Edgar Bronfman Sr. widely extended his family's holdings overseas into oil, real estate, and a $9-billion stake in the chemical giant DuPont. He also made the Bronfmans the most celebrated name in Jewish philanthropy. As president of the World Jewish Congress, he pressured Soviets to release Jewish dissidents. Who else would have the clout to recruit Senator Alfonse D'Amato to hold hearings on Swiss banking profits made at the expense of the Nazis' Jewish victims, and persuade the Clinton administration to force them to pony up $7 billion in reparation forty years after World War II?

The biggest—and some say prettiest—apartment at 960, taking up the full twelfth floor of the building, today belongs to socialite and ballet-patron Anne Bass, the chic Indiana-born, Vassar-graduated ex-wife of Fort Worth billionaire Sid Bass. Her divorce settlement broke all U.S. records in 1989, when she made him pay plenty for wanting to trade her in for a new missus, the Iranian-born Mercedes Tavacoli Kellogg, who also famously bolted out of her marriage to Ambassador Francis Kellogg. Anne's take, which by 2000 had grown to a personal worth of $690 million according to *Forbes*, which that year listed her among a handful of "Near Misses" (you needed $725 million to make the magazine's "400"), included more than one million shares of Disney, the couple's considerable art collection, and the palatial Fifth Avenue apartment her former husband bought in 1984 from Joan Whitney Payson for the then record price of $6 million.

Mrs. Payson, a member of one of New York's most aristocratic old families—the horse-racing, horse-breeding Whitneys, who gave the city the Whitney Museum—knew a thing or two about how to have fun in this life with one's money. Among her acquisitions, besides the sensational apartment at 960, were Van Gogh's $49 million *Irises*, the New York Mets baseball team, and the legendary Kentucky thoroughbred farm, Greentree Stables.

Back in the early 1970s, Mrs. Payson's purchase of the apartment made news for the $900,000 she paid to the estate of Andrew Mellon's daughter Ailsa Mellon Bruce, of the Pittsburgh banking millions. The somewhat eccentric Mrs. Bruce had moved into it after selling her other huge and extraordinary apartment in the building to Newport heiress Sunny von Bülow. That purchase would later catapult the building into tabloid fame, when the two attempted-murder trials of Claus von Bülow became the most talked-about society scandal on the East Coast and eventually was turned into a movie, *Reversal of Fortune*, starring Jeremy Irons.

Anne Bass is hardly the only one to end up with an enviable apartment at 960 Fifth Avenue after her husband quite publicly took a shine to another woman. Like Anne Bass—who quickly got into the social swim of things in New York by throwing great benefit parties for the likes of Peter Martins, the handsome Danish dance star who succeeded George Balanchine as head of the New York City Ballet, and for world-famous heart surgeon Dr. Michael de Bakey, who heads one of her favorite Texas charities—Lady

Patricia Rothemere, better known by her nickname "Bubbles," an effusive London social figure, started her second act in this building. The former wife of powerful British press lord Vere Rothemere, she took up residence at 960 Fifth Avenue after he left her for a young Chinese beauty in the 1980s and moved to Paris. Bubbles Rothemere wasted no time. Almost instantly, with her big smile, in her big, floating, silken gowns and colorful turbans, she became one of the prominent international hostesses, and toast of the town in her newly adopted city.

Contrary to persistent gossip, this is not the building where silver-screen star Gloria Swanson, immortalized by Billy Wilder's *Sunset Boulevard,* was kept in great style by Joseph Kennedy, patriarch of the political dynasty. Swanson's maisonette was in fact at 920 Fifth Avenue, on another block of this street of dreams.

This loftiest peak of Manhattan's residential real estate, however, has always sheltered its share of well-provided-for widows and divorcées. One of those was Brownie McLean, famous for the parties she gave in the building and the role she played in the April in Paris Ball, which for three decades reigned as America's biggest and most glamorous international charity event. Usually, the apartments of these widows and divorcées are outstanding articulations of personal style, as these often attractive, artistic, and fashion-conscious women know how to surround themselves with the tasteful things of this world they now can afford to indulge in to their heart's content. Two such polished, pedigreed creatures currently live at 960, though each keeps a relatively low profile. One of them is Kit Gill, a supermodel of the 1970s who appeared in the pages of *Vogue* and *Harper's Bazaar* but is perhaps best remembered as every New York designer's favorite runway star—a tall, slim show-stopper with all-American outdoorsy elegance, especially notable for her long, leggy thoroughbred stride. Her brother-in-law, independent filmmaker Tom DiCillo, was the first to discover the screen potential of future movie stars Brad Pitt and Catherine Keener in such well-received indies as *Living in Oblivion, Johnny Suede,* and *The Real Blonde.* The other is the pretty art historian Patricia Altschul, third wife and widow of financier, philanthropist, and art collector Arthur G. Altschul. Son of a senior partner at Lazard Frères & Co., and one of the most successful financiers of his time, Arthur cut quite a swath in New York's megabucks world of deal- making as a general partner of Goldman Sachs, while simultaneously serving as chairman of General American Investors and head of the Altschul family's Overbrook Foundation, which has administered over $150 million to charitable causes in recent years. Patricia and her husband traveled a lot in pursuit of their mutual passion for American art, but also created one of the world's most important collections of French neo-impressionism, or pointillism.

Art collecting, in fact, is remarkable among current owners at 960. Wealthy Denver oilman and former Inexco chairman Erving Wolf lives in a grand simplex filled with museum-caliber furniture—mostly by Frank Lloyd Wright. Wolf's son is married to Maya Lin, designer of the Vietnam Memorial in Washington, D.C., whose surface simplicity melds intellectual complexity into works of enduring power. Her latest project—also a few words carved into stone artworks—in honor of explorers Lewis and Clark—stands in the water at a Columbia River confluence point where the Nez Perce, Sioux, Cheyenne, and Shoshone tribes all gathered.

Charles Lazarus, founder and chairman of Toys "R" Us and Kids "R" Us, and his wife, Joan, amassed amazing examples of art nouveau, art deco, Tiffany lamps, early twentieth-century furniture, paintings and drawings by the Blue Rider group of German expressionists as well as the Austrian expressionist Egon Schiele. Henri Fraise, part of a big, successful French clan who divide the year between Paris and New York, all living in the top buildings in Manhattan; Dr. John Weber of Newport, who was married to Campbell Soup heiress Charlotte Colket Weber; Palm Beach society leaders and multimillionaires Emilia and Pepe Fanjul; and Ned Evans, who seesaws between New York and a beautiful horse farm in Virginia, all maintain apartments at 960, decorated with the finest eighteenth-century French and English antiques and European paintings. Retail giant Andrew Saul is a daring and eclectic contemporary art collector. Kentuckian Wendell Cherry, former chairman and cofounder of Humana Inc., the vast health-care company, who bought the von Bülow duplex in 1988 for $6.5 million, possessed some iconic works by Modigliani. One of them, a stunning depiction of Jeanne Hébuterne, Modigliani's last lover and muse—a twenty-two-year-old who was so disconsolate over his early death that she soon after committed suicide—was recently consigned by Wendell Cherry's widow Dotty to Sotheby's where it sold at auction for $21,008,000. And few residents at 960 forget the many wondrous objects, such as the rare Meissen group of Harlequin and Columbine parrots dating back to 1746, accumulated by Judge Irwin Untermeyer in his far-famed apartment that had a colossal sixty-by-twenty-five-foot salon. So valuable was the stuff he eventually bequeathed to the Metropolitan Museum that the illustrious C. Douglas Dillon, who also lived at 960 and was at the time head of the Met's board of trustees, asked Claus von Bülow, who was at that time head of the building's co-op board, to let some of the priceless porcelain and precious furniture travel down the passenger elevator instead of the back way.

Presently, two major New York art dealers reside at 960. They are man-about-town Richard Feigen and Robert Ellsworth, who is a brother-in-law of C. Douglas Dillon. The former head of Dillon Read & Company, which was later purchased by Citigroup, Dillon served as ambassador to France under President Eisenhower and was secretary of treasury in President Kennedy's cabinet. An avid collector of eighteenth- and nineteenth-century paintings, this most versatile Wall Street financier, though by nature shy, was for decades, until his death at ninety-three in 2002, one of the biggest play-ers on the city's cultural, economic, and social scene. Though this man of patrician graces was born into great wealth, he was, in fact, only twice removed from the meager existence of his Jewish immigrant grandfather from Poland. It was his father, Clarence Dillon, who founded Dillon Read. The young international banking house made headlines around the world in 1925, with the biggest-ever deal in the history of the automobile indus-try. Following the sudden, untimely deaths of brothers John and Horace Dodge, in 1920—one from influenza, one from pneumonia, just months apart—through a shrewd and brilliantly negotiated package by Clarence Dillon's financial firm, the widows received the then astronomical sum of $146 million for the company, which is still a strong brand today. This much money was unheard of in an era when a brand new Ford cost some-where between $260 and $660. Douglas Dillon's intellect was apparent to his parents very early on, and they began to shape it by enrolling him in elite private schools. At Pine Lodge School in Lakehurst, New Jersey, he became close friends with his schoolmates Nelson and Laurance Rockefeller and John Rockefeller III. He later graduated from Harvard. For twenty years, the Dillon family had owned Chateau Haut Brion vineyards, which produce a fine Bordeaux wine. This prepared Dillon for his future ambassadorship and also kindled his interest in art. After his stint in government, he returned to Wall Street, but when he was elected president and later chairman of the board of the Metropolitan Museum of Art, where he had been a trustee, the work came to fascinate him so much that he spent most of his time there during the next decade. He donated much of the fine artwork he had personally collected to the Met and is credited with nearly single-handedly building the museum's Chinese painting collection.

Probably no other single habitat in America can boast of such an impressive coming together of highly cultivated art lovers and discerning aesthetes. But perhaps nothing attests to the attractiveness and desirability of 960 Fifth Avenue more than the fact that it was the choice of residence for that *ne plus ultra* of timeless, elegant, but unpretentious and distinctively upper-class American taste, Mrs. Henry Parish II. Better know as Sister Parish, the internationally celebrated interior decorator had worked her magic on a series of grand houses and apartments, including the Long Island estate of Mr. and Mrs. William Paley and the Park Avenue home of Brooke Astor. Her *joie de vivre,* love of romance, and intuitive sense of luxurious comfort established her as the last word in evoking both fastidious grandeur and patrician coziness. It was to Sister Parish that first lady Jackie Kennedy turned when she needed an official decorator for the White House. Mrs. Parish got a terrific kick out of a newspaper headline at the time: "Kennedys Pick Nun to Decorate White House." A woman with an Edwardian aura and a Social Register background, who had bucked the caste system by setting herself up in business during the Great Depression, she had a profound sense of her own family's influence and of the lighthearted, flower-upholstered country houses of her childhood summers in Far Hills, New Jersey, and Dark Harbor, Maine. Yet she was driven by a slightly irreverent, irrepressible spirit of her own, favoring robin's egg blues, coral pinks, and apple greens for formal rooms—when most European interior designers dictated subtle hues known as "demitones." With her equally creative partner, the Tennessean Albert Hadley—who had a thorough understanding of the sleek, tailored, modern idiom, and a flair for such unexpected touches as silver-leaf ceilings and zebra rugs—Parish-Hadley Associates soon became America's preeminent design firm. Sister, by the way, named her youngest daughter "Apple," sixty years before Gwyneth Paltrow bemusedly chose the name for her firstborn baby girl.

"We were blessed to have Sister living here," reminisces one resident at 960. It was Sister who created this "wonderful, very low-key lobby. And then the building's board asked her to decorate the Georgian Suite, our very own four-star restaurant that has its special entrance—and separate address—3 East 77th Street." The building's in-house restaurant—actually two separate dining rooms and a fully staffed kitchen with a proper chef in a starched white toque—is indeed splendid. With its white Georgian pillars and lovely egg-and-dart molding, it is both formal and intimate, conducive to congeniality—Sister Parish's style—and could easily be the private dining room of an embassy. There is often a palpable excitement in the room among the various power people who live in this A-plus domicile, as they lean into the elegantly set, candle-lit tables, sip champagne, and engage in animated talk. In the past, friends of the building's residents—hosted with the chef's felicitous five-course meals—have included German Chancellor Helmut Schmidt and Prime Minister Raymond Barre of France. Claus von Bülow is generally credited with bringing the talented and polite Alain Tripeau over from France, where he had been previously the private chef in the great houses of the Patiño and Rothschild families. His most popular specialty among apartment owners is his foie-gras-and-truffle-stuffed chicken, Poularde Chimay. The kitchen staff is capable of pleasing tenants in infinite ways: baking up a batch of croissants for breakfast, whisking up to the apartment a fancy plate of *crudités* at cocktail time; delivering dinner on a tray; providing all the elements, including waiters, for a sit-down dinner for twelve in one of the upstairs suites or a dinner dance for 120 downstairs at the Georgian Suite. At Christmas, little girls in lace-frosted velvet dresses and boys looking like modern versions of Little Lord Fauntleroy scurry across the two dining rooms. Edgar Bronfman hosts a formal Passover meal each spring during the holidays. And once a month, the chef prepares dinner for the tenants to dine together. Perhaps because of the building's private restaurant, perhaps because these congenial neighbors have lived together longer—since apartments are not frequently sold or bought—there appears to be more special synergy between apartment owners in this co-op than in most New York structures of vertical cohabitation.

In the smooth social stew of quite diverse individuals under one roof at 960, one controversial protuberance, albeit for only a short time, was Pierre A. Rinfret, a millionaire economist who attempted to unseat two-time incumbent Mario Cuomo in New York's gubernatorial race of 1990. His gaffes during the campaign became legend. This anything but humble candidate bragged about his five university degrees and two Fulbright scholarships. He claimed to have been a consultant for more than two hundred leading corporations and advisor to three U.S. presidents. But he turned out to be an embarrassment for the Republicans. He raised little money and seemed to have only a tenuous grasp of the issues. Even though Cuomo's popularity was flagging at the time, Rinfret lagged far behind in the polls. Two weeks before election day, he threatened to quit the race and go sailing. He alienated prominent politicians of his own party, who in turn called him "a buffoon" and "a laughing stock." To his credit, he vanished from politics but was not vanquished. He continued to publish his lists of Famous and Infamous Crooks and Dedicated Public Servants, featuring capsule profiles of notables he met because, he claimed, "I have seen the compromising of integrity for personal gain and I have seen the good get raped every which way by thieves, liars and cheats. I have seen careers destroyed because individuals stood up against the cheats and the phonies." It is rumored that Rinfret bought his 960 apartment, which had belonged to Judge Untermeyer, for under $100,000, at a time in the early 1970s when the bottom was falling out of New York's real estate market, and that he sold it for $8 million in the early 1990s. It was one of the colossal duplexes, with a gigantic dining room that matched his ego and a living room that once was one of several private ballrooms in the building.

"It's just about the best building in Manhattan," says real estate maven Alice Mason, who put 960 at the top of the list of her five personal favorite co-ops in a *W* magazine interview. "It was built as a co-op, so a lot of people had apartments designed according to their own plans. Judge Untermeyer's apartment, which I sold years ago, had 20-foot ceilings in the library, living and dining rooms, with three master bedrooms each on the floors above and below. Several other people in the building built two-story living rooms. The von Bülow apartment which I sold to Wendell Cherry, had 15-foot ceilings." "This is the crowning achievement of architect Rosario Candela," comments Kirk Henckels, Harvard-educated director of Stribling Private Brokerage. "These grand apartments facing Fifth in the principal portion of the building, most of which have different layouts, are extremely sophisticated, complex, interlaced spaces. And in the back of this, fronting 77th Street, there are about 50 smaller pied-à-terre size units, all of which share the private dining room and exercise room." Until recently, there was maid and laundry service for the entire building. Shirts were washed, ironed, and brought to the back door within two hours. "And the apartment house has the best on-site managing agent. I don't see how you could do better."

In recent years, even the smaller apartments were occupied by socially prominent families such as John and Noreen Drexel of Newport and

Alexander Mellon Laughlin, who is currently the head of the co-op board at 960. The late Hedy Kravis, first wife of financier Henry Kravis, and a gifted decorator, had put together several smaller units facing East 77th Street into a very attractive spread.

More than mere snob appeal explains the concentration of so many aesthetically oriented millionaires at 960 Fifth Avenue. What makes this building so special is that it has a level of quality and detail not seen today, and obtained even in the 1920s, when it was built, only at a very high price. Most of the city's spectacularly large apartments were created in that period. The complex went up in 1927, at a time when apartment suite planning had developed into a high art, and Rosario Candela, the architect who generally gets credit for it, was at the apex of his creativity. The building was officially designed by Warren and Wetmore (the main architects of Grand Central Terminal), along with Rosario Candela, plus Cross and Cross as supervising architects for the famous developer of the era, Anthony Campagna. (Campagna was the developer of one of New York's most prestigious international hotels, the Pierre, also on Fifth Avenue.) To make room for this co-op of sedate grandeur, one of the fanciest private palaces on "Millionaire's Row"—as the series of opulent family mansions belonging to the likes of Astors, Vanderbilts, and Rhinelanders on old Fifth Avenue were known—had to be sacrificed to the wrecker's ball. This was the bombastic 130-room mansion of U. S. Senator William Clark, a copper king from Montana. The structure was as famous for its elaborate, white, wedding-cake stonework tower as for its over-the-top gold-leaf-decked interior.

According to Robert A. M. Stern, dean of the Yale School of Architecture and currently the lead designer of a full-block neoclassical apartment going up at 15 Central Park West (where the Mayflower Hotel used to be and where hedge fund mogul Daniel Loeb has already signed a contract to pay $45 million for the penthouse), the new complex was inspired by New York's great old apartment houses like 960, built by the two most influential architects of the 1920s, James Carpenter and Rosario Candela. "How they distributed people in the apartments, how they strung a lot of rooms together through long corridors, sometimes enfiladed, and other ways. How they handled service was quite ingenious. So was the way the various apartments inside interlock in clever ways. They had very elegant distribution of rooms through foyers and staircases and lines of sight, or blocking lines of sight and then shifting you off axis."

Although Candela's apartments are more often likened to the smaller palaces of Europe—specifically the manner in which one room opens onto the next, and again into the next and so forth through great double doors—Yale's Stern is less interested in the antecedents of Candela's ideas than in his innovations. "He had a mathematical turn of mind. Loved to put puzzles together. He was a cryptographer during World War II and broke the Japanese code. He preceded by decades what was thought so revolutionary about Le Corbusier's interlocking apartments."

The greatest glory of apartment houses like 960 that were going up mostly in the 1920s, and shaping the character of Fifth Avenue as it exists today, was actually not the face they presented to the world. Although they possessed attractive facades in a variety of historical styles, and decidedly embellished the streetscape, their real contribution to architectural history and urban sociology lay in the inventiveness of their floor plans. After decades of uncertainty, the societal changes following WWI had finally made apartment living an acceptable alternative to private town houses. Rosario Candela and his contemporaries, most notably his predecessor, James Carpenter, understood that, if this promise was to be fulfilled, the planning of apartments had to be so skillful that the very fact that these were multiple dwellings had to be obscured. So they perfected a sort of blueprint that separated the apartments at Fifth Avenue and Park Avenue's supreme addresses from those of ordinary New Yorkers' flats. Accordingly, the entrance hall or gallery was the pivotal point of the apartment. In a large unit, it became the fourth room in a series of reception spaces that included living room, dining room, and library, giving immediate visual orientation to those rooms. In smaller units, the foyer was the circulation hub for the entire apartment. To many architectural historians today, Candela stands as the preeminent designer of luxury apartments in America. His buildings, it is said, were the grandest in a decade that was itself the greatest for building in New York.

Born in Palermo in 1890, Candela came to America in 1909 to work with his father, a plasterer. He entered Columbia University's School of Architecture at nineteen, with hardly any knowledge of English. But from his very first luxury building in 1922, the somewhat baroque Clayton Arms on Broadway and 92nd Street, to his last, the sleek, white, modernist courtyard apartment on the northeast corner of Madison Avenue and 72nd Street, his touch was sure and true. Working successfully with a group of Italian-born builders and developers—Gaetano Ajello, Anthony Campagna, and Michael Paterno—Candela moved progressively eastward from Riverside Drive and West End Avenue to Fifth Avenue and Park Avenue, just as the luxury apartment trend had moved across town. By 1927, he had twenty-five buildings to his credit. Meanwhile Ajello, a fellow Sicilian who gave Candela his first job, stayed on the West Side, building more ornate buildings with his signature pilaster-framed entrances, some of which have been designated landmarks. Candela's buildings on the other hand grew simpler and more sedately grand on the outside, while inside his veritable jigsaw puzzle of simplexes, duplexes, triplexes, maisonette apartments, roof garden apartments, and penthouses with private elevators that opened directly into the apartments could fulfill any millionaire's dreams. When 960 Fifth Avenue was completed in November 1928, the interior of the thirteen-story limestone building had been sold as raw space to many of its residents. But that alone does not account for the unique design of the building, in which duplexes and simplexes were juxtaposed on floors of inconsistent and unusual heights. Knitting together the pieces, Candela's careful mix of layouts for the various apartments allowed extra ceiling height to be given to most of the entertaining rooms. Much of the beauty inside, as a result, comes from the drama that many of the individual units feature more than one level, with, say, a three- or four-step drop into the living room or drawing room. The largest apartments have five bedrooms and fourteen windows on 77th Street, and ten windows on Fifth Avenue for their three big entertaining rooms—living room, dining room, and library. Critics applauded Candela's respect for privacy within the apartments (two family members could simultaneously entertain two different sets of visitors) and his eye for significant details. Candela was the consummate conceptualizer. He added duplicate water connections to street mains and multiple switches for ceiling lights. He loved finely turned staircases and separate wine cellars. One particularly expansive duplex, specifically designed for Dr. Preston Pope Satterwhite inside the original 960, became known far and wide as the grandest living quarters to be found in an American apartment house. It contained seventeen rooms, including a two-story, sixty-by-twenty-five-foot living room that had a truly extraordinary, ceremonial, triple-run double staircase leading to the master bedroom. Too bad; this bedroom was occupied solely by Dr. Satterwhite, a widower.

By 1929, a mystique had grown up around Candela's apartments, as if he had a monopoly on luxury. If there was one New Yorker of the 1980s who understood luxury in all its ramifications and fine points, that was the overwhelmingly urbane, sharp-witted, somewhat mysterious society figure Claus von Bülow. A physically imposing Danish aristocrat, always impeccably—almost dandyishly—turned out in his bespoke London suits, Battistoni shirts, and exquisite custom-made shoes, he was a former barrister in the employ of the legendary oil billionaire Paul Getty, working as his personal troubleshooter. He was well-read, well-versed in classical music, eighteenth-century art, and decorative history. He was an epicure and a highly stimulating raconteur. One noted Manhattan hostess described him as "not so much too good as too grand to be true." Externals were important in Claus von Bülow's life, and when he married the Grace Kelly look-alike Sunny von Auersperg, the former Martha Crawford, who had previously been the wife of an Austrian prince and was one of America's richest heiresses, it seemed natural that the couple would live in one of the grandest apartments, even by Fifth Avenue standards. Nearly every object in the fourteen-room, eighth-floor apartment overlooking Central Park was of museum quality. This was in addition to the couple's ravishing mansion, set on ten acres overlooking the sea in Newport, Rhode Island. This, Clarendon Court, the iron-gated Newport house with a sweeping curved courtyard, was the location of the two alleged murder attempts—the attempts to inject his diabetic wife with deadly doses of insulin—of which Claus von Bülow was accused and for which he was tried twice. Prosecutors were convinced von Bülow wanted to murder his wealthy wife in order to inherit millions and marry the younger, comely, soap-opera actress and socialite Alexandra Isles with whom he was having an affair.

In February 1982, von Bülow stood trial on national television. The state's case rested on circumstantial evidence, a mysterious black bag filled with drugs, a maid's observations, and testimony from Sunny's two grieving children from her previous marriage. On March 16, 1982, von Bülow was found guilty and sentenced to thirty years in prison. However, the British-educated lawyer and Danish businessman, whose parents divorced when he was still a young boy and whose mother spirited him off to England during the German invasion of Denmark because she disapproved of the father sympathizing with the Germans, decided to fight back. He hired high-powered Harvard law professor Alan Dershowitz to appeal his case.

Dershowitz managed to discover several inconsistencies in the medical and scientific evidence presented at the first trial. Two years after the first verdict, the Rhode Island State Supreme Court reversed von Bülow's conviction. Armed with new medical evidence, his attorneys were able to persuade the jury that von Bülow was a man wrongly accused. In May 1985, he was found not guilty.

One resident at 960 remembers the von Bülows' apartment filled with costly artifacts that had rich back stories. Claus von Bülow used to regale guests with stories about the portrait of King Christian VII of Denmark, which hung in the sprawling drawing room, and how he had died of syphillis and drink. He liked to explain that the marble of the dining room table, which everyone mistook for green malachite, in fact was blue azurite, and that the silver-framed photographs of Sunny were taken by the famous photographer of movie stars, Horst. As revealed by John Richardson and Dominick Dunne in various *Vanity Fair* articles, both old acquaintances of the von Bülows, early in their marriage the couple seemed to make an effort to live up to their sumptuous surroundings at 960 Fifth Avenue. They entertained lavishly among life-sized portraits from the 1700s by Sir Joshua Reynolds and George Romney, a Langlois commode "every bit as fine as ones at Buckingham Palace," great silver pieces by Paul Storr, half-a-million-dollar candelabras, million-dollar antique tureens, delicate Longton Hall sauce boats, Chelsea bonbon dishes, and elaborate bouquets in the random-looking English fashion that were Sunny's personal, creative touches. Yet happiness sadly eluded this couple who seemed to have everything. In spite of the French couture gowns, this once smashingly beautiful woman,—who in Richardson's words was "much more literate and serious and good-hearted than most poor little rich girls"—and the charming, amusing, courtly Claus—who at 6 feet 4 inches in his sable-collared overcoat was hard to miss as he entered the most glamorous parties on two continents—blew it. Their friends from around the world—princes like Dodo Ruspoli, princesses like Ann-Marie von Bismarck—who were invited to their magnificently appointed quarters were bewildered when an evening's invitation would be abruptly canceled at the last minute. They were saddened that such an attractive couple, with three children, were losing affection and respect for each other and sinking into boredom, mistrust, reclusiveness, and eventually tragedy. During the murder trials in Rhode Island, some of the Old Guard families closed rank. One of the most respected grand dames of the resort, however, testified as a character witness for Claus. Meanwhile, his distinguished neighbors at 960 Fifth Avenue generally took a dim view of the long-running scandal, with its daily unsavory tidbits served up by both the *New York Post* and the *News*. When Claus allowed his new mistress, a flamboyant Hungarian divorcée named Andrea Reynolds, to move in—and supposedly wear Sunny's jewels—he brought the wrath of the reticent, publicity-hating residents of 960 upon himself. The charismatic Cambridge-educated Dane, who for eleven years had served as head of the co-op board in Manhattan's most exclusive building, was unmistakably made to feel that being accused of murder, even if he was eventually found innocent, was unacceptable conduct in such a building. Before he would be asked outright to leave, Claus's pride, presence of mind, and inbred aristocratic reserve kicked in. He sold the duplex. He is presently living quietly in London. Meanwhile, Sunny von Bülow—her always well-coifed hair regularly cut and curled, her nails manicured weekly, her favorite random mix of fresh-cut flowers in a vase next to her bed—languishes in a coma after more than twenty years, in a private room at the exclusive top-floor pavillion of a New York hospital.

740 Park Avenue

· 6 ·

---

740 PARK AVENUE

ALL THAT PARK AVENUE STANDS FOR

*I*F THERE IS one building that sums up the saga of New York social aspiration, and the rewards at the tippy top of the American dream, that building has to be 740 Park Avenue. Considered by many of today's New Yorkers the end-all and be-all, the glittering prize of corporate success, good connections, decorous demeanor, and sheer wealth, this splendid seventy-five-year-old art deco co-op on the northwest corner of 71st Street and Park Avenue, is all that. But the building is also a microcosm of lives lived large in a city of ever-shifting demographic and economic realities. It contains an overarching story of the making, showing off, and squandering of fortunes in changing times.

The latest wave of cash-rich American successes attracted to the multi-million-dollar dwellings at 740 Park Avenue are, like David Ganek who, in May 2005 paid $19 million for the duplex apartment of Rand V. Araskog, the former chairman of ITT Industries, high-profile hedge fund moguls. Besides trophy real estate, they collect major art—Monets, Picassos, Jackson Pollocks, Warhols bought at record-breaking prices at international auctions—plus such news-making purchases as the $8 million paid for the fourteen-foot tiger shark submerged in formaldehyde by controversial British artist Damien Hirst.

If these examples of the meritocracy boom on Wall Street, now basking in the efflorescence of art patronage, mirror their times, so the rich pageant of residents past colorfully reflect theirs. The cast of characters included courtly but canny John D. Rockefeller Jr.; debonair "Black Jack" Bouvier, father of Jacqueline Kennedy Onassis; Francis P. Garvan, the socially prominent prosecutor of one of New York's most sensational murder cases, railroad millionaire Harry Thaw's murder of architect Stanford White; vivacious jet-set princess and Standard Oil heiress Peggy Bedford Bancroft d'Arenberg D'Uzes, who, like those other vibrant Parisian party-lovers, the Aly Khan and Porfirio Rubirosa, met her end prematurely in a late-night car crash in the Bois de Boulogne; the flamboyant chairman of Time Warner, Steve Ross; the socially ubiquitous chairman of Norton Simon, David Mahoney; the Ecuadorian Noboa family of the Bonito banana billions; Singapore entrepreneur C.C. Wang; His Royal Highness Nawaff bin Abd al-Aziz bin Abd Rahman Al Saud, one of the forty-three sons of Saudi Arabia's King Abdul Aziz bin Abdul al-Rahman Al Saud, known as King Ibn Saud, and a brother of both the late King Fahd and his successor, King Abdulah, who in 1992 sold his apartment to Austrian financier Wolfgang Flöttl, who was married to the granddaughter of President Dwight D. Eisenhower, Anne; Revlon chief Ronald Perelman, who left the building when he gave up his first wife, Faith Golding; and those highest flyers of the 1980s go-go market, with their lavishly spending, photogenic trophy wives, buyout king Henry Kravis and takeover tycoon Saul Steinberg.

But perhaps almost as amazing are the co-op board turndowns in this building, for among them were Elizabeth Taylor, Joan Crawford, Barbra Streisand, and Neil Sedaka. Clearly, the board at 740 Park was wary of show business celebrities. The only well-known film person who lived in the building was the screenwriter of such hits as *Butch Cassidy and the Sundance Kid:* William Goldman. And whether formally or informally, there was also anti-Semitism evinced in the building during its early years.

Part of the magnificent assemblage of six of the most extraordinary status apartment buildings ever produced by a New York architect, this seventeen-story structure, with its two chic, gleaming, green-gray marble doorframes and geometric brass entrances subtly flanked by art deco columns, is considered Rosario Candela's most inspired work. According to architectural historian Elizabeth Hawes, the building represented "all that Park Avenue stood for on the eve of the Depression: solidity, security, and the height of luxury." This leitmotif runs through the interiors and is expressed via exquisite detailing—moldings, parquet floors, balustraded stairways, and unusually impressive entry halls.

740 Park Avenue was the pride and joy of Candela, whose most significant trait was designing buildings from the inside out—placing windows where they received light, balanced a room, and allowed for the most attractive arrangement of furniture. He liked unpredictable patterns of windows and perfected the use of architectural setbacks on the top floors, which add so much beauty and drama today to the penthouse towers and the overall elegance of rooflines on both Park Avenue and Fifth Avenue. At the time, Rosario Candela was so highly regarded as an architect of upper-crust high rises that the apartment suites in his buildings needed no promotion. They literally sold themselves.

The building started going up in September 1929, just before the stock market crash, when bankruptcies were rife and demand for palatial apartments was weak. It replaced the Presbyterian Hospital Nurses Home, a row house, and the Park Avenue houses of George Brewster and builder James Lee.

The Brewsters were descendents of the leader of the Plymouth Colony. James Lee, a real estate developer, was the grandfather of Jacqueline Kennedy Onassis. Once finished, the building became a magnet for the richest, oldest families in the country: Social Register couples named Borden, Schermerhorn, Hoppin, Scoville, and Thorne, as well as a procession of heirs to such classic American brands as Gulf Oil, the New York Central Railroad, Anaconda Copper, Chrysler, Havemeyer Sugar, International Harvester, Campbell Soup, Seagram's liquor, Saks Fifth Avenue, Avon products, and Estée Lauder cosmetics. Outside the walls of their homes at 740 Park, these men and women, who included the top executives of Chase Bank, American Express, and U.S. Rubber, were shaping America both economically and culturally.

740 Park Avenue was the childhood home of Jacqueline Bouvier, and the adult home of the department store tycoon Marshall Field and the founder of *Look* magazine, Gardener Cowles—two New York, postwar-era exemplars of both substance and style.

The building, which boasts some of the most exquisitely laid out triplex apartments, is also known as 71 East 71st Street, the side entrance being the preferred address used by some of the building's more low-profile, Old Guard residents. One of these was the late Isabel Morris Ledyard, a New York blue blood whose husband was both president of the New York Public Library and the personal attorney of J. P. Morgan.

In truth, the apartments with the 71st Street address, in the west wing of the building, have some of the more preferred views, looking out toward Fifth Avenue and the greenery of Central Park rather than onto Park Avenue, which in some people's minds is a four-lane highway, albeit one with a flower bed in the middle.

The crowning apartment in the complex, which from the start was billed as "the most expensive, the most exclusive, simply the best apartment house in the world," was the spacious duplex, expanded to a triplex, and reconfigured into a duplex, where John D. Rockefeller Jr. lived from the 1930s to the 1970s.

The building started out as a co-op, then during the Depression, when there were not enough patrician bodies to fill the place, became a rental until 1952, when it was bought by Rockefeller from New York real estate tycoon William Zeckendorf. Rockefeller is remembered as the building's savior, for he offered residents the option to buy their apartments. The John D. Rockefeller apartment at one time had thirty-seven rooms, fourteen bathrooms, eleven working fireplaces, forty-three closets, and his and hers saunas. Another apartment in the building employed a service staff of sixteen. At the height of the Reagan years, the Rockefeller apartment, redecorated by Juan Pablo Molyneux, became a much photographed mega-bucks showplace. It belonged to 1980s corporate raider Saul Steinberg and his tall, stylish, brunette wife, Gayfryd, who sat on several high-profile charity committees and liked to entertain. In 2000, Steinberg sold the former Rockefeller duplex to Stephen Schwarzman, head of the Blackstone Group and currently one of the most fabulously rich Wall Street deal makers, for what was then a record price for a Manhattan apartment: $37 million.

The Blackstone biggie, whose stature as the chief of one of the country's most efficient money-making machines has been enhanced by sitting on all the right charity boards, including those of the New York Public Library and the New York City Ballet, enjoys all the accoutrements of success these days: a corporate Gulf stream plane and Sikorsky helicopter; a place in the South of France; socializing with New York's most glamorous media catalysts, people such as Mike Nichols, Paula Zahn, and Ahmet Ertegun. A man of determined vigor, recently he was heard shouting "yahoo" as he was about to collect $42 million on his empty East Hampton, ocean-front lot from Yahoo!'s CEO Terry Semel. According to the *New York Post,* neighbors of the sociable Schwarzman were incensed when he mowed down trees to increase the 15.8-acre spread's expanse of ocean view, thereby adding to its marketability. Meanwhile, Schwarzman has acquired the late Carter Burden's lovely Mark Hampton-designed bayside estate in Water Mill, Long Island, for $34 million.

Schwarzman is one of contemporary New York's most ambitious and successful players. A self-made Yale graduate with a degree from the Harvard Business School, he makes $100 million a year. In 2005, he bought a fabled Fatio mansion in Palm Beach, which once belonged to financier Patrick Lannan but was originally built for E. F. Hutton. Soon after he famously got into trouble with the resort's watchdog preservationists for tearing down part of the designated landmark treasure. Schwarzman, who is married to an energetic, outgoing lawyer named Christine (briefly married to Austin Hearst, a scion of the Hearst publishing company), is the latest head of the John F. Kennedy Center for the Performing Arts in Washington, D.C. The Blackstone Group, with its $27 billion worth of private equity funds and its propensity to cash in its stakes quickly, sprinkles more than $700 million a year across Wall Street.

Henry Kravis, whose company competes with Blackstone and who, like Saul Steinberg, made millions through leveraged buyouts, lived at 740 for several years, starting in the mid-1980s. The apartment that he bought with his publicity-loving second wife, the lissome, brunette fashion designer Carolyne Roehm, who had been an assistant to Oscar de la Renta before Kravis provided the funds to launch her own line of well-received clothes, had belonged to George Ohrstrom, a private equity investor, and his fine-boned equestrian wife, Sandra, a former fashion model. Although Sandra Ohrstrom did not want to move out when the couple divorced, her husband wanted to sell the apartment, because it was around the summer of 1985 that both the price of apartments in the building began to appreciate considerably and maintenances were starting to escalate in major ways. The building was becoming what it originally was meant to be. By this time, Kravis had formed the merchant banking firm of Kohlberg, Kravis and Roberts, and his fortune was estimated at $300 million. Kravis was just beginning to emerge as a public figure, and although Steinberg and Perelman already lived at 740, he encountered considerable resistance. Some say that Carolyne being a designer might have also figured into the equation. It was ultimately John French, an early venture capitalist from an old Southern family with a history of financial ups and downs, who got the Oklahoma-raised Kravis approved by the building's co-op board. It helped that Kravis, like French, was a staunch supporter of Ronald Reagan. Carolyne, like Gayfryd Steinberg, brought a lot of attention to the building. The Kravis wedding, at which live doves were released to take flight, made the newspapers. So did the lavish decorating by the design firm of Denning and Foucade, which installed faux-marble walls and huge Sargent, Sisley, and Pissarro paintings. Carolyne also gave an opulent dinner party, for which she rented the Temple of Dendur at the Metropolitan Museum. All this brought a burst of publicity upon the couple in such glossy publications as *Manhattan, Inc., Esquire, W,* and *Town & Country* magazine, but most famously in an issue of *Fortune* devoted to trophy wives, titled "The CEO's Second Wife." It turned out that Henry Kravis, a quiet, serious businessman, didn't like all this noise. In 1993, the marriage broke up, and though Carolyne was hoping to keep the apartment at 740 Park, Kravis gave her the couple's Connecticut house instead. But when a year later Henry Kravis married French-Canadian economist Marie-Josée Drouin, he bought a triplex penthouse for his new bride at 625 Park Avenue. Built by that other famous luxury-apartment architect of the 1920s, J. E. R. Carpenter, the new Kravis apartment was once owned by cosmetics queen Helena Rubinstein and later by Princess Ashraf Pahlavi, the twin sister of the Shah of Iran.

The marital discord, divorces, and remarriages in the building are legendary. One famous story, of an estranged wife who refused to surrender the couple's apartment, had the husband changing the locks one night while she was out. Arriving home while the family fortress was still in the process of being resecured, the wife immediately returned fire by calling in her own troop of locksmiths. The result was not appreciated by the neighbors: warring hardware trucks were parked in front of the building. In the end, the husband won. He now lives in the apartment with a new wife.

According to real estate agents, the co-op board at 740 Park will not even consider a prospective buyer whose net assets are less than $100 million. Among 740's residents are some of the richest men in the world: David Koch of Koch Industries, the second largest private company in the United States; George David, chief executive of United Technologies; much-married hedge fund manager and descendent of Declaration of Independence signer Charles Porter Stevenson; Kent M. Swig, cochairman of Terra Holdings, which owns Brown Harris Stevens and Halstead Property; fabulously wealthy Greek shipping heir Spyros Niarchos; Courtney Ross Andrews, widow of the man who merged the two media giants Time Inc. and Warner Bros.; the patriarch of one of South America's richest and socially prominent clans, Julio Mario Santo Domingo, and his wife, Beatrice.

So rare is it that one of the dream dwellings in this building comes on the market, and so coveted are they, that they are usually swooped up right away. An example in 2006 was the relatively small gem of a penthouse, with only two bedrooms, that had belonged to the late Enid A. Haupt, an heiress to the Annenberg fortune who was once editor-in-chief of *Seventeen* magazine as well as one of America's most generous philanthropists; she gave the magical, glass-domed conservatory to the New York Botanical Garden in the Bronx. Located on the seventeenth and eighteenth floors, with terrace views on both levels of both Park Avenue and Central Park, and notable for its resplendent elliptical staircase, the apartment almost immediately sold for the high asking price of $27.5 million to John A. Thain, the chief executive of the New York Stock Exchange. Thain, who hails from a small Illinois town, was president of Goldman Sachs before he took over the stock exchange in the wake of the furor over the $139.5 million pay package of Richard A. Grasso, who was ousted from his job in 2004 as stock exchange chairman.

Cosmetics billionaire Ronald S. Lauder, who has one of the most spectacular art-filled apartments in the building, is rumored to be leaving the place to the mother of his children Jo Carole Lauder, now that the couple have announced they are divorcing. It was Ronald Lauder, a major benefactor of the Museum of Modern Art and the founder of the Neue Galerie, his own exceptional Fifth Avenue museum for German and Austrian art, who is said to have helped hedge fund mogul David Ganek, a former protegée of Steven A. Cohen, founder of SAC Capital Advisors, and Ganek's attractive wife, Danielle, who was brought up in Switzerland, to pass the picky co-op board at 740 Park. Like Steven Cohen, who last year bought a Jackson Pollock for $52 million, and like Ronald Lauder, who in the spring of 2006 paid $135 million at a Sotheby's auction for the 1907 Gustav Klimt painting *Adele Bloch-Bauer I,* David and Danielle Ganek have become increasingly visible art collectors. According to William Neuman, in an article in the *New York*

Times, the couple last year pledged to donate thirteen prints by the photographer Diane Arbus to the Metropolitan Museum of Art.

Through apartment owners who descended from planters, puritans, and patroons, whose grandfathers sailed on the *Mayflower* or rode horseback alongside George Washington, and until the hedge fund bubble may or may not burst, the fascination of a building like 740 Park is that, from its earliest days as a Republic, the United States has been known as "a democracy of opportunity which created an aristocracy of achievement."

· 7 ·

The San Remo

CELEBRITY ENCLAVE

Screen goddesses Marilyn Monroe and Rita Hayworth were once hiding from a curious public behind the window shades of the twin towers of this huge apartment complex, which has perhaps the most pronounced and distinctive silhouette on the Central Park West skyline. When viewed from the East Side of Manhattan, from across the park, the San Remo, rising majestically to a height of thirty stories with its pair of elaborately pointed spires, dominates everything around it. The building is an integral part of the panoramic drama that encircles and defines the unique essence of the great carpet of greenery at the heart of Manhattan.

Today, the San Remo is one of New York's main celebrity enclaves. Besides Marilyn Monroe, who lived there after her divorce from playwright Arthur Miller, and Rita Hayworth, who died there of Alzheimer's disease in 1989, the San Remo's ornate cartouche-topped entrance has guarded the New York homes of Steven Spielberg, Steve Martin, Apple Computer's Steve Jobs, Dustin Hoffman, Paul Simon, Elaine May, Tony Randall, Diane Keaton, Demi Moore, and Bruce Willis. The co-op's board of directors infamously turned down Madonna's attempt to purchase an apartment in the building

The San Remo

just before she married Academy Award–winning actor Sean Penn in1985. In 2005, the Irish rock star and lead of U-2, the noted humanitarian Bono, who has been enlisted by billionaires Bill Gates and Warren Buffet to work with them on their world-changing mega-foundation, had no trouble passing the scrutiny of the building's co-op board.

This is one of the really special co-op buildings on the West Side of Manhattan, among the most coveted residences on Central Park West, which, according to architecture critic Paul Goldberger, is "the best street of large scale in New York, better than Park, better than Fifth." A Central Park West resident himself, Goldberger feels the stretch of avenue between Columbus Circle and West 90th Street is architecturally unmatched. "The architecture is just more interesting. The average anonymous building on Park or Fifth is not as good as Central Park West."

Indeed, while Park Avenue revels in the clear message such numbers as 640, 720, 740, 770, or 778 automatically convey—what Tiffany stationers would instantly recognize as "a beautiful address"—most of the top residential complexes on the West Side have names. And they are great names, reverberating with glamour, grandeur, a longing for faraway fantasies, fun, and fizz. They are called Majestic, El Dorado, Kenilworth, Osborne, Apthorpe, Ansonia, Century, and Alwyn Court.

Designed by Emery Roth, the San Remo went up in 1930 and was the first of the four twin-tower buildings on Central Park West. Back then—and now—this architectural landmark at West 74th Street has always been viewed as the epitome of elegant New York's skyscraper living.

Bearing the official address 145 Central Park West, it was named after the town of San Remo on the Italian Riviera, a fashionable resort since time in memorial and, in the second half of the twentieth century, famous for its international music festival. This gargantuan apartment house replaced a hotel of the same name. The original San Remo was one of the popular, high-spirited, "family hotels," along with the Olcott and the Majestic, which were originally filling out Central Park West near the Dakota.

These great hotels—along with their East Side counterparts, the Savoy and the Netherlands, were, in truth, late nineteenth-century antecedents of apartment compounds. Their successes boded well for communal living. Most famous of these turn-of-the-century exemplars of exhilarating urban living was the original Waldorf-Astoria, covering a block on 34th Street and Fifth Avenue, where the Empire State Building is today. It was the most famous hotel in America, providing a luxurious white-tie-and-tails society atmosphere in its Palm Court restaurant, luminous galleries, and lounges. The amenities suggested exclusivity, but the guests—politicians, divas, and tourists from small towns all over the United States—came from all ranks of society. "The poorest man living in or visiting New York, provided he is well-dressed, may sit about those corridors, night after night, spending never a cent, speaking to no one, and he would be allowed to stay," wrote E. I. Zcisloft in 1899, in a book called *The New Metropolis*. Hotels like the old Waldorf-Astoria and the original San Remo did a lot to create a positive view of city life. They paved the way for newly successful urban dwellers to embrace discreetly ornamented, pragmatically ordered apartment houses that acknowledged certain aristocratic aspirations of the day.

Into this turn-of-the-century atmosphere arrived Emory Roth, a thirteen-year-old orphan from Hungary, who came all by himself to be apprenticed to a cabinetmaker. Soon after he arrived, he went to Chicago to work as a draftsman at the World's Columbian Exposition, and then for a while to Newport, Rhode Island, where he worked on the interiors of the most famous of the palatial "cottages" of the Gilded Age, the Vanderbilt family's Breakers. It was at the Breakers that this young man, who had no formal architectural training, only happenstance employment, good instincts, and a series of enriching educational jobs, learned to understand the housing requirements of rich Americans and, more importantly, the complex organization needed for serving a multitude of people living under one roof.

According to architectural historian Elizabeth Hawes, "Roth was a new breed of architect in New York. He had a peculiarly American kind of energy born of optimism, pragmatism and dreams. In an age when his confreres were gentlemen, and got their commissions through family, clubs and social connections, he was a businessman. He formed an early association with the brothers Leo and Alexander Bing, who had launched a firm that sold plots to speculative builders. Quick to grasp the principles of building costs and operating expenses, Roth established himself as an expert in real estate."

Long before Fifth Avenue luxury apartment architects James Carpenter and Rosario Candela, Emory Roth had important buildings to his credit. Among them was the Belleclaire Hotel at 77th and Broadway in 1903, and the apartment house 570 Park at 61st, Street which went up in 1915. Both were luxury pioneers in their respective neighborhoods. Near the Ansonia, which, strictly speaking, was an apartment hotel, home to such fabled theatrical personalities of the era as Florenz Ziegfield and such music legends as Arturo Toscanini, Igor Stravinsky, and the Menuhin family, was Emory Roth's Belleclaire. There, actors and poets and soldiers met to discuss life so exuberantly that novelists Henry James and Edith Wharton used it in their fiction as backgrounds. They recognized these hotels as seedbeds of a new social attitude. In the wake of these successful West Side establishments arrived a spate of even grander new hotels on Fifth Avenue: the St. Regis, the Gotham, and the Plaza.

The San Remo benefited from a law passed in the spring of 1929 that allowed high towers on plots greater than 30,000 square feet. Rising to twenty-seven floors, the tower residences were ten floors higher than the rest of the apartment houses along either side of Central Park and were rivetingly topped by two templelike peaks decorated with tiers of columns, ornate lanterns, and copper finials.

The best apartments are in the south tower, which consists of five thirteen-room duplexes that boast glorious 22 x 35 foot living rooms. Originally the north tower had 10 six-room simplexes. Below the towers, there are approximately ten spacious apartments on each floor. An interesting feature of the building is its unusual window design. Typically, each had the usual swing-out casement plus a smaller transom above and below. The top one swings out, and the bottom one swings in, all contributing to a multiple variety of ventilation options.

When the Great Depression hit New York, the brand-new San Remo was only partly filled, and because it was mostly financed by the Bank of the United States (records are shrouded, and there's strong indication that the ledgers were burned), when that bank collapsed spectacularly in 1931, the San Remo, along with the Beresford, was foreclosed. But by the mid-1930s, several prominent show business people made the fabulous towers their privileged retreats. They included one of the Warner brothers, Albert Warner; Loew's vice president Joseph Vogel; and the vaudeville comedian turned popular radio and movie star, Eddie Cantor.

In 1972, the San Remo was converted from a rental building into a cooperative apartment house. Whether renting, subletting, or owning, the list of its famous residents is formidable. It includes prize fighter Jack Dempsey, who lived in a fourteen-room tower apartment for thirty years; Princess Yasmin Aga Khan, who is Rita Hayworth's daughter; movie star Raquel Welch, who for a while subleased singer Barry Manilow's place; Zero

Mostel, while he starred in the Broadway musical *A Funny Thing Happened on the Way to the Forum;* concert pianist Misha Dichter; song writer and performer Peter Allen, who was briefly married to Liza Minnelli; the photographer Diane Arbus; and Broadway lyricist Fred Ebb, who worked with composer John Kander on such hit musicals as *Cabaret* and *Chicago.* The duo also wrote the famous title song for Martin Scorcese's film *New York, New York,* which, thanks to a later recording by Frank Sinatra, has become a seemingly immortal part of New York City's soundtrack.

Although the San Remo is a co-op full of famous people, it also has certain unspoken rules about the nuances of fame. Apparently degrees of overexposure, or too high a profile, can hurt a prospective buyer. Madonna didn't quite cut the mustard in the eyes of other celebrity residents at the storied Central Park West fortress. Yet the Irish rock star Bono had no trouble making the grade. He bought an apartment belonging to the founder of Apple Computer, Steve Jobs, who had hired famous architect I. M. Pei to redesign the suite. After waiting seven years and spending $15 million, the computer king lost interest in the renovated bronze-doored dazzler, and Bono effortlessly, and happily, moved in. Co-op boards also tend to dislike designers; however, Donna Karan, who is a well-known serial renovator of her homes, managed to live in the building for a while in the 1980s.

As to why Madonna was rejected by the blue-chip San Remo co-op board, many versions of the episode have been put forth over the years. There were apparently two reasons for the decision.

"People were worried about security issues for such an international megastar—then at the height of the success following her early videos such as 'Like a Virgin' and 'Material Girl.' There was the issue of her bodyguards. Controlling the paparazzi and so forth," remembers one San Remo apartment owner. She doesn't mention that during the month of her San Remo interview, Madonna's photographs in *Playboy* and *Penthouse* were on all the newsstands. "But very importantly, Sean Penn, who was about to become her husband, refused to come for a co-op board interview. We didn't like that at all."

Nowadays, floor for floor, the San Remo—a photogenic icon recognized worldwide—is Hollywood's most prestigious stronghold in New York. Bruce Willis, Dustin Hoffman, and the so-called King of Hollywood, Steven Spielberg, and his Queen, the actress Kate Capshaw, call the place home.

Marriage and remarriage are sometimes curiously finessed among these super-rich New York apartment aficionados. For example, when Governor

Nelson Rockefeller divorced his first wife, Mary Todhunter Rockefeller, to marry his second wife, Happy, he so dearly loved one floor of his old apartment at 810 Fifth Avenue that, when he purchased a new place for his new wife, it was an apartment on the same floor in the building next door at 812 Fifth. This way, he could break through two outside walls to join the two apartments. Meanwhile, his first wife, who kept the top floor of the Governor's old digs, never had to run into the second wife in the elevator. In fact, Mary "Tod" remained on the floor above Happy Rockefeller for the next forty years. Similarly, when comedian Steve Martin married the actress Victoria Tennant, he bought two apartments at the San Remo and combined them. When a few years later the couple divorced, and she remarried, he separated the apartments again with a thick, soundproof wall, and the two continued to live side-by-side, though they were never again on speaking terms.

Everybody comments on the good condition of these 1930s apartments. Emery Roth was famous for his metal kitchen cabinets, beautiful hardware with bullet hinges, and his pristine tile bathrooms. He would do each bathroom in a different color tile. In an interview with William Newman of the *New York Times*, Kirk Henckels, the director of Stribling Private Brokerage, described an apartment in the building that was put up for sale at the beginning of 2003 by the family of Nadia Jaglom, who lived there from 1940 until she died at 105 in 2004. Mrs. Jaglom's grandson particularly remembers the building's pleasurable showers, also Emery Roth specialties. "It was a stall shower with multiple shower heads, like six or eight, three on each side, one at the bottom and one above. I used to love going in there as a kid. You can imagine that when it was built everyone probably thought it was the coolest thing anyone had ever seen." Mrs. Jaglom outlived her husband by three decades. The Abraham Jagloms had moved into the San Remo soon after they arrived in America from Europe in the late 1930s. While living at the San Remo, they raised a family and compiled an impressive art collection of works by Renoir, Degas, and Bonnard. Her apartment was on the tenth floor and had ten windows facing Central Park. Seven other windows in the flat overlook West 75th Street.

Soon after the Jaglom apartment went on the market, at an asking price of $11.9 million, the owners of the two apartments on either side contacted real estate man Kirk Henckels to say they also wanted to sell. The result of combining the three suites is one of those rare opportunities for creating a sprawling, spectacular eight-thousand-square-foot apartment with twenty-two rooms, including seven bedrooms. By January 2005, the price for all three in combination was set at $23.5 million. But by June, the Russian-born financier who agreed to meet the $23.5 million for the three combined apartments was rejected flatly by the board. According to an insider, the board members' mantra was, "We don't want this to become a building of billionaires."

· 8 ·

4 EAST 66TH STREET

ELEGANT RESTRAINT AND REVERSE SNOBBERY

*T*HERE ARE VERY accomplished, very social people who do not want to live on Park or Fifth avenues—and even if they do, insist on the building's side-street address. This is because they find the screaming status of a Fifth Avenue address not unlike wearing a designer label on the outside of a dress. Manhattan insiders, however, know that these so-called "discreetly social" buildings are every bit as high-luxe, glamorous, and exclusive as the big, beautiful numbers on the two elite boulevards.

Two sterling American families who preferred these more subtle ways of telling people about their New York gold-coast homes were the Roebling family, who built the Brooklyn Bridge, and the Morris family, who descended from Gouverneur Morris, a signer of the Declaration of Independence, and were the first to have their own racing colors in America's thoroughbred horse world. They all lived at 4 East 72 Street. Likewise, today the chairman of Estée Lauder, Leonard Lauder, and his wife, Evelyn, live at 2 East 67th Street. These are both actually A-plus, blue-chip Fifth Avenue-style apartment houses, beautifully appointed and endowed with marvelous Central Park views.

4 East 66th Street

Perhaps the best-known of these outstanding side-street addresses is 4 East 66th Street. The proud, palatial, but deliberately restrained—almost austere—Fifth Avenue building, on the southeast corner of 66th Street, is reticent about shouting out its top-flight location and imperially vast, haughtily self-contained apartment units. Actually, this is 845 Fifth Avenue, but at the insistence of its very private, very rich inhabitants, the building has a 66th Street canopy and main entrance. Some say this is a form of reverse snobbism. Not that East 66th Street is small potatoes. Just across, in the residential complex at 1 East 66th Street, lives Princess Firyal of Jordan. One block away at 45 East 66th Street, in one of the most eclectically ornate, landmark corner buildings on Madison Avenue, is the home of former Mayor Rudolph Giuliani. And a little farther east, 131 East 66th Street is one of the best apartment houses in town, featuring two-story living rooms with mezzanine balconies. This was the former New York home of Baron Philippe de Rothschild and is the current home of Vice President Al Gore's daughter, Karenna Gore Schiff, and her M.D. husband, and also home of artist-socialite Wendy Vanderbilt.

Until his death at age ninety-four in 1965, the august presidential advisor Bernard Baruch—whose phenomenally active life and times spanned the post–Civil War South, where he was born, and the Atomic Age, when he was named by President Truman to head the United Nations' Atomic Energy Commission, after serving as chairman of the War Industries Board—received a procession of world-renowned personages in his grand second-floor apartment at 4 East 66th Street. With its many low windows, Baruch's place had a front-row-center view of the beauty of the changing seasons, playing out on the treetops of Central Park.

David Schine, the young lawyer who, along with Roy Cohn, captured the spotlight during the McCarthy hearings in the 1950s, and a decade later died in a plane crash, also owned an apartment at 4 East 66th Street with his wife, Hilevi, a former Miss Universe.

Today, some of the biggest names on the *Forbes's* richest list have superlative apartments in the building. One of these is Sid Bass, whose Fort Worth–based empire, built on the legendary Texas oil fortune of his uncle Sid Richardson, includes the venture capital firm Hawthorne Finances, Iomega Oil and Gas, and, together with his brothers, the largest shareholdings in the Walt Disney Company. Bass and his shapely, couture-clad wife, Mercedes, who grew up in Switzerland and sits on the board of the

Aspen Institute, are major supporters of Carnegie Hall and in December 2005 gave $25 million to the Metropolitan Opera. It was the single largest gift ever bestowed on New York's legendary cultural treasure. Mercedes Bass has, in the last few years, also been very supportive of fellow 4 East 66 residents and music lovers Ezra and Cecile Zilkha's many cultural philanthropies. Ezra Zilkha, a courtly gentleman from Iraq, whose banking interests extend from London to Caliornia, New York to the Middle East, and his gracious wife, Cecile, are today at the very top of New York's global pyramid. Philanthropically magnanimous, and socially impeccable, they give 4 East 66th Street a special cachet. Cecile Zilkha and Mercedes Bass usually chair the opening night benefit for the concert hall and opera and the famous, annual fund-raising dinner on the Met stage, where the world's greatest tenors and sopranos mingle with a Who's Who of global society. Also in the building lives Veronica Hearst, the tall, dark-tressed, Dutch-born widow of Randolph Hearst, whose family's newspaper-magazine-television empire spans the earth. Before Randy Hearst, the father of kidnapping-victim Patty Hearst, Veronica had been married into two colossal South American forunes, the Beracosas of Venezuela and the Uribes of Colombia. Because of Mercedes, Veronica, and Cecile, each frequently photographed and married to a big-name beneficent businessman, the building is sometimes, with tongue-in-cheek, referred to as "the House of Angels."

One of the beloved Society hostesses of the Saratoga horse circuit, the late Kay Jeffords lived at 4 East 66th Street for decades. Her husband, Walter C. Jeffords's family, the Philadelphia horse-racing clan, were the owners of perhaps the greatest American thoroughbred, Man O'War, which never lost a race in his entire career and whose bloodline courses in many of the top champions of today. Kay's valuable English antique furniture, memorabilia from the thoroughbred establishment and fabulous British sporting paintings—including the second-most-valued Sir Alfred Munnings in the world—were sold at one of the most successful auctions at Sotheby's in the fall of 2004.

Among the most popular, bona fide society couples of their time, Kay and Walter "Jeff" Jeffords were constantly on the go between their many far-flung residences: their horse farm in Pennsylvania; the much photographed, Saratoga-season, Victorian party house; an apartment in Texas; a place in Palm Beach; and houses in Maine. Their apartment at 4 East 66th Street is the one that had belonged to Bernard Baruch and also included Baruch's office suite on the building's main floor. The charismatic couple both used the office, keeping their secretary, who was with the family for over thirty years, perpetually on her toes. For many years, Walter Jeffords was president of the 4 East 66th Street building's co-op board.

The Jeffords bought their apartment from Bernard Baruch for what was, in 1965, the astronomical sum of $200,000. But by 1996, the building's eleventh floor apartment was sold for $14 million.

There is a certain irony at play that, seventy years after these superb limestone-clad urban palazzos were built, they still embody what V. S. Pritchett called "the glamour of wealth and respectable certainty." When their owners or inheritors of these co-ops cash in, part of what they're selling is exclusivity. In the early 1900s, they were closed to anyone who was not born or did not marry into the "right" families. Now, economic ups and downs have opened the doors. And the people who bought some of these sought-after floor-through jewels for as little as $100,000 in the 1970s are trying to close the doors even tighter than in the old days. Why? Sometimes they are jealous and resentful of people who have become so much, much, much more successful financially. And because the very notion of exclusivity sells. The prestige of a building can jack up the price of a sale. "It is really infuriating how unreasonable key decision-makers sitting on co-op boards can get," comments a Manhattan realtor specializing in A-plus properties.

What are the criteria for getting into an A-plus building today? Payment in full cash, usually. Impeccable social credentials—which means good schools, private clubs, a summer home in the right place, philanthropic contributions to the right causes. And having somewhere between $50 and $500 million in assets, a substantial portion of which is liquid.

A building, by law, does not have to give a reason for turning down a prospective active buyer. As one building board president commented, "We're not a co-op board that has a rigid viewpoint: every person that might want to live here is judged on his own merit." If boards don't like that you come to the board interview in Bermuda shorts, or wear emeralds the size of eggs or speak with whatever speech patterns they found unappealing, you will never know that those were the reasons the doors were shut in your face. Keeping up the glamour, after all, means excluding anything not thought to be glamorous. Yet, people keep subjecting themselves to these potential turndowns, because what Edith Wharton wrote over one hundred years ago in her novel, *House of Mirth,* still pertains: a Fifth Avenue address is definitely "a rung in the social ladder."

In 1920, the greatly admired designer of 4 East 66th Street, J. E. R. Carpenter, winner of the 1916 Gold Medal Award of the American Institute of Architects, fully understood a prevalent impulse among America's upper-class families for a tastefully quiet but quality-detailed way of living that could only be described today as understated chic. Accordingly, his subdued eleven-story limestone creation contains one single, utterly refined, eighteen-room apartment to a floor. Only the widely spaced windows on Fifth Avenue hint at the exceptionally enormous pair of entertaining rooms inside each apartment. They have extra-high thirteen-foot ceilings. And then there are the beautiful long galleries within. Here, vast areas meander into exquisitely capacious sitting rooms and the kind of enormous party space of bygone times that takes your breath away.

James E. R. Carpenter, along with Rosario Candela, has become synonymous with the great apartment houses of New York City. They created a new paradigm of apartment living. They defined luxury in a way not equaled since their day, and the well-proportioned rooms, inspired individual layouts, planning and design principles they pioneered are still strongly influencing contemporary apartment house architects. According to the consensus of scholars Andrew Alpern, Christopher Gray, and David Netto, Carpenter's and Candela's contributions to the architecture of New York City are as significant as the city's great office skyscrapers. Between them, they designed several dozen of the city's most exquisite residential structures.

It was James E. R. Carpenter who laid the foundation for other people to build higher and more elaborately in New York. Carpenter, who started more than a decade before Candela, is usually credited with having initiated and perfected the "off the foyer" apartment design. The two talented men augmented each other and enhanced America. Yet Carpenter was always quick to acknowledge that the first steps were taken in that direction by William A. Boring, who with Edward Lippincott Tilton designed the Ellis Island Immigration Center in 1895 and later became the dean of Columbia University's School of Architecture. Carpenter, a discerning, elegant, pipe-smoking Southerner from Tennessee, had attended the Massachusetts Institute of Technology, and worked for three years for McKim, Mead & White before studying at the École des Beaux-Arts in Paris. He had already designed such notable structures as the five-star Hermitage Hotel in Nashville, the Ridgely Apartments in Birmingham, the Hurt Building in Atlanta (now designated a historic landmark), and the American National Building in Pensacola. All this before he brought his well-honed skills, in 1907, to a New York about to embrace apartment living. Carpenter, who died suddenly of a heart attack in 1932, had designed an estimated five hundred buildings across the United States. He indefatigably and successfully fought a New York City regulation that limited the height of residential buildings on Park and Fifth avenues, thereby paving the way for Candela's fanciful wedding-cake setbacks atop Park Avenue high rises. Carpenter also designed four Manhattan office skyscrapers, perhaps the most significant being the silvery, art deco, fifty-two-story Lincoln Building across from Grand Central Station on 42nd Street.

720 Park Avenue

· 9 ·

---

720 PARK AVENUE
770 PARK AVENUE
778 PARK AVENUE

THE CREAM OF PARK AVENUE

*F*EW HIGH-FASHION concepts carry the invincible cachet of a Park Avenue penthouse. Material manifestation of living at the top of the social hierarchy, it is still the oyster, the champagne, the caviar of metropolitan living. While there are pricey penthouses in other cities, especially in Chicago, Miami, Denver, Las Vegas, and Los Angeles, New York is still penthouse central. The matchless architectural setbacks, with their magical cascading terraces in the sky, atop the tall, thin Park Avenue palazzos Rosario Candela created around 1929 (when a new law allowed apartment houses to rise higher), are, to this day, the apexes of Manhattan real estate. More than three-quarters of a century after they went up, these penthouses are at a premium among contemporary cliff dwellers. In a borough where cooperative or condominium ownership is the predominant mode of living for accomplished professionals and established families, those dream apartments are more than status symbols, they are breathtaking properties with sometimes 360-degree views, plenty of light, unique layouts, and highly desirable outdoor space. Located just below—or sometimes on top of—the roof, it's possible for them to have wood-burning fireplaces, splendid skylights, and

770 Park Avenue

778 Park Avenue

high ceilings. And of course, there are no upstairs neighbors. These crowning apartments, and usually the other apartments below them—some of them height-of-luxury maisonettes—in a handful of Park Avenue buildings, enfold the cream of Manhattan's lifestyles. And the people who own them represent the substantive top layer, as well as fascinating froth, of the culture of the city.

At any rate, Candela's buildings are still housing some of New York's most energetic folk. In particular, 778 Park Avenue, on the northwest corner of East 73rd Street, is commonly known as the pick of the crop. One of Candela's best buildings, it is the address of New York's most social and affluent. *National Review* editor, syndicated columnist, television debater *non pareil*, and best-selling novelist William F. Buckley and his wife, Pat, live at 778 in a sixteen-room "maisonette"—those opulent residential plums meaning "little house"—that are actually spacious duplex or triplex urban mansions embedded in the larger Park Avenue or Fifth Avenue buildings surrounding them. The Buckleys' place, which has a private entrance on 73rd Street, is considered one of New York's ultimate dwellings.

Brooke Astor, "the Queen of New York Society" who went from an elegant, hatwearing, white-gloves-and-pearls, vibrantly active woman, to a "locked-away" recluse at the age of 104 in the midst of an acrimonious and bitter battle by her family over her millions, for a long time lived at 778 Park in a timeless Parish-Hadley decorated floorthrough apartment. Her huge lacquered burgundy and gold library houses over three thousand leather-bound volumes. Her "Welcome to New York" party for newly elected President Reagan, with a guest list of the city's most luminous personalities, and the good time she had giving away her husband's millions to the New York Public Library and other worthy institutions, have earned her a large following, wide fame, and highly protective prominent friends like Annette de la Renta, Henry Kissinger, and David Rockefeller.

Wedding gown designer Vera Wang has a fabulous apartment in the building, which was featured in *Vogue* magazine. (Her brother, Kenny Wang, who worked with their late father, Singapore tycoon C. C. Wang, also has a home in the complex.) Various members of the Croesus-rich Jonathan Tisch family, who are the most generous supporters of New York University, have lived at 778 for many years in various apartments, as has real estate developer Sherman Cohen, whose lavish spread was decorated by Peter Marino.

Former American Express chairman James Robinson also lives there. The late Roone Arledge, creator of Wide World of Sports and president of ABC

News, who had perhaps a more profound impact on the development of TV news and sports programming than any other individual, was a co-op owner here for decades. Claudia Cohen, the *News* columnist and real estate heiress, moved into the building while she was married to Revlon chief Ronald Perelman. The owner of the Carlyle Hotel, the late Peter Sharp, was also a longtime resident.

One of the full floor, six bedroom apartments, with beautiful fireplaces in the entrance gallery and dining room as well as the living room, is owned by Susan and John B. Hess, chairman and chief executive officer of Amerada Hess, an oil and gas company that conducts exploration and production globally. While an undergraduate at Harvard, Hess studied in Beirut and became fluent in Arabic and Farsi. As a young executive managing exploration and production operations in the oil fields of Canada and the Gulf of Mexico, he was brought together with various leaders of the oil industry and at one gathering surprised everyone when he introduced Abu Dhabi's oil minister, Mana Said al-Otaila, in faultless Arabic. He is the grandson—on his mother's side—of David Wilentz, who prosecuted the kidnapper of the Lindbergh baby. When in 1995 Hess took over the company, he was walking in the footsteps of one of New York's giants, Leon Hess, who built Hess Oil in the 1930s from a tarry black substance most oil companies at the time had little use for after refining: residual fuel oil. He realized that utilities and other big users were switching from coal to number 6 residual oil whenever they could get it. Leon Hess, who later gained fame for saving the New York Jets football team from bankruptcy with a group headed by MCA head and New York sports legend Sonny Werblin in 1963, owned the team until his death, when the family sold it to Johnson & Johnson heir Robert Wood Johnson IV. During his sixty years of immense success in the energy business, Leon Hess granted a newspaper interview only once. John Hess, unlike most of today's high-profile CEOs of leading, publicly traded companies, has shared his father's aversion to the media.

The seventeen-story building has sixteen units, including three duplexes, which means there is only one tenant per floor. Aside from its very, very large apartments, the building's outrageous prices guarantee something else: a limited pool of applicants. The building is proud of having had almost no embarrassing turndowns. On the other hand, sometimes nothing comes available for as long as five years.

When Rosario Candela designed 778 Park with its wedding-cake tiers on top, he was echoing a silhouette that he had designed eight months earlier in 1929, considered the greatest of all apartment construction years in New York City. It was the final display of architectural fireworks before the Great Depression descended on the Empire State. On Park Avenue, 770 and 778 are bookended buildings, vertical landmarks to the new multiple-dwelling law that went into effect that year allowing apartments to rise to nineteen stories—provided the top floors were set back—seven more than the previously permitted twelve-floor limit. Candela's buildings, which had been extravagant inside but relatively subdued, though elegant, lime-stone structures on the outside, suddenly began to fly. The first of these Candela apartment houses to suggest the high quality of the good life inside was 770 Park Avenue, on the southwest corner of 73rd Street. It climbed to twelve stories, then it burst into a series of terraced setbacks to create a gradual, upwardly narrowing penthouse tower. When both 770 and 778 were completed, the pair, sufficiently alike with their towers, framed 73rd Street on the west side of Park Avenue like two sentinels guarding the way to the greenery of Central Park.

What made 770 so different from anything before it was not only its clusters of penthouses on top but also its unusual fenestration, which was judged harshly by one architectural critic of the time as "a distressing amount of half-baked" concepts, and by another as "a pile-up of mansions." The irregularly spaced windows hinted at floor plans of the duplex apartments within. Actually, they were rather ahead of their time, articulating the tenet "form follows function."

Most of the terrific apartments at 770 contain between eleven and fifteen rooms, with one line of slightly smaller eight-room units, but also a totally unconventional arrangement for each of the penthouses on different setbacks on top.

The late Gianni Agnelli, the head of Fiat, and his wife, Marella, born a princess and one of the most stylish women in the world, kept a U.S. residence at 770 Park for decades. This magnificent apartment, 17-A, was later bought by the CEO of Vornado Realty, Steven Roth, and his Tony-winning Broadway, producer wife, Daryl. It is being redesigned by the prestigious French decorator Jacques Grange. The second- and third-floor duplex apartment once belonged to Yul Brynner and his jet-setter wife, Doris. Michael Lynne, head of New Line Cinema, owns a splendid eighteenth-floor penthouse in the compound. It has a spectacular living room with floor-to-ceiling windows facing east, south, and west, and a very large, festive dining room.

And this was the building where the co-op board famously and inexplicably blackballed CBS Television's *60 Minutes* anchorman Mike Wallace and kept him from buying a home in the place. Wallace, stunned, eventually moved into a brownstone down the street.

One of the most attractive of the fifteen-room duplexes at 770, with a curved wrought-iron staircase and hand-painted Chinese murals in the dining room, belongs to Edgar Cullman Jr., a Philip Morris heir, and is decorated with the traditionalist flair of his wife, Elissa, who, with the late Hedy Kravis Ruger, Henry Kravis's first wife, was half of the stylish decorating firm Cullman & Kravis, Inc. Others who presently own apartments in the building are Moishe Safra of the banking family; Marlene Hess, whose father founded Hess Oil, and her husband, Jim Zirin; and Kathleen Troia "KT" McFarland, a 2006 GOP candidate for U.S. senator; Hassan and Sheila Namazee, major Democratic fund-raisers especially for Al Gore; and David and Lisa Schiff, whose physician son is married to Al Gore's daughter, Karenna.

Earlier in 1929, before 770 and 778, before the building spree that dispensed "the Park Avenue style" of amusing "little roof spaces" attached to some exceptionally expansive multifloor apartments, Rosario Candela joined architects Cross & Cross and completed another eighteen-floor extravaganza, 720 Park on the northwest corner of 70th Street. The top of the building is an unusually complex mix of bays, battlements, buttresses, setbacks and stickouts. The terraced penthouses were built to specifications of their first owners.

Perhaps the most talked about of these was the huge two-floor apartment of the head of Macy's department store, Jesse Isidor Straus. It had a forty-foot entrance gallery and a library of nearly one-thousand square feet, with a baronial stone fireplace and chimney breast. There was a separate wine and vegetable closet, a valeting room, a sewing room and a colossal kitchen, larger than most modern living rooms. Following Straus's death in 1970, the fabulous apartment went begging at a price of $500,000 for two years. Unsalable, it was divided into two units, and the glorious library cut into several smaller rooms.

Though the rooms throughout the building are slightly smaller than at 740 Park, which was the subject of a 2005 book by Michael Gross subtitled *The Story of the World's Richest Apartment Building,* many people consider the apartments inside to be perhaps even more terrific in architectural details, and more relevant in design to today's lifestyles. Famous realtor and party-giver Alice Mason puts the building among her top five Manhattan favorites in a *W* magazine interview: "The moldings are even more extravagant than in 740. Both were designed by Candela. His buildings are best because of the proportions and appointments. 720 has extremely large dining rooms." A 1994 article in *Town & Country* also rates 720 Park Avenue among the five best buildings in the city. "The lobby is a series of spaces unfolding from intimate to grand: a small vestibule, a larger one, then a proper library/sitting room with a fireplace," enthuses Steven M. L. Aronson.

In the recent superactive real estate market, apartment buyers have been willing to pay as much as 20 percent more per square foot for a property at the top, brokers say. Usually the people who won't settle for anything less than the topmost floor are at a point in their careers where they want something that makes them feel like the "master of the universe," the big kahunas of the power game that they feel they have become. Living in some of the higher apartments at 720 feels like a helicopter ride over Manhattan. The penthouses have terraces on three sides, and views uptown and downtown as well as from the East River to the Hudson River.

Residents consider the tenor of the building more low-key and less showy than 740. "Practically everyone here has a museum or some major cultural contribution." Emily Fisher Landau, who is a member of a wealthy real estate family, is a well-known art collector and philanthropist with a private museum in Long Island City. Mary Louise Black, who is on the board committee at the Whitney Museum, a few years back opened a museum of contemporary art at Bard College. James Marcus is the former chairman of the Metropolitan Opera Association. Suzanne Usdan has a performing arts center on Long Island. Peter Aron was the life force behind New York's South Street Seaport Museum, and Paine Webber chairman Donald Marron, who is vice president of the board of the Museum of Modern Art, and his wife Katie gave several fund-raisers in their apartment for the first President Bush. One of the first big fund-raisers for President Clinton was also given in the building by Barbara Lee Diamonstein, chaiman of the Landmarks Preservation Foundation, and her husband Carl Spielvogel, chairman and CEO of Backer Spielvogel Bates Worldwide Inc. and a board member of more primary nonprofit institutions than anyone in the city.

Among the glittering society names—women whose faces appear regularly in magazine and newspaper accounts of Manhattan's top charity events, are Cynthia Phipps, who is an avid squash player in the building's private squash court; Louise Savitt Melhado Grunwald, widow of Henry Anatole Grunwald, the illustrious editor of *Time* magazine who later became ambassador to Austria; and Audrey Gruss, considered one of the city's reigning beauties, wife of tycoon Martin Gruss, who has his own Palm Beach polo team. Diana Quasha, another photogenic 720 resident frequently appearing among the most decorative people in the party pages of glossy magazines, is the wife of Alan G. Quasha, chairman of Harken Energy, which back in the late 1980s acquired George W. Bush's oil company and took him on as a director and consultant. The Quashas sold their fabulous duplex penthouse at 720 in May 2005 to Cleveland billionaire Randolph D. Lerner.

Listed with Sotheby's International Realty for $12 million, the apartment on top of this elegant Park Avenue citadel is one of the finest in the city, featuring all the luxurious architectural touches, delightful terraces, bay windows, and spatial surprises that Candela specialized in. Randy Lerner, who is on the *Forbes's* list of the world's richest people, is chairman of the credit card company MBNA and owns the Cleveland Browns football team. Others of note who own apartments at 720 today are Frederick Melhado, Louise Grunwald's former husband, and his wife Virginia; and former Revlon chairman Michel de Bergerac, whose brother, Jacques Bergerac, was the last husband of Ginger Rogers.

Over the years, 720 has always been thought of as one of the quintessential Park Avenue buildings jam-packed with sparkling society names— people Cole Porter liked to call "the rich rich." They've included some great, patinated, East Coast establishment names, descendents of New York's early seventeenth-century Dutch and English families: the famous dowager Mrs. Horace Havemeyer; Hope Auchincloss Whipple; Mrs. Woolworth, with her floor-through apartment in the front tower adjoined to another floor-through in the back tower that belonged to her daughter Countess Combemale; Seagram's liquor head Edgar Bronfman's late sister, Minda, who was the Baroness Alain de Gunzburg; and San Antonio newspaper publisher, and former ambassador to Germany under President Johnson, John McKinney, whose European wife, Marielle, gave some of the most memorable and exclusive parties in the couple's treasure-filled, terraced, tower triplex.

Which is better: Fifth Avenue or Park Avenue? The answer, realtors to New York's upper crust agree, is that while Fifth Avenue's very, very top buildings have incomparable ballroom-sized entertainment rooms facing Central Park, many Fifth Avenue units darken into railroad apartments in the back. Park Avenue apartments are arranged in more square-shaped fashion, providing more light from more sides. When all is said, Park Avenue probably has a greater total number of truly outstanding units.

Park Avenue as an elite boulevard—a dramatic urban canyon of penthouse rooflines and high-rise residences that epitomized civility, sophistication, and luxury—was actually a Johnny-come-lately to Fifth Avenue's reputation as the foremost boulevard of glamour and wealth, solidity and respectability. Park Avenue developed in several stages generally related to the railroad, which, beginning in 1834, ran up its center. According to Christopher Gray, "although the tracks were at first at grade level, increasing development in the neighborhood led the owner Cornelius Vanderbilt, to sink the tracks in 1872–1875. Steam engines still belched coal smoke up through the vents, but it was still an improvement and builders erected brownstone rowhouses on the side streets directly off Park Avenue."

At a time when upper-crust housing was pushing up along Fifth and even Madison avenues, a Park Avenue home was anything but chic. People who lived on the corner of Park Avenue inevitably took side-street numbers for their addresses. But by 1903, collisions in the smoky tunnels below required legislation to electrify the trains entering Manhattan. Electric power reduced not only the smoke but also the noise, and soon the avenue became a site of promising real estate. The magnificent apartment houses designed in the late 1920s by James E. R. Carpenter, Rosario Candela, and John W. Cross of Cross & Cross still epitomize the ultimate aspiration. In these tower suites, the most successful people from all over America continue to want to live and look down on the avenue's famous medians, where tulips burst into bloom in spring, and evergreen trees atwinkle with lights make New York's Christmas season one of the most beautiful in the world.

· 10 ·

THE BERESFORD

FROM MARGARET MEAD TO JERRY SEINFELD

*I*N 1998 THREE seismic shifts occurred in the life of Jerry Seinfeld, star, co-creator, and executive producer of NBC's *Seinfeld,* one of the most popular and successful sitcoms of all time on American television. That year, the superbly cast ensemble show about a quartet of scheming, anxiety-ridden, easily irritable, not entirely likable but very funny near losers on Manhattan's Upper West Side—in which Jerry Seinfeld played a caricature of himself—after nine hilarious seasons went off the air. Also that year, following a lengthy and slightly scandalous dalliance with a pretty student named Shoshana Lonstein, who was in secondary school at a prestigious private girl's prep when the fortyish actor met her in Central Park, Seinfeld began dating Jessica Sklar. They had met by chance at the Reebok Sports Club and had started a romance, even though she had just married Eric Nederlander, a scion of the powerful Broadway theater-owning family, who contemplated suing Seinfeld for busting up his marriage. Finally that same year, Jerry Seinfeld bought a $4.35-million duplex from revered concert violinist Isaac Stern at the Beresford, the landmark, triple-towered, celebrity-filled co-op at 211 Central Park West.

The Beresford

Known as much for its world-famous tenants past and present—Rock Hudson, Beverly Sills, Mike Nichols, Tony Randall, Sidney Lumet, Glenn Close, and John McEnroe, to name a few—as for its commanding architectural presence, the immense chunk of elaborately embellished apartment house, taking up a full 200 feet of city block at a prime location, is one of New York's most striking urban monuments. This is especially true at night, when the Beresford's three towers are lighted with beacons. When viewed from inside Central Park, the Beresford gives the impression of a turreted, hilltop, Renaissance fortress. In fact, this last of the city's luxury apartments to be inspired by classicism is a glorious pile of Italianate elements sagaciously composed for modern living. A giant twenty-two-story cube of granite, marble, limestone, terra-cotta, and brick, surmounted by three almost baroque, domed cupola towers, its extremely large, elegantly appointed, very comfortable apartments surround an open inner courtyard, much like a castle does.

Emery Roth was envied when he was given the opportunity by the HRH Construction Company to create an apartment building on this imposing site at the corner of West 81st Street and Central Park West, facing Central Park on one side and Manhattan Square, with the venerable American Museum of Natural History, on the other. But Roth's thoroughly original creation with its three short trademark corner turrets (two of them actually cover water towers), multitude of terraces, and profusion of extravagant yet dignified touches, has lived up to the challenge. The Beresford's multiple lobbies—each small, but rich with marble and bronze ornamentation—lend an opulent intimacy and glamorous ambience to this gargantuan complex of sixteen-room duplexes, mansion-size triplexes, and some comfortable smaller suites.

Celebrities may be drawn to this building for its almost contradictory character. It has the look of a special place for special people. Yet while the four entrances to the building are powerfully grand, the four lobbies—two on West 81st Street, one on Central Park, and one on West 82nd Street—are quite cozy and residential for a building of such large scale. This contrasts greatly with the more customary arrangement in other high-life high rises on Central Park West, such as the Century and the Majestic, where big, rambling lobbies interconnect several elevator banks. What adds such sheltered privacy to lifestyles at the Beresford is that the building's elevators serve only one or two apartments apiece at each landing. Inside each residential suite, however, the overall feeling is one of spaciousness—the most luxurious commodity in New York City apartments and no doubt something of great appeal to Hollywood luminaries, who are used to more expansive domiciles on the West Coast. At the Beresford, each apartment has a splendid central entrance and circulating gallery, so the usual long, corridor-strung rooms of New York apartments are unnecessary. This further adds to the spaciousness within. Not that each room isn't capacious to begin with. Living rooms are as large as 20 x 36 feet, some bedrooms measure 18 x 28 feet, and on some of the building's upper terraced levels, ceilings go up to a lofty twenty-two feet.

But the real grandeur, according to architectural author Andrew Alpert, "comes in the embellishments Emery Roth bestowed on the Beresford, one of his three greatest residential masterpieces to go up in the late 1920s." For example, the four entrances have "grandly conceived and boldly executed framing. Broken pediments, strongly modeled cartouches, and delicate bas-relief are carved in the limestone and are complemented by bronze lanterns and doors. Rising from there is the beige brick bulk with prudently plain casement windows (any repetitive embellishment would have been overwhelming and would have distracted from the strength of the composition). A multitude of skillfully placed elements articulate, emphasize and enhance the basic building form. These are belt courses, balustrades, iron railings, rosettes and cartouches (including one large one proclaiming 'Erected in 1929'). At the terraced setbacks the ornamentation gets more profuse, encompassing obelisks, finials, colonettes, pilasters, corbeled consoles, garlands, angelic cherubs, stark skulls, ram's heads and still more balustrades, pediments and cartouches."

Roth was in love with Greek and Roman temples and Renaissance palaces. He was a classicist, not a modernist; however, he had an intuitive attraction to height and he understood contemporary yearnings and high-density urban living.

From as early as 1905, the firm of Bing and Bing, among the top apartment house builders in the city, gave Roth practically all their buildings to design. It was, however, in 1925, as buildings and spirits began to soar, that Emery Roth expressed in stone what was in people's imagination about the modern age. His forty-one-storied Ritz Tower, on the northeast corner of Park Avenue and 57th Street, was the first residential skyscraper in New York and the tallest such structure in the world. Its sheer verticality dazzled architects and critics, who described it as "sky-puncture," "home five hundred feet high," and an inspiration for a new attitude toward an aerial city. The ornate towers of Roth's San Remo also articulated his affection for classicism and his fidelity to his times. They seemed to lift the building into an almost vertical mode, just as New York City had revised its last legal restraints on height. It was his exaltation in a newly open sky.

Roth's fondness for elaborate enclosures for the water tanks and elevator bulkheads and his concern with the aesthetics of the roof would in time lead to the high-fashion penthouses and gardens in the air. In *New York, New York—How the Apartment House Transformed the Life of the City (1869–1930)*, Elizabeth Hawes puts forth that Roth's genius was his ability to adapt the details of classicism to modern building forms: "He made elegant compositions of the new size and the old spirit. If he was modern it was because he liked the city, its gregariousness and its drama. His buildings showed his urbanity and broadcast the romance of cohabiting height for miles around."

At the Beresford, too, in Andrew Alpern's words, "The grand finale to [his] stone symphony were the fully orchestrated triple towers." Actually, they enclosed octagonal pavillions. The northern one was originally open, and its exuberantly ornamented, mission-tile roof, lighted at night by tall copper lanterns and unusual oeil-de-boeuf windows, is part of the startling apartment of former tennis star and television sport broadcaster John McEnroe, who lives there with his wife, the singer Patty Smythe. McEnroe's is one of three apartments in the Beresford with the much coveted tower rooms that have drop-dead panoramic views. The southeast corner tower suite is owned by *Cosmopolitan* magazine editor Helen Gurley Brown and her film-producer husband, David Brown. Theirs is an especially grand apartment, with a double-height studio living room and additional rooms on three separate levels below. It formerly belonged to theater and film director Mike Nichols before his marriage to Diane Sawyer. The third dramatic tower apartment, on the building's southwest corner overlooking the splendid Rose Planetarium of the American Museum of Natural History, is another "wow" of Manhattan real estate. It is an exceptional four-story home in the clouds, with an added fifth-floor grand attic with high ceilings, massive beams supporting the domed roof, and three oval windows. It was bought in 2004 by the chairman and chief executive of Coach, the leather-goods company, Lew Frankfort, and his wife, Roberta, from Bob Weinstein, cofounder and former cochairman of Miramax Films. The asking price was $14.5 million, but because the building is a co-op, city records do not show how much was actually paid to Bob Weinstein, who with his brother, Harvey, formed a new film production company in 2005 after they split with the Walt Disney Company and left behind their former studio, Miramax. Incidentally, Harvey Weinstein, the other half of Miramax, creatively responsible for such films as *Shakespeare in Love* and *The English Patient,* until recently lived near the Beresford at 88 Central Park West. This is one of New York's under-the-radar celebrity hives, safe haven to rock star Sting and his wife, Trudy Styler; song writer and recording star Paul Simon; *Saturday Night Live*'s Lorne Michaels; actress Celeste Holm; and the *Rolling Stone* magazine's original backer and current publisher of *Interview,* Jane Wenner. Harvey Weinstein's 88 Central Park West apartment—a nine-room duplex that was combined with an adjacent seven-room apartment—went to his ex-wife, Eve Chilton Weinstein, after their divorce in 2005. In October 2006, film star Robert de Niro and his wife bought it for $23 million.

Contextualism is a tricky thing in Manhattan. It doesn't require that a building vanish into the surroundings, but it does mean that a structure has to fit into the mind-set of its neighborhood. New York is unlike other cities around the world where social status is determined largely by what side of the tracks people live on. Still, there are distinct neighborhoods all over Manhattan that define people's social and financial status, ethnic background, and sometimes even age and sexual preference. Furthermore, within those neighborhoods—Chelsea, Carnegie Hill, or Tribeca—there are specific enclaves that speak volumes about the nuances and delineations of special turf in the most exciting, but also the toughest, town in the world.

Central Park West may house the greatest number of entertainment-world eminences (today, Madonna, Mia Farrow, Isabella Rosselini, and Kevin Bacon and Kyra Sedgwick are examples of those who are scattered along the avenue, in handsome apartments outside the major concentration of celebrities at the San Remo, the Dakota, and the Beresford). What has made addresses along the West Side more sought-after than ever is that CPW has always blended a certain flashiness with a bit of frumpiness. The usual comment is that Central Park West is a little "more human" than the elite boulevards of the East Side. The charm of the place has always been in the mix. In contrast to the more homogeneous power elite on Park Avenue and Fifth Avenue, CPW's blue-chip buildings may be somewhat more glitzy and show biz, but they also are inhabited by a wider assortment of today's creative meritocracy—culturally innovative, intellectually influential, idea-marketing, change-effecting individuals like literary agents, museum curators, newspaper publishers, composers, choreographers, and, yes, also some social lions.

Katrina van den Heuvel, editor of the *Nation* and granddaughter of MCA founder Jules Stein, in a *W* magazine interview with James Reginato, remembers growing up in a sprawling Central Park West apartment. "We lived on the second floor, so we could hear the subway rumbling. Thanksgiving, we could reach out our windows and practically touch Bullwinkle. Merv Griffin lived across the hall. My mother had a disco ball in the front hall. Mia Farrow, who lived upstairs, kept adopting a new kid every year."

Though best known for the show biz luminaries protected inside its gates, the Beresford was granted special gravitas by one of the great American stars of academia, the often controversial anthropologist Margaret Mead. She lived at the Beresford for decades until her death in 1978, having moved there while she was curator of ethnology at the American Museum of Natural History across the square and serving as director of research in contemporary cultures at Columbia University. She had just returned from her famous field expeditions researching primitive societies in New Guinea, Samoa, and Bali, the results of which were published in the 1930s, but she continued to speak out on modern social issues and serve on government and international commissions into her seventies. She was particularly devoted to the study of child-rearing patterns in various cultures, and in analyzing the problems of contemporary American youth. Although she authored seven books, her last two, *Culture and Commitment, A Study of the Generation Gap,* and her memoir *Blackberry Winter*—both penned at the Beresford—garnered the most favorable reviews and widest readership.

Vitally contributing to America's cultural sparkle from one of the Beresford's 175 apartments, where he lived with his wife, Phyllis Newman, for almost forty years, was Adolph Green. It was where, with his creative partner, Betty Comden, who lived down the street, he wrote parts of the movie *Singin' in the Rain* and the books and lyrics to such urban frolics as *On the Town, Wonderful Town, Bells Are Ringing,* and *Subways Are for Sleeping.* These smash Broadway shows and movie musicals shaped the world's view of New York as the most charming, the most romantic city on earth. Comden and Green worked with such musical legends as Leonard Bernstein, Morton Gould, Andre Previn, Arthur Schwartz, and Howard Dietz. Among their best-loved songs are "Just in Time," "Make Someone Happy," "The Party's Over," and "New York, New York," the high-octane number unforgettably performed in the MGM film by the sailor-suited trio of Gene Kelly, Frank Sinatra, and Jules Munshin. For years, Newman and Green were fixtures on New York's glittering theatrical and social scenes. Comden and Green, one of the longest-running creative partnerships in theater history, collected Tonys and Grammys, were elected to the Songwriter's Hall of Fame, and in 1993, on the fiftieth anniversary of their song "Ohio" from *Wonderful Town*, were thrown an extravagant party by the governor of that state.

Further adding to the Beresford's heft of cultural output has been artist Elizabeth Strong-Cuevas. Preferring to be called "Bessie," she is the daughter of the Chilean Marquis de Cuevas, who for a while headed the legendary Ballets Russe de Monte Carlo and is a Rockefeller on her mother's side, but doesn't want anyone to know it, since she carved out recognition on her own in New York's highly competitive art world. And of course Isaac Stern, who, with his Guarnerius del Gesu violin, continuously performed and recorded an exceptionally wide-ranging schedule and regularly toured with Emmanuel Ax, Jaime Laredo, and Yo-Yo Ma. Their chamber music tours together resulted in highly successful recordings of piano quartets by Beethoven, Brahms, Fauré, Schumann, and Dvorak. While he lived at the Beresford, the Academy Award–winning documentary *From Mao to Mozart* was made about a trip he took in 1980 to China. This came on the heels of another highly successful film, *Journey to Jerusalem*, about a performance of Mendelssohn's Violin Concerto that Stern gave following the Six Day War—atop Mt. Scopus, with the Israel Philharmonic conducted by Leonard Bernstein. But Russian-born Isaac Stern's commitment to music's transcendence as a way to bring the human family closer together involved him in civic activities beyond music. He became an originating member of the National Endowment for the Arts, and, as president of Carnegie Hall for over thirty-five years, he spearheaded the drive to save the great concert hall from demolition. His humanitarian efforts earned him the highest honors from around the world: the Order of the Rising Sun from Japan, the Legion of Honor from the French Republic, Israel's Wolf Prize, the Commander's Cross of the Danish government's Order of Dannebrog, and America's Presidential Medal of Freedom.

The father of three and grandfather of five, Isacc Stern moved to Connecticut when he sold his Beresford duplex co-op in April 1998 to Jerry Seinfeld.

Like Steven Spielberg at the Beresford's sister building, the San Remo, after Spielberg paid $7.3 million for the thirteen-room apartment to *Saturday Night Fever* producer Robert Stigwood, Seinfeld hired "architect to the stars" Charles Gwathmey to renovate the place. The Spielberg renovation, with its never-ending jackhammering, drove his neighbors—some of them writers and editors—absolutely crazy. Because the renovations went on for three ear-splitting years, Gwathmey's interior face-lift made the gossip columns regularly. So much so that Spielberg offered to rent offices for his fellow San Remo denizens so that they could pursue their screenwriting and wordsmithing in peace and quiet.

Because these power tools play such havoc with the lives of fellow New Yorkers in these aerial arrangements of communal living, in recent years co-op boards in these prestigious buildings have adopted stringent regulations regarding renovations. Installation of a new bathroom sink or construction of a new bookcase needs to be approved by the board, and with a new buyer, the co-op asks for a submission of renovation plans. Jerry Seinfeld promised the board that his renovations would be finished in four months, even though they included tearing down the existing staircase, sealing it up, and then creating a brand-new shaft between the floors in another part of the apartment to create a glamorous new staircase of imported marble. Naturally, after the four-month time limit, the interior architecture was far from completed. Jerry Seinfeld kept charmingly apologizing for the fact that his contractors hadn't finished, but after another month the Beresford's co-op board began to fine him $500 a day for not meeting the deadline.

Jerry Seinfeld meanwhile had married Jessica Sklar on Christmas Day 1999. And by the time the costly renovations on the duplex were finally finished, they had a baby daughter, Sasha, who was born in November 2000. Evidently, Jerry and Jessica thought the three-bedroom duplex was not enough for their budding family, because almost as soon as Gwathmey's work on the duplex was done, they bought a second apartment next door from Broadway producer Edgar Lansbury—Angela Lansbury's brother, who, with Yoko Ono, put some of the $8.6 million he made on his Beresford home into the 2005 musical in which seven different actors—some of them women—played the role of rock legend John Lennon.

When it came to renovating the former Lansbury apartment, the Beresford board wasted not a minute and made even stricter rules: All renovations had to be completed within ninety working days, excluding weekends. If the gutting and spiffing-up exceeded that period, penalties would start at $1,000 a day for the first month and after that would double to $2,000 a day.

By the time the Seinfeld renovation was over, reports Steven Gaines in his book *The Sky's the Limit*, the Beresford was enriched by hundreds of thousands of dollars, so much of the anger was dispelled. As for Jerry Seinfeld, he could easily afford the tab. In 2004, *Forbes* magazine reported his earnings for that year alone as $267 million, which made him the highest-earning celebrity of that year. Even though the sitcom ended in May 1998, *Seinfeld* continues to generate revenue. In fact, it makes more in syndication than most current shows. And Jerry continues to work. He returned to stand-up comedy. His process of developing and performing new material for his special brand of laughter-making he calls "observational comedy" was chronicled in the 2002 documentary *Comedian,* and he's written several books. Though not attributed to him, it is widely believed he is the real author of Ted L. Nancy's *Letters from a Nut* and Ed Broth's *Stories from a Moron,* since no one has ever seen these authors publicly, whereas Jerry Seinfeld has been heavily involved in pitching the works. Seinfeld has also written a children's book called *Halloween.* The neighbors seem to have forgotten the long-running renovation drama, after the Seinfelds added two more babies to their family: a son, Julian, was born in March 2003 and another son, Shepherd, came in August 2005. Jerry Seinfeld has endeared himself to his neighbors with his friendly, chatty charm on the elevator and in the building's private gym in the basement. Jessica, too, has proven that the Seinfeld humor has rubbed off on her. Recently, when a *New York* magazine reporter asked her how she put up with the eternal hordes of red-carpet photographers screaming, "Jessica! Over here!" she endearingly quipped, "Oh, it's fine. I just think it's funny that they shout just as loud to every single person, so even D-listers like myself have to stop and pose and pretend like we think they care."

Today, the Beresford may be home to moguls and superstars, yet it also typifies the peculiar conditions of New York City's complex civilization.

Well into the 1920s and 1930s, the majority of New York's West Side apartments were designed for families with children. The wondrously interesting apartment houses like the Beresford that rose along Central

Park to create one of America's most resplendent skylines had staggering room counts by today's standards. In them, twelve-room apartments were the norm. Gradually, with the disappearance of servants, New Yorkers' smaller families and the crushing financial problems affecting Manhattanites during the Depression, many of the larger suites were subdivided to suit changing ways of life. Many of the wealthy families who moved into Emery Roth's glamorous Beresford and San Remo did so because they were rental buildings, whereas some of the elegant East Side edifices were organized as cooperatives—elite, exclusive, and "restricted," which meant they could, in the manner of clubs, exclude anyone they deemed "undesirable," which in those days often meant "Jewish." Kept away from Fifth and Park avenues by social pressures, affluent and influential Jewish New Yorkers looked more and more for luxurious lodgings on the Upper West Side. Emery Roth himself lived there. Completed a mere month before the stock market crash of 1929, the Beresford had a very hard time fighting off the Great Depression. "It succumbed in 1940, and was sold in tandem with the San Remo apartments for the incredible sum of $25,000 over the mortgages (for both buildings)," writes architecture historian Andrew Alpern.

As the political climate darkened in Europe in the late 1930s, wealthier Jewish families got out of the troubled continent and they, too, found their way to "nonrestricted," fabulous Manhattan towers on Central Park West, like the Majestic, the Eldorado, the Century, and the Beresford.

Peter Osnos, publisher and chief executive officer of *Public Affairs*, recalls how his parents, who grew up in Warsaw and spent much of the 1930s in Paris, happened to be in Poland when the war broke out in 1939. Only through acts of great courage were they able to escape.

"They made their way across Romania, Turkey and Iraq and found refuge in Bombay, where they lived until securing visas to the United States. A troop ship transported them across the Pacific, and in the spring of 1944, they arrived by train in New York," Osnos remembers. His parents were in their thirties, and he was "barely six months old with an Indian birth certificate that declared 'Caste: Polish.'" His parents originally split an apartment with two other families on the corner of Broadway and 86th Street, with furniture from the Salvation Army. "It's hard to believe that they were barely a decade from their harrowing escape, when they were able to buy a summer home on a lake in New Jersey," and less than another decade later prosperous enough to move into an eighth-floor apartment in the

Beresford. During this time, the Beresford had also had its ups and downs. Recovering after World War II, it went on to become a cooperative in 1962—among the first on Central Park West. Peter Osnos's parents paid $40,000 for apartment 8B, which, while relatively modest by Beresford standards, "had the splendor—the enormous rooms, the beautiful moldings, the door and elevator men, the view of the park that represented the lifestyle that they had expected for themselves before they were forced to leave everything behind when they fled the Nazi onslaught of Europe." He realized how important it was for them "to reclaim graciousness in their lives to match the courage and energy they had expended in rescuing themselves.... Every time I pass the place," which he thinks is more splendid than ever, beautifully maintained, and worth every penny poured into it. "I pay my respects to its enduring beauty and the tradition of urban good living that it represents," and he thinks of his parents, "whose own strength and style it served so well."

The flight to the suburbs after World War II dealt another terrific blow to the Upper West Side. It brought about the serious deterioration of many neighborhoods. These increasingly slummy streets, plagued by warring juvenile gangs, increased crime, and ethnic conflict were the inspiration for Leonard Bernstein's classic *West Side Story.* But by the late 1960s, the renovation and rebuilding were underway, first triggered by the arrival of the throbbing cultural activity around Lincoln Center and, in the 1980s and then again with the new millennium, by a tremendous number of new luxury high rises—particularly the Trump International Tower, the Time Warner Center, and the Zeckendorf brothers' new, block-long 15 Central Park West apartment complex, where the Mayflower Hotel used to be.

Most people who pass by the Beresford at night can't help but wonder about who might be living in those three intriguingly lighted tower apartments. Yet, as astonishing a luxury perch as the expanded tower triplexes of John McEnroe, Lew Frankfort, and Helen Gurley Brown may be, the most breathtakingly glamorous apartment in the Beresford is said to be the nineteenth-floor, southeast corner penthouse right below the Browns, next door to where lyricist Adolph Green had composed his legendary musicals. This is the former penthouse of Rock Hudson, epitome of the dashing Hollywood leading man of the 1950s and 1960s.

The movie star whose string of box-office hits with Doris Day featured a series of snappy New York bachelor pads had, in real life, acquired one of

the ultimate penthouse suites on Central Park West. Though not a huge Beresford mansion-sized home, the nine-room beauty has a private elevator opening directly into the apartment. Its two spacious setback corner terraces are tastefully embellished with ornamental ironwork, decorative terracotta floors, potted shrubbery, corbeled consoles, finials, and stone obelisks. The magnificent view to be enjoyed from the conversational groupings of wrought iron garden chairs and sun-chaises encompasses the Great Lawn, the reservoir, Shakespeare's Garden, the Delacorte Theater, Belvedere Castle, the Swedish Cottage, Turtle Pond, Rowboat Lake, the Sheep Meadow, and, beyond that, the whole skyline stretch of Fifth Avenue high rises along the other side of Central Park.

The penthouse made news for several years, when, right after the actor famously died of AIDS in October 1985 at fifty-nine, the spread was sold for a then staggering price of $2 million. Following the sale of Hudson's New York City home, a private trust was reported to have purchased Hudson's twenty-five-acre Beverly Hills estate for $2.89 million. The buyer of the nineteenth-floor Beresford penthouse has ripped out every inch of his three-bedroom place. Nicholas J. Clay, chief executive of Avica Technology, a digital cinema company in Los Angeles, bought the apartment in 1998 and redid the inside to "make it more of a family apartment and bring the unit up-to-date." It still has a private elevator, two bedrooms, and an upstairs study that is a vestige of a time before Rock Hudson, when the apartment was a full duplex. "I really wanted to hold on to it because it was such a gem," said Clay. "It ultimately came to a point where we weren't using it." There were multiple bidders for the suite when it came on the market in the summer of 2005, but it was actress Glenn Close and the man she had been seeing for a year, David E. Shaw, founder of a biotechnology company for veterinarian diagnostic devices in Maine, who bought the Rock Hudson penthouse for around $6.5 million.

One Beekman Place

· 11 ·

One Beekman Place

RIVERFRONT PRIVILEGE
SINCE COLONIAL TIMES

$\mathcal{F}$ROM THE EARLIEST existence of a social pecking order in this vibrant metropolis, down through the centuries, the high desirability of the cliff-top riverfront site of One Beekman Place was recognized by New York's wealthiest cosmopolitan elite.

Located at the end of a tranquil, tree-lined row of townhouses, which over the years were owned by such super-rich personages as philanthropist Mary Lasker, who planted all the trees and flowers in the center of Park Avenue, and Mexico's most powerful media Midas, the handsome and glamorous Emilio Azcárraga, this bucolic corner, high above the bustling East River Drive at East 50th Street, and looking like an exclusive garden district of a European capital, has been synonymous with the wealthy at play.

The Beekman family—Colonial New York's richest merchant clan, which had intermarried with the Anglo-aristocratic Livingstons and the Dutch-manorial Van Rensselaers—built their waterside mansion on this site back in 1764. At that time, the frolicsome combination of river access and idyllic setting became New York Society's favorite picnic grounds. Soon the Beekman estate on the strip along the river gained something of a cachet resembling that of an exclusive beach resort.

Margaret Beekman, in her youth, was not just an heiress; she was the heiress of New York. She was the sole surviving child of Colonel Henry Beekman, who owned 240,000 acres of land along the Hudson, known as the Beekman Patent. It was her eldest son, Robert R. Livingston Jr., a drafter of the Declaration of Independence but better known as Chancellor Livingston, who, as New York State's highest legal official, administered the oath of office at George Washington's inauguration as the first president of the United States on the steps of Federal Hall, at the corner of Wall Street and Broad Street in downtown Manhattan, on April 30, 1789. One of Margaret's sons-in-law was the Revolutionary War hero General Richard Montgomery, who died during the storming of Quebec. Another of Margaret Beekman's sons, Edward Livingston, better known as "Beau Ned," was, despite his patrician background, intellectually enraptured with the idea of democracy. He served as mayor of New York City, became U.S. senator from Louisiana and was secretary of state under President Andrew Jackson.

Hundreds of illustrious New York surnames have been joined to the Beekman clan, among them Roosevelt, Astor, and Schuyler. But they also married people with names like Duyckink and Schwartz, Smith and Jones. According to the old adage, social eminence is determined by three criteria: pedigree, property, and cash. In an ever-changing New York of constantly new, ambitiously climbing, and enormously talented people trying to parlay wealth into social position, the Beekman family did pretty well for over two centuries.

The Beekmans stubbornly held on to their precious terraces and gardens along the East River until the towering steam plants of industrialization made them give up the fight and sell in 1922. But they should have held on, because by 1930, John D. Rockefeller Jr.'s son-in-law David M. Milton was set to build the luxurious sixteen-story co-op that, with $1 million borrowed from his father-in-law, would become One Beekman Place. In key with the site's reputation as a privileged playground, the apartment house featured a waterside complex of tea rooms, gym, swimming pool and squash courts.

Because Milton's wife, Abby Rockefeller, was dubbed "the wealthiest young woman in America" by the *New York Times,* and because the newspaper soon after reported that the young couple were taking an eighteen-room triplex with a 33 × 25 foot living room at One Beekman, in a manner typical of how status-conscious New Yorkers react to such publicity, the other twenty-three duplexes in the building were almost instantly sold.

Among the early tenants were Ambassador David K. E. Bruce and his first wife, the former Ailsa Mellon. One of the most gifted and seasoned diplomats of his generation, Bruce's great charm, wit, and smooth ability to cool heated situations led him to a distinguished career that included heading three of America's premiere embassies, in London, Paris, and Bonn. A tall, exquisitely dressed man with a slight limp and a trace of a Tidewater accent, Bruce was the son of a U.S. senator from Maryland who had won a Pulitzer Prize for a biography of Benjamin Franklin. Although David Kirkpatrick Este Bruce was a Democrat, the diplomatic assignments he took were nonpartisan. He served presidents Truman, Eisenhower, Kennedy, Johnson, Nixon, and Ford. While he and his stylish second wife, Evangeline Bruce, presided over some of the most glittering diplomatic parties, such as the lavish traditional Fourth of July celebration at the Paris embassy for the American community there—for which he pitched in considerable personal funds—Bruce had also handled some of the most vexing diplomatic crises. He led the American delegation at the stalemated Paris peace talks to end the war in Vietnam. He became the first head of the U.S. liaison office set up in China in 1973 and served sixteen months as the U.S. delegate to the North Atlantic Treaty Organization.

One of David K. E. Bruce's neighbors at One Beekman Place was Major General William J. Donovan, for whom Bruce served as right-hand man during World War II during the formation of the Office of Strategic Services, the intelligence-gathering organization that later evolved into the Central Intelligence Agency.

There also were other Rockefellers in the building from the beginning. One of them was Abby Milton's brother John D. Rockefeller III and his wife Blanchette, the beautiful Vassar-educated daughter of Elon Huntington Hooker, a chemist and hydrodynamic engineer who founded the Hooker Electrochemical Company in Rochester, New York, and also ran for governor in 1920. A woman of elegant restraint but vital civic involvement, her accomplishments ranged from her main interest, the Museum of Modern Art, to education and medicine. The Blanchette Rockefeller Neurosciences Institute in Morgantown, West Virginia, was established in her memory by her son Jay Rockefeller, the U.S. senator from West Virginia, who grew up at One Beekman Place.

Another famous political figure, former New Jersey Governor Christine Todd Whitman, spent her early years at One Beekman. Both her father, Webster B. Todd, and grandfather, John R. Todd, were contractors working with the Rockefellers on the plans for Rockefeller Center, not only with architects Corbett, Harrison & MacMurry, but also with Sloan & Robertson, the architects for One Beekman.

Along the way, One Beekman Place duplexes were occupied by two of the twentieth century's most notorious playboys: Rita Hayworth's one-time husband Prince Aly Khan and A & P supermarket heir Huntington Hartford. These infinitely loaded, incorrigible *enfants terribles* took advantage of the fact that each duplex had two separate entrances, with an elevator stop on two different floors. These fast-living cads shamelessly delighted in an endless stream of pretty young things coming and going to their lairs at all hours of the night and day, and they could easily juggle the female traffic. One newly arriving beauty would be greeted by the houseman downstairs, while the previous young lady would be quickly ushered out of the bedroom by the host and sent on her way through the upstairs elevator exit.

This story comes from a German-born beauty, now married in Palm Beach and wishing to remain anonymous, but one who clearly knows her way around the building, for back in the late 1950s she dallied with both Aly Khan and Huntington Hartford. Aly warned her, "Don't try to make me jealous. It won't work!" And he gave her another tip: "When I take you to a restaurant, you can order anything you want. But you must eat what is on your plate. I can't stand women who order the most expensive thing on the menu and then just swish the food around the plate with their fork."

Another famous ladies' man, Sacramento-born, self-made television producer Mark Goodson, was a flamboyant host in his spectacular One Beekman Place apartment, where he entertained some of the most attractive starlets and journalists of the 1960s. A few of them, like Barbara Walters, became TV legends. Goodson, whose radio and television career lasted more than half a century, devised and produced dozens of game shows, including some of the longest-running ones in TV history, such as *What's My Line?, The Price Is Right,* and *Family Feud.* With all his shows, Goodson personally selected the hosts and panelists. He made household names out of John Daly, Arlene Francis, Dorothy Kilgallen, and Bennett Cerf. He was also responsible for bringing to television such familiar game show elements as buzzers, bells, and "returning champions."

A highly literate and articulate man, Goodson sometimes expressed regret that the game show business was essentially without status. When he wanted to buy his Beekman Place duplex, he got whiff of the fact that he would probably be rejected by the co-op board. Without hesitation, he decided to use his media muscle. He called up Blanchette Rockefeller, at the time a major figure in New York City's art circles and an important contributor to the city's community services, and threatened to publicize the fact that he was kept out by an anti-Semitic building full of Rockefellers. Goodson assured her he would sabotage her brother-in-law Nelson Rockefeller's gubernatorial campaign if he were turned down at One Beekman Place. He got into the building.

Among today's co-op owners at One Beekman Place are fashion designer Arnold Scaasi and his partner, the book agent, cable TV book show host, and social catalyst Parker Ladd. Add striking brunette Barbara de Kwiatkowski, a former model and one-time girlfriend of such coveted examples of the New York male as wildlife photographer Peter Beard and the late CBS chairman William Paley. She is the widow of swaggering Polish entrepreneur Henryk de Kwiatkowski, who made a fortune leasing and selling aging airplanes to developing countries and owned Calumet Farms, the storied home of nine Derby-winning thoroughbreds in the Kentucky bluegrass area. While Barbara de Kwiatkowski had to give up their house in the Bahamas to Henryk's four children from a previous marriage, after his death in 2003, she got a big chunk from the sale of the Kwiatkowski estate in Connecticut, Conyers Farm, which sold for a headline-making $50 million.

In 2005, television star Jane Pauley and her famous cartoonist husband, Garry Trudeau, creator of the long-running Doonesbury comic strip, bought a triplex maisonette with a two-story living room that opens onto a garden overlooking the East River. And finally, there's opera patroness Princess Titi von Furstenberg, a Texas oil heiress who divides her year among homes in Paris, Salzburg, and New York. She grew up in Houston, a member of the Blaffer family of Humble Oil, playing with the young Howard Hughes, both their families having benefited from the giant gusher of the 1930s, Spindle Top, which made them all Texas "giants."

Princess Titi, the stepmother of Egon von Furstenberg, was one of the determined forces behind what was perhaps the most dramatic removal by a Manhattan co-op board of a legendary American character from a famous luxury building: the 1982 eviction of seventy-year-old supermarket heir Huntington Hartford from his fourteen-room duplex.

Although most co-ops spell out causes for eviction and for what constitutes inappropriate behavior in their buildings, it is very rare that a shareholder in an A-plus apartment house is forced to leave over a "morals issue." The eccentric, silver-haired playboy, publisher, museum-founder, resort entrepreneur, show-business impresario, and self-appointed culture warrior against the high-modern New York aesthetic of the 1960s and the prevalent taste for formalist functionalism and abstract art, after squandering much of his A & P inheritance, had, in 1982, sunken into a dissolute, druggy existence. Once one of the richest men in America, who also had homes in Cap d'Antibes, Palm Beach, London, and owned a 240-acre estate in Los Angeles, at one point Huntington Hartford could afford anything his heart desired. Foremost among these were much younger women. Four of them became his wives. At one time he palled around with Errol Flynn, the Duke of Windsor, Salvador Dali, and the Beatles. His exploits were covered in newspapers around the world. Magazines showed him with a bevy of beauties night after night, at such glamorous New York and Hollywood hot spots as El Morocco, the Stork Club, and Ciro's. For the 1962 opening party of his new resort in the Bahamas, Paradise Island, two thousand guests were flown down on private jets. There was major press coverage of everything he did, such as the 1954 opening of the Huntington Hartford Theater, the first legitimate theater in Los Angeles in three decades, and Hartford's founding of a 145-acre artists' colony in the Santa Monica Mountains, where Edward Hopper and Pulitzer Prize–winning composer Ernst Toch were artists in residence. His short-lived but thoroughly unique glossy magazine, *Show*, launched in 1961, made quite a splash and became a collector's item. And when, in 1964, he opened his controversial New York museum, the Gallery of Modern Art, in an Edward Durell Stone Venetian-Gothic-inspired structure at 2 Columbus Circle, which bore the personal imprint of Hartford's taste for swank interior decor and figurative art—especially Pre-Raphaelite and surrealist paintings—he went against every fashionable aesthetic of the day. It was dismissed by critics as "an adventure in vanity."

Less than twenty years later, fellow residents at One Beekman Place, according to a former resident who had been married to two prominent movie actors, became increasingly concerned by the procession of druggy, spaced-out, teenage women coming through the lobby to visit the aging Hartford. Neighbors worried about the decadent goings-on in the apartment, which they felt had become a flophouse for undesirable hangers-on, and called the police on several occasions. After a particularly nasty night in the Hartford duplex, when a young woman—supposedly Hartford's secretary—was reportedly assaulted by him and his fourth wife with hair scissors, the building decided to put him out. All the tenants signed the petition to evict him, except one. That was quiz show producer Mark Goodson. He said he just didn't have the heart to throw a man, down on his luck, out of his home and into the street.

Huntington Hartford, who for a while lived in total obscurity in Brooklyn, then in seclusion in upstate New York, at this writing is ninety-five and living in the Bahamas, where he is being taken care of by his daughter Juliet, from his third marriage.

820 Fifth Avenue

· 12 ·

820 Fifth Avenue

ONE MAGNIFICENT APARTMENT TO EVERY FLOOR

*P*ICTURE IT: ONE of those Hollywood swells—say, Cary Grant, tapping a cigarette he is about to light with infinite panache against his jewel-encrusted, gold cigarette case—or Robert Montgomery perfecting a martini in a frost-gathering silver cocktail shaker. Think of Joel McCrae in white tie, flinging open a pair of tufted-leather Art Deco doors and springing a surprise announcement in what is clearly an ineffably enviable Manhattan apartment, noisy with the hum of gaiety and glittering with lights.

Everything about the allure of money, breeding, taste, wit, and glamour in those ritzy 1930s movies depicting the New York high life could have been pitch-perfect evocations of what it once was like, and still is, inside 820 Fifth Avenue, one of the three most expensive apartment houses in New York.

Yet money—even hundreds and millions of dollars—is not enough to get you into this glistening, gray, twelve-story limestone palazzo surrounded by a meticulously landscaped patch of blossoming cherry trees, well-kept shrubs, and lush grass on the corner of East 63rd Street. The splendor of lives insulated by luxury is only barely suggested by the building's elegantly subdued finishing touches, such as its subtly gleaming copper cornice and a pair of highly polished, thick, bronze filigree doors guarded by two doormen in dark gray uniforms with tuxedo stripes running down the sides of their trousers.

This is one of the best addresses in the world. 820 Fifth has been the home of such golden couples as CBS chairman William Paley and his Best-Dressed-Hall-of-Fame wife, Babe; Ann and Gordon Getty of the California oil billions; Kathryn and Arthur Murray of the famous dancing schools; former governor of New York and U.S. presidential candidate Al Smith; Eberhard Faber, whose name has been on billions of pencils and crayons; Peruvian former secretary general of the United Nations, Javier Perez de Cuellar; and legendary Greek shipping Midas, Stavros Niarchos.

Truly a rarefied universe, this is one of the few buildings left in New York where each grand eighteen-room apartment—only twelve of them, one to each floor, and every floor a veritable museum—has never been subdivided since it was built in 1916 by the master architects of the time, Starett and Van Vleck. "If you can judge a person by his handshake, you can feel the character of a building in its hardware. A solid brass door knob on a solid-core door tells you that the house itself is solid," reports Lauren Ramsby. The March 14, 1994, issue of the *New York Observer* describes the entry to the building, which has not much more decor than two bronze-and-glass lanterns and a lovely bronze mirror. "A door can take only so much brass, a room can take only so much chandelier ... the building is recognized as not only solid but steadfast, having largely avoided the yuppie invasion of the Upper East Side," in the 1990s, when young men on Wall Street were suddenly raking in seven times the commissions their fathers made.

From the lobby, where an armed guard sits 24/7, twin elevators—one reserved for parties in progress, though at times used for less frolicsome purposes—open directly onto the breathtakingly big, forty-three-foot-long entrance gallery with parquet de Versailles floors, the opulent first impression to each apartment. With the exception of the maisonettes, the layouts at 820 Fifth are all identical. In the wake of this entrance hall of immense square footage—lavished on most floors with art and decorative objects that reek of money beyond belief—follows a series of beautiful entertaining or public reception rooms, each opening into the next through sets of double doors, and beautifully flowing from living room, sitting room, library, dining room, each with its own fireplace with at least nine generous windows on each floor, facing Central Park. These voluminous apartments—where the rooms resemble those found in European chateaux—seldom change hands because they are unique even among the greatest A-plus buildings of New York. Most Fifth Avenue buildings have their bedrooms in the back. Here, the spacious master bedroom has a wonderful park view, and the layout of the rest is such that a separate hallway leading to the huge 400-square-foot kitchen, which has four sinks, and to seven servants' rooms in the back, allows the staff to go about their tasks pretty much unseen by the apartment owners.

To attain this address is "probably the longest gauntlet to run," comments Steven M. L. Aronson in a 1993 *Town & Country* article. "Here it's not just the magnitude of one's wealth that weighs but its loftiness." The price of admission to 820 Fifth is chic, pedigreed, legendary money as opposed to instant wealth made through funeral parlors, fast-food chains, or parking lots. There is still a lingering whiff here of that 1890s social arbiter, Ward McAllister and his idea of New York's Four Hundred—the people in society who count. McAllister's dictum of separating the "nobs" of breeding and position from the rest of New York's achievers does seem to permeate the unwritten laws that govern who gets in and who does not when it comes to this building.

Entertaining smart, showing off one's class through astute art collecting, exquisite furnishings, and beautiful clothes, and giving deliciously novel dinner parties or private balls—which generations of "Fifth Avenoodles," as old newspapers used to call the furiously social people on the avenue—still matters in this building. The residents at 820 are committed to their *juste milieu*—their special way of life. Some things have changed, however. Years ago, only fabulous wealth with illustrious family genealogy—a name like Du Pont, Goelet, or Cushing—could get you into the building. Today, big money with occupational prestige can do the trick. For example, among present apartment owners are the attractive and very social William and Donna Acquavella, who own an important Madison Avenue gallery and are active on the benefit circuit both in Manhattan and in their Southampton summer quarters, and the senior partner of the pedigreed and infinitely powerful international financial firm Lazard Frères, Michel David-Weill. It is David-Weill who now has the dazzling ninth-floor apartment where that great giver and enjoyer of parties, the late William S. Paley and his beautiful swanlike wife, held forth and entertained the cream of New York among their Gaugins, Cézannes, and Picassos—which Paley later bequeathed to the

Museum of Modern Art—in a style that was celebrated in newspaper columns and glossy magazines around the world.

Today a potential owner must have at least ten times the net worth of the apartment, which means that he must have no less than $150 million in liquid assets. And this is one of the "all cash" buildings. No one can buy a co-op here with a mortgage. Yet not all credit-worthy individuals get in. For example, Ronald Perelman, the owner of Revlon, was embarrassingly turned down at 820 Fifth. So was another man worth hundreds of millions of dollars, and without an explanation: gas-and-oil heir Frederick Koch. Quite astonished by the rejection, Koch, already residing in a prestigious Fifth Avenue abode, expanded his digs by adding another to it next door at 825 Fifth.

And by the way, this is a city that does not forget. With nearly nine-million people, with nine-million stories in the crowded city, you still have to behave in New York. The things you do to others can come back to haunt you. The man whose call you never returned, the people you might have slighted in some business deal, may be sitting on the co-op board of the apartment of your dreams. And, oh wow, revenge can be sweet! That's exactly what happened to Asher Edelman, another billionaire kept from buying an apartment by the co-op board of 820 Fifth Avenue. Edelman, a Wall Street arbitrageur, was often described as "a feared corporate raider" in his fierce skirmishes to wrest control of companies he had invested in from entrenched management. Edelman, who did buy a supreme apartment at 120 East End Avenue, later retired to run an art museum in Switzerland. Newspapers speculated that one reason for his retirement was increased government scrutiny of corporate raiders in the late 1980s.

"This is a very nervous building," Town & Country's Aronson quotes an aspirant to 820 Fifth Avenue, which he dubs "a club for serious art collectors."

The discreet and inconspicuous simplicity of the exterior that safeguards the anonymity and privacy of its residents hardly hints at the mindboggling possessions and museum-caliber treasures contained within each eighteen-room suite. World famous experts from all continents are constantly coming in to restore masterpieces of Impressionism, fabled eighteenth-century French furniture, giant golden Buddhas and precious Tang horses from China, patching up cracks in the splendorous artifacts and architectural touches inside these walls.

The late Chauncey Stillman, a longtime resident of the building and a descendent of Roger Williams, the founder of Rhode Island, owned one of the most priceless Florentine cinquecento treasures—the world's only Jacopo da Pontormo in private hands.

Although art dealer William Acquavella is president of 820's co-op board, the all-powerful grande dame of the building is Jayne Wrightsman. The slim, stylish, chiseled-featured brunette is the octogenarian widow of Charles Wrightsman, an immensely rich if at times difficult Oklahoma oilman. His two daughters, Charlene and Irene, married two famous international playboys of the 1950s, Igor Cassini, also known as the society columnist Cholly Knickerbocker, and the handsome Australian and best friend of Errol Flynn, the bobsledding Olympic champion Freddy MacEvoy. Jayne Wrightsman is said to have met her then newly divorced husband back in Los Angeles, while working behind the perfume counter of a department store. She admirably made it her business to educate herself in the art of connoisseurship and all things French, after her oilman husband presented her with a palatial twenty-eight-room Palm Beach house soon after their wedding. With the help of the world-famous Parisian decorator Stephane Boudin, she turned the villa into one of the resort's showplaces and entertained the likes of the Duke and Duchess of Windsor, auto-industry power broker Ernest Kanzler of Grosse Pointe and Hobe Sound, and the very social Woolworth Donahue clan, who had inherited the five-and-dime-store fortune. She also headed several noteworthy Palm Beach charity balls and became one of the closest friends of Jacqueline Kennedy—another Francophile and art lover, who put her in charge of acquiring fine antiques when, as First Lady, she decided to redecorate the White House. Jayne Wrightsman and her astute advisors, who included the savvy Parisian *antiquaire* Bernard Baruch Steinitz, will live on in the minds of future generations of art appreciators through the Wrightsman Collection of eighteenth-century art and furniture and the handsome wing she bequeathed to the Metropolitan Museum of Art, twenty blocks up Fifth Avenue from her home.

The Wrightsmans' tenure at 820 Fifth, however, was not without its drama. On April 1, 1986, gossip spread like wildfire among the A-plus domiciles of Fifth Avenue, that a very pretty blonde had jumped to her death from the roof of the building at 820. There were only two smashing blondes living at 820 at the time: the British-born, platinum-tressed Valerie Sabet, married to a close friend of the Shah, Iranian financier Hormoz Sabet; and tawny, blond, former top model Kit Gill, wife of businessman Robert Lieberman. It turned out the suicide was the twenty-three-year-old sous-chef working for the Wrightsmans.

The Wrightsmans had so many servants that Mrs. Wrightsman bought a couple of the extra servants' rooms on top of the building and later bought two doctor's offices on the ground floor, to serve as sitting rooms for her chauffeur and her butler. However, realizing that she already had a whole brownstone around the corner on East 64th Street for her huge staff, she soon sold the doctor's offices to Lily Safra, wife of the Lebanese-born investment banker Edmond Safra, who lived in the topmost apartment on the twelfth floor, for her married daughter from a previous marriage.

Nothing revealed Jayne Wrightsman's unimpeachable control over the building more than the fact that the clothing designer Tommy Hilfiger was able to enter the hallowed portals of 820 and secure for himself the much-coveted fourth-floor gem of an apartment that had been for over seventy years in the hands of the Old Guard Social Register family, the Cranes. It was originally the home of Mrs. W. Murray Crane, the widow of U.S. Senator Winthrop Crane of Massachusetts, who, along with Blanchette Rockefeller, was one of the co-founders of the Museum of Modern Art as well as a founder of the Dalton School, a prestigious progressive school on New York's Upper East Side attended by several children of movie stars. The apartment had been lived in for many years by her daughter Louise Crane, a well-known poet and a considerable philanthropist in her own right. Louise Crane gave much of the family money, which incidentally came from the manufacturing of porcelain toilet bowls, to endow music and art projects throughout the city. When Louise Crane died in 1998, her apartment went on the market for $13.5 million. So rare is it that anything opens in the building, that almost immediately potential buyers appeared at the doorstep. One of them was a Johnson & Johnson heiress, Libbet Johnson. But the deal fell through when Libbet Johnson wanted to buy a second apartment in the building and combine the two. Horrified that Johnson's ambitious construction work might take years, Mrs. Wrightsman and the co-op board nixed the deal.

If there is one group of New Yorkers most discriminated against in Fifth Avenue and Park Avenue co-ops, it is fashion designers. Though the men and women who live in these high-priced high-rise buildings probably spend more money on finely made fashionable clothes than anyone anywhere, they tend to think of designers in the snobby British way as "trade." They dismissively refer to them as "garmentos."

What got Tommy Hilfiger into the building at 820 Fifth Avenue was a very clever, very seasoned real estate broker, Alice Mason. For many years known to New Yorkers for giving monthly dinner parties for the city's movers and shakers whose names regularly appeared in boldface in newspaper columns, Mason put together a very seductive board package for the designer whose sportswear empire was built mostly from baggy pants that were such a favorite with hip-hop musicians and would-be rappers. What emerged from the letters of recommendation, some lovingly written by childhood friends from Hilfiger's upstate New York hometown, some by such substantial business figures as Leonard Lauder, head of the cosmetic empire Estée Lauder, which distributed Hilfiger's blockbuster perfume, was the profile of a highly successful, self-made young man who was married to his first girlfriend and was the father of three appealing children. But what snagged Jayne Wrightsman's attention in the application package was that Tommy Hilfiger—like Wrightsman herself—was a fellow benefactor, of all things, of the Metropolitan Museum. Jayne Wrightsman is totally devoted to the institution, traveling with curators to Europe and the Far East, and giving generously to the museum not only financially but also with her time and art expertise. A few years before his quest of a supreme address in the most discriminating of New York buildings, Hilfiger had made a generous million-dollar-plus donation to the Costume Institute of the Metropolitan Museum. Amazingly, Hilfiger's other major charitable gift was to another of Wrightsman's pet charities, the Fresh Air Fund, which allows inner-city children to experience summer camp.

Although Hilfiger was approved by the board, he never moved into 820 Fifth. Just a few months after closing on the coveted fourth-floor apartment of the Cranes, his $2.5 billion business started to come apart with the end of the craze for baggy pants. And so did his marriage of twenty years.

Meanwhile, as a result of a much-written-about occurrence in December 1999, Lily Safra became one of the world's wealthiest widows. When Mrs. Safra heard that Tommy Hilfiger decided that a downtown apartment would be more fitting for his altered lifestyle, and the fourth floor apartment was about to come on the market—this time for $18 million, she immediately snapped it up for her daughter.

The mysterious death of Edmond Safra, founder of Republic Bank, the fabulously successful investment operation that handled much of the Middle Eastern wealth coming out of the oil-producing countries, was widely reported by the likes of Dominick Dunne in *Vanity Fair* and the European media. The story goes that Safra's male nurse, Ted Maher, had set fire to Safra's Monte Carlo penthouse, allegedly to rescue the world-renowned banker and make himself look like a hero.

Safra, who was worth $2.5 billion and entertained the likes of the Reagans and Kissingers, the president of Turkey, and Russian Ambassador Shevardnadze in his sumptuous 820 Fifth apartment full of Dresden china, Augsburg silver, and Venetian glass, died of asphyxiation, locked in his Monte Carlo bathroom. Speculations have surrounded his death ever since. Three-times widowed, Lily Safra, who also has homes in Venezuela, Switzerland, the South of France, and London, where she is a close friend of Prince Charles and his wife Camilla, is founder of the Edmond J. Safra Philanthropic Foundation, which has been a particularly generous funder of stem-cell research. She also sits on the board of the Museum of Modern Art.

Another well-known widow at 820 Fifth Avenue was Phyllis Schmertz, a slender, dark-haired young woman from Hewlett Harbor, whose husband, New England Whalers president Robert Schmertz, owned the Boston Celtics basketball team and gave his name to the World Hockey Association's Coach of the Year Award. Tragically, Bob Schmertz died a mere six and a half weeks after their wedding. Phyllis Schmertz remarried a few years after her husband's death, this time to a titled Englishman, Earl Sondes, whose previous wife was another American, the socialite Sharon McCluskey. This second marriage happily lasted for ten years, until the British aristocrat was diagnosed with terminal cancer. Today, Countess Sondes presides over one of Britain's great historic houses, Lee's Court, in Kent, and enormous surrounding estates. She has vowed never to marry again but to devote her time, energy, and land holdings to innovative agricultural programs that help less fortunate people in developing countries to improve the use of their land.

There are two other fascinating aspects of this shining Fifth Avenue palazzo of the super rich. One is that the building is a beacon of self-sufficiency. Just like a hospital, it has its own generator. One resident found that during the last New York blackout, as he was groping his way home, everything was dark on the street except his building. "The lanterns in the front were on." The building also has its own parking lot, clearly a luxury in a city of outlandish cost for such prime real estate. It is situated right behind the apartment house, on 63rd Street, where a town house used to be that 820 bought and tore down. But because no car may be left unattended overnight, the lot is used mostly by personal drivers, ready and waiting for one or another prominent resident.

Over the years, these grand and glorious apartments, which had belonged to General Motors chairman Alfred Sloan, tobacco billionaire Pierre Lorillard, horse breeder and racer Alfred Vanderbilt, and Robert Goelet, the former head of the New York Historical Society and one of the quiet Old Guard, who owned much of the mid-Manhattan land under such landmarks as St. Patrick's Cathedral and Rockefeller Center, gradually found new owners. Currently, the Belgian ambassador occupies the tenth floor. Stavros Niarchos's heirs sold his apartment recently to Goldman-Sachs mergers and acquisitions cochairman Jack Levy and his wife Fran, for $15 million. And the former co-CEO of Warner Bros., Terry Semel, who is now head of Yahoo!, purchased the Gettys' seventh-floor apartment, which had the distinction of coming with its own wine cellar in the basement. Among other present owners are two very social couples, H. Frederick Krimendahl and Emilia Saint-Amand and Ara and Rachel Hovnanian, and the beloved widow of Ambassador William A. M. Burden. Mrs. Burden's unique modernist apartment was designed back in the 1950s by her husband's fellow Museum of Modern Art trustee, the late Philip Johnson. The Burdens and William Paleys were close friends, but Mrs. Burden was not the mother-in-law of Amanda Burden, socialite daughter of Babe Paley and chair of the New York City Planning Commission under Mayor Michael Bloomberg. After divorcing Carter Burden, the nephew of William Burden, Amanda went on to became the ex-wife of Steven Ross, who brought about the merger between Time Inc. and Warner Bros. to create the media giant Time Warner, and then she became the ex-girlfriend of Public Television's Charlie Rose. For some fifty years now, Mrs. William Burden's 820 Fifth modernist apartment has been the site of an intimate society tradition: her annual New Year's Day dinner. All the courses feature vintage New York family recipes, and those lucky to be invited wouldn't miss the affair for anything.

820 Park Avenue

· 13 ·

820 PARK AVENUE

A STACK OF PRIVATE MANSIONS
REACHING FOR THE SKY

$\mathcal{D}$RIVEN BY ONE man's hubris and fantasies of baronial Upper East Side living, this unique fourteen-story Holland-brick tower, culminating in fortress-style balconies and mock mansard roofing, on the northwest corner of Park Avenue and East 75th Street, was one of the most unusual experiments in early apartment building.

Mindful of the Zeitgeist—a time of major lifestyle transition in the city—Albert J. Kobler, head of the highly successful syndicated Sunday magazine *American Weekly,* put up the building in 1927. He wanted to mesh a persistent longing among leading New Yorkers for the way life used to be in those distinctive Georgian and Federal town houses on Manhattan's pretty side streets with what was the happening thing: the emergence of the powerful canyon of status high rises that Park Avenue would ultimately be.

What propelled 820 Park Avenue's ascent was a fear of the potentially class-leveling effects of a row of relatively same-looking, big, compartmentalized buildings and a desire for the kind of heraldic individualization that shows off cultivation and achievement. The idea was to create a series of vertically stacked "private mansions" of Gothic grandeur that conveyed permanence, social standing, and power.

Indeed here, right away, came to live some of the most powerful men in New York. Among them was Herbert Lehman, who, after joining his family's investment banking firm of Lehman Brothers, became a leading liberal in New York State politics. He was strongly instrumental in destroying the long, convoluted, and corrupt sway that Tammany Hall bosses had held over New York's Democratic Party, and he served as governor of New York from 1932 to 1942. He was named director general of the United Nations Relief and Rehabilitation Administration during World War II and was elected as a Democrat to the U.S. Senate from New York, an office he held from 1949 to 1957. He was posthumously awarded the Presidential Medal of Freedom.

Another nationally prominent figure who moved into 820 Park Avenue a few years after its completion was automobile manufacturing giant Walter P. Chrysler. One of the wealthiest men in America at that time, the Kansas-born railroad engineer whose fascination with early "horseless carriages" took him to Flint, Michigan, had made Buick's name synonymous with soundness and quality before founding the Chrysler Corporation, the third largest North American automaker. Named Man of the Year by *Time* magazine in 1928, he was greatly admired for his foresight in realizing that research and development were key to the auto industry. He kept his company prosperous by launching new vehicles, starting with the introduction of the Plymouth, then the DeSoto, and, after many months of haggling, the purchase of the Dodge Brothers Corporation. He did allow himself at least one show of vanity. His gift to the New York skyline is to this day everybody's favorite, silvery, Art Deco spire: the landmark Chrysler Building.

A third titan to become ensconced in one of 820 Park Avenue's mansions in the sky was that brilliant promoter, entrepreneur, and financier Joseph H. Hirshhorn, whose drive, energy, and faith in Canada's mineral potential led to a remarkable career on Wall Street and billions of dollars in profit for the uranium and gold mining industries in both Canada and the United States. An avid collector of Rodin, Mary Cassatt, Jackson Pollock, and Franz Kline, Hirshhorn donated to the federal government the first modern art museum in Washington, D. C., the Hirshhorn.

The original force behind the multiple mansion concept, A. J. Kobler was one of New York's most flamboyant and successful publishing figures of the

Roaring Twenties. He started out as an ad salesman in 1910 for the Hearst newspapers, but by 1917 he was so good at it that William Randolph Hearst appointed him publisher of the highly popular *American Weekly* magazine. Kobler claimed to have increased the Sunday supplement's circulation from 2 million to 25 million in just a couple of years.

Unbudgingly ambitious, Kobler soon wished to compete with the ostentatious New York residences of two other bigwigs of the newspaper world, his boss, William Randolph Hearst himself, and Arthur Brisbane, one of Hearst's high-profile assistants, who had just built two apartment houses that included sumptuous suites for his own use: the 1926 Ritz Tower at 57th Street and Park Avenue, where Brisbane took a handsome duplex for himself, and another building at 1215 Fifth Avenue, where he created a lavish triplex penthouse that was the talk of the town.

Initially, in 1923, Kobler bought an existing stone mansion on the northwest corner of 75th Street and Park Avenue. He filled it with art and antiques and had it photographed by *Arts & Decoration* magazine, which called his treasures "priceless" and described the house as being reminiscent "of baronial castles of England."

Always a fashion-conscious man, Kobler was in tune with what was coming up. He saw that the great family houses on Fifth Avenue and Park Avenue were no longer considered smart. They began to look like relics of another era. In the year 1927 alone, three Vanderbilt mansions came tumbling down. By contrast, the new high-rise apartments going up in their places looked solid, and their uniformity, side-by-side, looked bold, modern, commanding. They had an aura about them, as if they had always been there and always would be there. So Kobler decided to demolish his stately new house in favor of a dramatically different kind of dwelling.

He hired Harry Allen Jacobs, who had just built the Gothic-flavored Friars Club on East 55th Street and whose specialty had been the sumptuous town houses of such super-rich New Yorkers of the era as Otto Kahn, Martin Beck, and Adolph Lewison. Jacobs's mission was to create a new kind of skyward aggregate of mansions, which would elevate the families inhabiting them high above the "detrimental propinquity" of the street noise and automobile pollution, and eliminate the security problems faced by street-level town houses.

Just prior to designing Kobler's fourteen-story apartment building of full-floor duplexes for five tenants—saving the ground floor for the lobby and the top three floors for Kobler's triplex mansion—Jacobs had predicted in a *New York Times* feature that soon "the private house will be forgotten and a thing of the past," because of taxes, problems with servants, and the construction of other tall apartment buildings in elite neighborhoods, most of which "are rather barrack-like and unattractive."

With the chance to design a special residence high in the sky, with fresh air, cool breezes, abundant sunlight, and expansive views, the previous generation's requirement for a totally private roof over one's head became less and less important as the decade of the 1920s proceeded. "How could the mansions compete?" asks author Andrew Alpern, an expert on architectural and real estate legal matters whose specialty has been the study of the luxury apartment houses of Manhattan.

Harry Allen Jacobs's design remains unorthodox to this day. The hazy orange-yellow base of the building is made of Ohio sandstone that, according to one geological expert, is 3 million years old. From the outside, the top three floors—Kobler's apartment—have a split personality: half Gothic castle, half slate-shingled, mansard roof house. The ironwork in the lobby is by one of America's most prominent metal workers of the 1920s, Samuel Yellin, and is a startling design of hammered medieval blades and a knight in armor.

At first, Kobler owned the whole building and leased each of the duplexes for around $30,000 a year. What was so appealing to the rich and powerful people who rented them was that, from the beginning, the architect gave tenants a chance to individualize their "mansions" within the framework of the building. Each floor had a different plan. Typical were twenty-room duplex units—each an extravagant home with a spacious library, royal-sized dining room, 38 x 22 foot living room, and five master bedrooms with six servants' rooms.

The upper-most triplex was Kobler's own spectacular mansion in the sky. It boasted vaulted ceilings, richly carved medieval doors, a great stone arch, sixteenth-century stone fireplaces, stained glass, a cavernous 37 x 39 foot drawing room, a massive three-story stairway, and a series of decorative ecclesiastic stone steps and Gothic windows reminiscent of European fortresses. His tapestries and chandeliers had illustrious provenances. Some were supposedly owned by Henry VIII, others once hung in the formidable palazzos of Italy's papal aristocrats: the Strozzi Palace in Florence and the Barberini Palace in Rome. Kobler, of course, was again competing with the interior decoration of William Randolph Hearst's Riverside Drive home and the abode of the other media giant, Arthur Brisbane, at 1215 Fifth Avenue.

But Hearst newspaper executives like Kobler and Brisbane were not the only ones creating awesome high-rise palaces in the city when 820 Park Avenue came into existence. No way could they eclipse the totally make-believe atmosphere at William Randolph Hearst's five-floor New York home, which was the crowning glory atop the Clarendon Apartments, the building Hearst bought at Riverside Drive and 86th Street. Here, the media magnate set an example of consummate luxury with an array of almost phantasmagoric, over-the-top riches: dramatic bronze statuary, ornate Renaissance art objects, rare Flemish tapestries, suits of armor, Egyptian mummies, Italianate landscaped roof gardens, choir stalls from French Gothic cathedrals, silver-filled Georgian dining rooms, and silk-bedecked Empire bedrooms.

This sweeping transitional period of rich and famous New Yorkers moving from family mansions to apartments did, however, meet with some resistance. And this resulted in a major trend of "individualized apartments" in the vein of 820 Park Avenue—duplexes, triplexes, and a variety of custom-staggered floor levels that were explicit expressions of epic eccentricity and wild extravagance. In a few famous instances, builders completely catered to an apartment-house shareholder's specifications, designing a whole building around the capricious demands of one unfathomably deep-pocketed man or woman who had actually purchased blocks of unshaped space. Mrs. William K. Vanderbilt I, for example, simply expected to transfer her domestic seat from her Fifth Avenue mansion to her new home on Sutton Place. Mrs. William K. Vanderbilt II demanded a separate address for her seven-bedroom triplex maisonette at 660 Park Avenue. Vincent Astor, who built the apartment house at 120 East End Avenue, reserved the entire thirty-five-room seventeenth-floor for himself. These were public figures of great wealth, and their one-of-a-kind apartments were extreme examples of the luxurious spaces carved out within multiple dwellings during the thrust of the apartment movement in the city.

The individualized apartment that has gone on record as the largest and most elaborate in New York history was that of Mrs. E. F. Hutton, better known after her second marriage as Marjorie Merriwether Post and the original chatelaine of the legendary Mar-a-Lago in Palm Beach, where Donald Trump's extravagant wedding to his Slovenian bride, Melania, took place in the spring of 2005. Mrs. Hutton had been vehemently resistant to selling her private mansion at 1107 Fifth Avenue, and when she finally gave up the property, she instructed the contractors Rouse and Goldstone to re-create her demolished fifty-four-room mansion on top of the towering new apartment structure. To ensure her privacy, the builder cut a separate porte-cochere, a circular drive-in entrance, into the side of the building on East 92nd Street, which led to a private elevator that whisked her and her friends to the three-story penthouse that was reminiscent of a Newport estate. It was complete with gardens that changed with the seasons, sun porches, gown rooms, silver rooms, children's play rooms, breakfast rooms, sitting rooms, a separate servants' wing, and a self-contained guest suite.

Throughout the city, interior decorators created the illusion that these incredibly wealthy apartment dwellers were living not in a large, new, impersonal apartment building, but in some personalized country house in the city, or in some imaginary Victorian-Gothic stronghold. Ironically, though these pampered people of great means had chosen to live in fifteen-story skyscrapers encased in steel, they were looking for the reassurance of the heavy and the medieval: stone arches and vaulted vestibules. Even though the fresh winds of an eclectic new style of apartment furnishing were already riffling through the high-rise rooms of many stylish New Yorkers, the comfort of these Victorian decorating conceits took a while to be replaced by the modernity of Art Deco, which particularly suited Manhattan high-rise living. Art Deco also suited to perfection the clean-lined, strong-contrast backdrops of black-and-white celluloid—the rave new entertainment that hit the world in the 1920s. The style gained terrific momentum through the sophisticated movies of the 1930s, which often depicted the excitement of modern city living and disseminated the glamorous image of the great New York apartment around the globe.

Among Alfred Kobler's original neighbors at 820 Park Avenue, besides Governor Lehman, were the Wrigley family, whose fortune was made through that great American brand, Wrigley's Spearmint Gum, and Herbert S. Martin, a vice president of the investment bank of S. W. Straus & Company. Martin, his elegant wife, and three sons lived in an astonishing duplex on the eighth and ninth floor, from which Martin famously fell or jumped in January 1930, not long after the stock market crash of 1929, according to a July 2, 2000, article in the *New York Times* by Streetscape columnist Christopher Gray. "He had previously had a nervous breakdown and was getting ready to go on a three-month vacation in Egypt and Europe."

Of Kobler's apartment, the March 1928 issue of *Art & Décor* gave this opinion: "There are no finer, more comfortable, more beautiful ways of living in the world than the New York apartment at its best. Now that houses are actually being built for duplex and triplex apartments so that all the space and isolation to be found in the large country home can be achieved, with much less care and responsibility, there seems to be no end to the popularity of this very modern way of living luxuriously in a large city. And when it is possible for the very structure of an apartment to be designed and executed as a gracious and appropriate background for the treasures that have been accumulated in the lifetime of very artistic people, it would seem as though the finer ideal of civilized life has been achieved."

This optimistic outlook reached a crescendo on the eve of the Great Depression. In 1941, four years after Kobler's death at the age of sixty, his palatial triplex at 820 Park was subdivided into six apartments. Most of the other duplexes in the building were also split up. Then, after the building went co-op, and particularly in the wake of phenomenal new fortunes made on Wall Street in the 1980s and 1990s, several residents have recombined some of the old duplexes and returned them to glory. A recombined duplex in the building today would probably fetch $15 million.

Governor Lehman's apartment was subdivided, and part of it—still a very generously proportioned "trophy" apartment—belonged for years to David Susskind, the influential television personality, producer, talk-show host, and New York bon vivant. Reynolds Tobacco heiress Judith Boyd owned another elaborate apartment in the building for many years. And before he was killed in a bicycle accident in Central Park, well-known New York gynecologist Dr. Mark Beckman lived at 820 Park and played weekly host to Seagram's chairman Edgar Bronfman, who came every Thursday to play pool with the physician.

Tenants have included Madison Avenue antique dealer Linda Horn and her husband, Steve; elegant gem emporium Seaman Schepp's owner Jay Bauer and his wife Binnie; Andrew Farkas of the Alexander's department store clan; and, until recently, popular Moroccan-born party giver Regine Traulsen, married to lawyer Bill Diamond, who held several prominent civic leadership positions during Mayor Rudy Guiliani's administration.

In October 2005, Cheng-Ching Wang, father of the fashion designer Vera Wang, who has lived for many years at one of the city's most prestigious prewar co-ops, 740 Park Avenue, bought a three-bedroom, three-bathroom apartment at 820 Park. This is four blocks uptown from his long-time New York home, which he had bought in 1983, for $350,000, from Campbell Soup heiress Elinor Dorrance Ingersoll and which the *New York Times* estimated as being worth over $25 million today. Word was that Cheng-Ching Wang, whose wife, Florence, was the daughter of a Chinese warlord, and whose own father was a general under Chiang Kai-shek, wanted to turn a new leaf after his wife's death. Unfortunately, he, too, passed away in 2006, before he could move into the building.

A proud, highly cultured man, the Singapore-based tycoon made his initial millions after World War II, distributing Western pharmaceuticals in Asia. He has been involved in enterprises of global consequence, not the least of which has been his investment in his daughter's phenomenally successful design empire.

· 14 ·

THE CHELSEA HOTEL

BUZZING BOHEMIA

*I*CONOCLASTIC, SUBVERSIVE, PSYCHOTROPIC, protectively thick-walled and seemingly never asleep, the Chelsea Hotel has been a cauldron of creativity—and sometimes destructiveness—for over a century. It has been home or temporary *pied-à-terre* to some of the most revolutionary innovators in literature, music, dance, painting, sculpture, movies, underground filmmaking, or just plain wild experimentation and seditious activity. The hotel's permanent residents have run the gamut, from Elizabeth Gurley Flynn, head of the Communist Party in the United States, to Charles James, the refined couturier to movie stars and the pampered upper-crust wives of America's captains of industry.

Self-destructive rock legend Janis Joplin, who lived at the Chelsea on and off before her premature death, hastened by drugs and alcohol, once quipped, "A lot of freaky things happen in the Chelsea, just like in the California communes. Only it costs a bit more."

No two rooms at the Chelsea are alike, and some larger suites these days cost as much as $168,000 to live in per year.

The Chelsea Hotel

Actually, the Chelsea Hotel was New York's very first co-op apartment house. The twelve-story, quaintly gabled and towered building at 222 West 23rd Street (between Seventh and Eighth avenues), with its characteristic lacy, black iron balconies, multiple chimneys for the many wood-burning fireplaces inside, and unique black-marble staircase, which runs from the lobby to the penthouse, was the creation of French-born architect Philip Hubert. The Chelsea began its life as a home for writers and artists in 1884, at a time when 23rd Street was fleetingly a prototype of what Broadway ultimately became.

Its original owners were ten successful painters and artists of the day. An advertisement in the *Real Estate Record* of 1883 describes the building as containing "brownstone-style flats for 40 families." By 1884, according to files in the Museum of the City of New York, the Chelsea had ninety-seven suites, ranging from three-room units to twelve-room apartments. Its top floor boasted New York's first duplex studios. The Chelsea is also reputed to have been the first New York building to feature penthouses and to plant the city's first roof garden.

According to architecture historian Christopher Gray, "The bloom of the co-op movement in the city wilted by 1885, and new legislation severely restricted construction of tall apartment houses. At some point the co-op was dissolved and by 1900 the building began to shift toward transient occupancy. In 1921, the Chelsea was acquired by the Knotts Hotel corporation. And again in 1942, when the hotel ran into financial difficulties, an investment group spearheaded by David Bard, the current proprietor's father, bought the hotel after a foreclosure sale."

Over the last half century the Chelsea has come to be best known for the two brilliant Celtic drinkers who both sailed off from the hotel to their deaths—the Welsh poet Dylan Thomas, and the former house painter, IRA terrorist Brendan Behan. Behan overcame his writer's block while living at the Chelsea to create the high point of his career, the autobiographical *Borstal Boy.* Dylan Thomas's final drinking binge took place at The White Horse Tavern in Greenwich Village. After quaffing down nineteen shots of whiskey on a chilly November evening in 1953, this intractable man, whose alcohol-soaked genius produced such great art as *Under Milk Wood* and *A Child's Christmas in Wales,* staggered out, collapsed, and was admitted to close-by St. Vincent's Hospital. The mellifluous, curly-haired poet, who was about to embark on a major lecture tour across the United States and who

had poignantly written "Do not go gentle into that good night," was so ine-
briated that he fell into a coma and went into that good night a few days later.
He was only thirty-nine at the time of his death from liver failure.

The Chelsea's roster of literary residents past and present is nothing less
than awesome. William Sidney Porter, better known as O. Henry, used the
Chelsea Hotel as one of his main bases to capture the essence of early twentieth-century New York in his wonderful short stories. He was a prototype
of many future Chelsea residents, a classic urban drifter and drinker. Before
becoming a professional writer, he had quite a checkered past. The son of an
alcoholic doctor from Greensboro, North Carolina, he started out as a gifted
cartoonist. His troubled early life included a journey to Texas and Honduras,
embezzlement from a bank, abandonment of his first wife and child, and
five years in the Ohio State Penitentiary. It was from prison that he began
to publish his 250 memorable stories under his famous pen name, before
becoming a free man and settling in New York City.

Mark Twain stayed at the Chelsea whenever he came to New York, which
was often. Thomas Wolfe wrote *You Can't Go Home Again* inside the Chelsea's
walls. The visionary poet, shipyard worker, and world-wanderer Hart Crane
set out from his Chelsea apartment on his final trip by ship to Mexico, from
which he mysteriously disappeared and was generally assumed to have
jumped overboard. Sherwood Anderson wrote *Winesburg, Ohio* at the
Chelsea, and Arthur Miller penned *After the Fall*, his fictionalized play-
memoir of his marriage to Marilyn Monroe. America's Tennessee Williams,
Russian-born Vladimir Nabokov, and India's R. K. Narayan scribbled away
as transient Chelsea lodgers, creating twentieth-century masterworks.
Arthur C. Clark holed up there during visits from his house in the jungles
of Sri Lanka, especially while consulting with Stanley Kubrick during the
shooting of Kubrick's epic adaptation of Clark's dazzling science-fiction
novel *2001: A Space Odyssey*.

Out of "hundreds of memories over the last quarter-century at the
Chelsea," a place he considered his second home, Arthur C. Clark's fondest
recollections were of fellow writer Charles Jackson, "a kind and gentle person who never repeated the success he achieved with *The Lost Weekend*." Jackson's harrowing novel about a New York alcoholic was a bestseller of the
1940s and became a highly successful film, earning an Academy Award for
its star, Ray Milland. It also helped put the popular Third Avenue watering
hole P. J. Clarke's—where the story was filmed—permanently on the city's

tourist map. Arthur C. Clark also likes to reminisce about a marvelous day "using Norman Mailer as the subject for my very first Polaroid roll (yes, roll!) I ever shot." Then there was the priceless moment of Clark's having dinner with fellow Chelsea residents Edith and Clifford Irving, at the height of the famous Howard Hughes fake-autobiography caper. Clark remembers during the meal "watching a character who claimed to be Howard Hughes being interviewed on TV. He was completely wrapped in bandages, just like Claude Rains in *The Invisible Man;* when forcibly unwound, he proved to be Mel Brooks (I think; if he wasn't, he should have been)."

Understandably, Clifford Irving's memories of those days are more bittersweet. "The Chelsea was my hideout and hideaway at a time when I went involuntarily public and needed a secure nest, friends, buffers. Stanley [Bard, the Chelsea's beloved proprietor] and staff understood. My wife and I were broke, too. Stanley arranged an auction of my wife's paintings in the lobby; Cliff Gorman, the comic, was the auctioneer. We must have sold a few canvases, and there was a fine party afterward. The tribe came through. When I got out of prison in 1974 I stayed there again. My sensuality had been stifled for sixteen months." He was reminded of a fire in the Chelsea during his previous stay in 1972. "It was a community event. No one was coming on with 'out-of-my-way-I've-got-to-save-my-ass.' Everyone wanted to help the older folks and kids out first, then the pet snakes and exotic cats. That awareness of tribal feeling was far more warming on that cold winter day than the flames." After his prison term, he claims, "I felt cold, out of it. Chelsea girls lit another fire."

Harvard-educated heir to the Burroughs adding machine and cash register fortune, William S. Burroughs stayed at the Chelsea when he created two in his peerless canon of inaccessible novels, *Naked Lunch* and *The Nova Express,* both full of paranoia, violence, and homoerotic imagery. While at the Chelsea, Burroughs was hanging out with Allen Ginsberg and Gregory Corso, who was the real working-class rebel and representative of criminality in the beat poets' circle. The abusive poet is best known for *Elegiac Feelings America* and *Mindfield,* published in 1989.

Author of *The Naked Civil Servant,* which was made into a movie with John Hurt, all-around eccentric British character Quentin Crisp, typically turned out in his androgynous tilted fedoras and triangular silk scarves, resided at the Chelsea for thirty-five years. Among other longtime apartment-dwellers were such groundbreaking publishers as Jake Baker, founder of Vanguard Press, who published Upton Sinclair's *The Jungle*, Thorsten Veblen's *The Theory of the Leisure Class*, and *The Letters of Sacco and Vanzetti*. Another one was the daring publisher Maurice Girodias, whose father published Henry Miller's *Tropic of Cancer* and who himself risked putting into print novels no one else had the guts to touch. One of these was *Lolita*. Among the others were *Naked Lunch* and Valerie Solarnos's *Scum Manifesto*, as a result of which Girodias had a small part in the film *I Shot Andy Warhol*, Valerie's biopic. Girodias died suddenly during a radio interview about censorship.

Living at the Chelsea intermittently, while conducting his on-and-off affair with French feminist Simone de Beauvoir, who was notably the long-time mistress of existential philosopher Jean Paul Sartre, was Nelson Algren. He was the author of several streetwise books of the 1950s, including *A Walk on the Wild Side* and *The Man with the Golden Arm*, the story of a heroin addict (played by Frank Sinatra in the Otto Preminger film).

The Chelsea's many raw layers of bohemia became sensationally exposed by the countercultural crosscurrents of the 1960s. On top of the old Bohemians—ex-labor radicals and aging vintage rebels—piled the new Bohemians, mostly hippies, sullen young writers, rock singers and their groupies, fast-living, prematurely rich, long-haired record company men, and untalented phonies, decadent trust-funders, and various hangers-on. Toward the end of the 1960s, especially after the Russian invasion of Czechoslovakia, there was also an international influx: Czech writers like Ivan Passer, who after a while went on to Hollywood, plus artists and craftsmen from Japan, Holland and France. For most of these genuinely creative people, the hotel became a stopover on the global avant-garde circuit.

Not to be overlooked were the army of "underground" filmmakers and Warhol superstars who lived at the hotel: Ultra Violet, Viva, Nico, Brigid Berlin, and Edie Sedgewick.

Above all, in the 1960s and 1970s the Chelsea was a hotbed of psychedelia and rock music. The great and tragic psychedelic blues singer Jimmy Hendrix regularly camped out at the Chelsea, as did Joni Mitchell, who wrote the song "Chelsea Morning" while staying there. Bob Dylan wrote his classic "Sad Eyed Lady of the Lowlands," and one of his children was born while he lived at the Chelsea. Patti Smith made her breakout album in the 1970s, when she and erotic photographer Robert Mapplethorpe lived together at the hotel and she took the portrait that was the album's attention-getting cover.

Though there was much high drama—raucous fights, fires caused by candles and cigarettes, and abuse of every imaginable hallucinogenic substance—there was only one murder in the hotel. But that was a headline-maker. It happened shortly after the temporary breakup of the British punk rockers the Sex Pistols. At the time, their lead singer Sid Vicious lived in the Chelsea with his very young girlfriend, Nancy. They lived in room 100 and spent all their money on heroin. According to the cult independent film of 1989 titled *Sid and Nancy*—in which, incidentally, Courtney Love, later to become ill-fated Nirvana legend Kurt Cobain's controversial widow, had a bit part—Sid allegedly killed Nancy at the Chelsea, then a few days later killed himself or simply overdosed on heroin.

When asked about Sid Vicious, Stanley Bard, the Chelsea's manager, is discreetly evasive. "Oh, he was a very polite fellow," he answers, sinking into one of the gray-velvet Art Deco chairs next to the huge, ornately carved Victorian fireplace in the lobby, which is crowded with painting after painting done by current and former Chelsea tenants. Although Bard doesn't say it, rumor has it that many of these works of art were accepted in lieu of rent during lean times for the various painters—by the gentle-mannered man, whose father ran the Chelsea for thirty-nine years before him and whose son, David, and daughter, Michelle, have worked with him for the last few years and will be ready to take over if and when Stanley departs.

"All the big music groups liked to stay here. Yes, there were a lot of drugs used, but there was never any selling of drugs here," he insists. The building's thick walls from the beginning attracted a lot of musicians, he explains. They wanted to be able to practice without bothering their neighbors. Stanley Bard does not divulge the names of current musical tenants. Nor will he share any colorful anecdotes involving past legends. For one thing, he's saving them for a book he wants to write about the Chelsea. "Eventually. Down the line. But I don't know when I'll have the time. My heart is still completely wrapped up in this place. And this place is still a great home for creative people, where their wish for anonymity is respected and protected. 'How informal, how pleasant it is to live here,' they tell me. And they're right. It's quiet. It's private and conducive to inspired work. The Chelsea has a proven record. It worked for the legends and it works for dedicated, driven talents working on fresh output now."

There still exists, to be sure, a relatively secret hair salon, run by an irre-pressible stylist named April Barton, in suite 303 of the Chelsea where—along with struggling actors and sculptors, many of the rockers, punkers, and heavy metal gods come to get their trims and wild dos. Among them are U-2 drummer Larry Mullen, Seattle grunger and Pearl Jam lead singer Eddie Vedder, Oasis's Gallagher brothers, and perhaps most famously, Elvis Costello.

Musicians of importance who composed at the Chelsea include the Canadian musician, novelist and artist Leonard Cohen, whose song "The Chelsea Hotel #2" was released in the 1960s. Then there were Gerald Busby, who scored several of Robert Altman's films, and contemporary composer Virgil Thompson, who had his hand on all the pulse points of the musical world, from opera down.

The list of artists who called Chelsea home is astounding: Willam de Kooning, Jasper Johns, Larry Rivers, Jim Dine, and Claes Oldenburg are just a few of the seminal figures who helped make New York the world's art cap-ital in the second half of the twentieth century. Bulgarian-born artist Christo moved into the Chelsea before he began his monumental wrappings around the world. And film folk galore inhabited the hotel—mostly the unconventional ones such as Jane Fonda, Sam Shepard, Donald Suther-land, Dennis Hopper, Milos Forman, and John Houseman, actor, teacher and cofounder, with Orson Wells, of the Mercury Theater. Also, he is believed to be the uncredited cowriter of Wells's *Citizen Kane*, voted by experts the greatest movie of all time.

Dancer turned cinéma vérité director Shirley Clarke and dancer-chore-ographer-turned-anthropologist Katherine Dunham were longtime resi-dents at the place. But perhaps the all-time most beloved resident of the Chelsea was George Kleinsinger, composer of "Shinbone Alley" and the famous children's symphony "Tubby the Tuba." His tropical apartment in one of the upper floors was legendary. Here, ferns, palms, waterfalls, a Chi-nese nightingale, toucans, monkeys, lizards, turtles, and snakes kept the composer company. One jealous monkey was known to have temper fits dur-ing great human conversations and would occasionally bite a visitor who was the center of attention. Kleinsinger's ashes were sprinkled on the roof of the Chelsea.

Stanley Bard remembers the night he gave Katherine Dunham permis-sion for a rehearsal of the Metropolitam Opera's *Aida*. The outcome managed to unhinge even the unflappable Mr. Bard, who is used to dealing with artists and their caprices. Bard says that Dunham merely requested that elevators be kept running late. That evening, the desk clerk hysterically called Bard at home. He reported that there were limousines pulling up out front, and lions and tigers marching into the hotel. Bard said, "You must be joking." The clerk was not. Dunham, however, assured Stanley that the lions (there were no tigers) were well behaved. Typically, none of the neighbors complained that night.

As one married couple who have lived at the Chelsea for thirty years shrug, "We feel like we're living in a movie here—a Fellini movie."

Quintessential New York reporter Pete Hamill once described the Chelsea Hotel as "a grand dark shambling pile, the color of dried blood, rising eleven stories above a street coarsened by time." But in recent years New York's Chelsea area has again burst forth as a hub for creative, high-energy enterprise and a neighborhood for the young and the hip.

Chelsea has now outpaced SoHo and Madison Avenue as the heart of New York's exuberant art scene, with the city's best-known galleries making their presence felt in the spacious former warehouses along Manhattan's far West-Twenties' cross streets. Google, the international search engine company, has its New York headquarters nearby. The same building also houses such dynamic companies as Nike, the Deutsch advertising agency, and Armani A|X.

A few blocks away from the Chelsea Hotel, the developers of the Time Warner Center are building a twenty-six-story condo called the Caledonia, complete with fitness club, meditation garden, and terraces with built-in barbecue grills. The pulsing beat of cool urban nightlife pervades such chic Chelsea restaurants as the Red Cat, Pastis, and Amy Sacco's Bette. Also nearby, where Chelsea intersects the Flatiron district, a couple of converted condominiums known as Altair 18 and Altair 20 have become a mecca for vibrant, young, talented people, especially fashion and media types.

Among Chelsea town house owners are the likes of actors Susan Sarandon and Tim Robbins. Just down the street from the Chelsea Hotel sits the ever-humming, four-story brownstone of Southern gentleman William Ivey Long, the hardest-working costume designer in show business. The four-time Tony Award–winner's wit and inventiveness have consistently raised the bar for musical theater glitz—most recently for Stephen Sondheim's *Frogs* at Lincoln Center and Broadway's *The Producers* and *Hairspray*.

Many people poke their heads into the lobby, but few strangers can ever penetrate beyond the Chelsea's check-in desk, which is forbiddingly ringed with a complicated Victorian iron railing and guards both the stairwell and the elevators. There is almost nothing else like it in the city.

Indeed, despite Chelsea's haute bohemian atmosphere, society and aristocracy have always liked the kind of typically quirky New York shelter and privacy it provides for those who choose to live there. Juliet D'Hamelcourt, a former lady in waiting to Queen Juliana of the Netherlands, kept an apartment at the Chelsea for several years. When Andy Warhol superstar Viva once mentioned to her that she was tired of her line of work and asked how she could apply to be a lady in waiting, the Dutch woman laughingly answered, "My dear, this is a job you have to be born into." Olivier Chandon de Brialles, a handsome professional car racer and an heir to the Moët & Chandon champagne fortune, was another well-born European who used to make his New York home at the Chelsea. At the time, he was engaged to top model Christie Brinkley. Still a resident is a quiet New York blue blood whose ancestors were in Manhattan when it was still called New Amsterdam. He is James Schuyler, a poet, novelist, Guggenheim fellow, and Pulitzer Prize winner.

Although the twenty-first-century Chelsea Hotel is home to several stockbrokers and families with children, it also boasts its share of boldface names. Among them are dance critic Clive Barnes; art critic John Russell and his famous art lecturer wife, Rosamund Bernier; the actor-writer-filmmaker Ethan Hawke; and that ubiquitous queen of the downtown night scene, Swiss-born fashionista Suzanne Bartsch.

And that Warhol girl, Edie Sedgewick, keeps on getting her fifteen minutes of fame. During her life, when she provoked Princess-Di sized press as the embodiment of 1960s New York, Edie Sedgewick had all the qualifications for tabloid stardom. She came from an old-moneyed Massachussetts family, but didn't seem to care. She had the looks: short-cropped platinum hair, decadently coal-rimmed eyes, huge kaleidoscope dangling earrings, clingy minidresses, and long legs clad in black tights. She enjoyed a remarkably brief moment as Manhattan's favorite party girl before dying of barbiturate intoxication in 1971 at the age of twenty-eight.

Over the years, much has been written and speculated about this wayward socialite and her rapid flame-out. Both Warren Beatty and Mike Nichols have contemplated making a film about her. Finally it looks like

Miramax has pinned down her heady life in a feature film called *Factory Girl*. Researching her role as Edie, famously wronged fiancée of the Jude Law "nanny scandals" and thus a perpetual tabloid item herself, British actress Sienna Miller visited the apartment on the first floor where Sedgewick lived. Sienna, whom *Vogue* magazine tagged "London's Most Stylish Bird" and "along with Kate Moss and Sofia Coppola one of the youthful sirens of highly personal, intriguingly mismatched dressing that's imitated by trend-conscious young women around the world," observed the flow of characters through the Chelsea's lobby. Watching a cowboy-hatted urban eccentric and a temperamental French artist in the corridor, she effused, "I love this place. I want to stay here!" She is not alone. The young, the riotous and the controversial of today are still in thrall to this myth-permeated red caravansary on cool-again 23rd Street.

1040 Fifth Avenue

· 15 ·

1040 FIFTH AVENUE

JACKIE'S HOME

*A*FTER THE SHATTERING assassination of President Kennedy in 1963, when she had to move out of the White House to make room for the family of incoming President Lyndon B. Johnson, Jacqueline Kennedy decided to return to New York, the city where she had been raised. She chose to take up residence in one of the quietly elegant, limestone cooperative apartment houses along upper Fifth Avenue. The building was particularly known for carefully hiding the luxurious nature of the apartments within its restrained exterior. Located on the corner of East 85th Street and facing one of the best-equipped Central Park playgrounds, it was also mere steps away from the culturally ardent former First Lady's beloved Metropolitan Museum of Art.

Soon after, the awning marked "1040" became the most photographed Fifth Avenue entrance. Every move, every outfit of the confident, fashionable, yet shy and vulnerable widow, who was to become the world's most famous woman of the second half of the twentieth century, was recorded by the paparazzi, especially Ron Galella.

The unshakeable Galella had previously perfected the art of celebrity-sighting with such famous subjects as a chinchilla-enfolded Elizabeth Taylor arriving on the arm of Richard Burton at the Grand Prix of the Arc de Triomphe, and Brigitte Bardot cutting up late one night at the Zoom Zoom nightclub in St. Tropez. Suddenly he focused almost exclusively on Jackie. As she began to emerge from mourning, he followed her to openings at art galleries, recorded her grabbing a hamburger with George Plimpton at P. J. Clarke's and lunching at the 21 Club with her sister-in-law, Patricia Kennedy Lawford. Galella trailed Jackie to a downtown movie house, where she had slipped in to see an X-rated Swedish film *I Am Curious Yellow,* and to Chinatown, where he first photographed her in the company of Aristotle Onassis at one of her favorite eateries, the Szechuan Taste restaurant.

Jackie did all the things Manhattan mothers do: She walked her children to school and took them bike riding in Central Park. She attended their school recitals and introduced them to the many stimulating cultural events and treasures New York City offers children. She tried to hide behind movie-star sunglasses as she walked John John to St. David's School and Caroline to Sacred Heart Academy five or six blocks up Fifth Avenue. But Galella was always there and usually snapped her the instant she stepped out of the building.

The Bronx-born Galella leapt into headlines himself by jumping out of bushes and cars to photograph Jackie and her young children when they did not expect it and did not want it. Galella, in fact, became an early symbol of the obsessive, relentless, American paparazzi who stalked, staked out, and ambushed his uncooperative subjects for the shots that celebrity magazines prized, but his targets came to despise. One of Galella's newsmaking encounters on a Manhattan street was with Marlon Brando, who, in 1973 knocked out several of the photographer's front teeth with a fast, potent punch as Galella was popping pictures of the reclusive movie star. Jackie's various court clashes with Galella began in the late 1960s and went on into the early 1980s. She accused him of making her life "almost unlivable." He accused her and her Secret Service protectors of interfering with his livelihood. However, he liked to boast, "A hard-won picture gives you a psychic reward."

In any case, Galella over the years helped perpetuate Jacqueline Kennedy Onassis's unique image: poised yet mysterious, a revered public figure yet a woman with private needs, a loving mother, and a courageous survivor who handled heartaches, pleasures, fame, wealth, and a love of learning relatively silently but with a remarkable sense of purpose and self-knowledge. In front of 1040 Fifth Avenue, over the decades, Galella also inadvertently chronicled her ever-evolving, always trend-setting style. There was her classic, understated, upper-class American elegance: casual khakis and T-shirts when with her children, sweaters and pantsuits as the working book editor she later became, no plunging necklines and only low-heeled shoes whenever she embarked on a festive night out. There was her own brand of international chic, particularly after she became Mrs. Aristotle Onassis: glamorous Givenchy coats and Valentino evening gowns, Pucci minidresses, mink coats, real jewelry from Tiffany's and Van Cleef and Arpels.

Later, when John F. Kennedy Jr. became America's unofficial dynastic prince and handsome heartthrob and dated movie star Darryl Hannah, more photographs followed the comings and goings in the building. The young couple were caught leaving 1040 Fifth Avenue on roller blades the morning after Jackie Kennedy Onassis died.

According to one longtime Manhattan luxury-real-estate broker, it was Bobby Kennedy who selected the building for Jackie. A liberal politician, he surely must have paused for thought that 1040 Fifth Avenue was at the time one of the "restricted" buildings, meaning no Jews allowed.

What comforted Bobby Kennedy about 1040 Fifth Avenue was that it was so close to the New York homes of so many of his Kennedy siblings. Patricia (Kennedy) and Peter Lawford lived at nearby 990 Fifth Avenue, and Jean (Kennedy) and Stephen Smith lived at 950 Fifth. What's more, Jackie's sister, Lee Radziwill, had just a few months before the assassination moved into 969 Fifth Avenue. All these relatives had children attending New York City private schools—mostly on the Upper East Side—and these younger cousins, especially Lee's son, Anthony Radziwill, and Jackie's son, John, were very close.

In the period immediately after President Kennedy's assassination, the low-key nature of the apartment house was the family's main consideration. There were actually several threats of violence against the young widow, and numerous credible kidnapping alarms involving Caroline and John that were taken quite seriously by the Secret Service assigned to them. Jacqueline Kennedy never ceased to worry about her children's safety. Her fears were understandable. She had lost two children through miscarriages and a third, little Patrick, shortly after his birth. She was always battling for her privacy, especially when it came to motherhood, which mattered to Jackie most. By the time John Fitzgerald Kennedy Jr. was born on November 25, 1960, the world knew the baby's father would be the next president of the United States, and media interest in the attractive young family was at fever pitch. Jackie was afraid, while still in the White House, that perpetual media attention would deprive her children of childhood. Jacqueline Kennedy was also superstitious. She was afraid that Caroline and John lived under the shadow of some terrible curse. It is a fact that, during the thirty some years since the assassination of President Kennedy, a member of the Kennedy family or someone closely associated with them has either died or been the victim of some horrendous accident on the average of once every two years.

Another worry of Bobby Kennedy's was how a stuffy Fifth Avenue co-op board would react to having twenty-four-hour Secret Service on duty in the building. Such a famous woman—despite the universal sentiment of sympathy for the beautiful young widow—might be turned away from such a deliberately low-profile building. His concern was not unfounded. Fame was definitely not a plus when it came to getting into these mostly Old Guard WASP buildings in those days. Most show business luminaries—with few exceptions such as Robert Redford, Sidney Poitier, Richard Gere, Paula Zahn, Mary Tyler Moore, Kevin Kline, Paul Newman and Joanne Woodward—were not permitted to purchase apartments in Fifth Avenue cooperatives over the years. A little more than a decade after Jacqueline Kennedy's purchase, former President Richard Nixon was brazenly rejected by the board of a similar elite apartment building, designed, as was 1040 Fifth, by the master of patrician apartment living, Rosario Candela.

Well versed in art and architecture, Mrs. Kennedy no doubt was familiar with the name of Rosario Candela. He was the ultimate specialist in rarified residential restraint. Architect Candela's Fifth Avenue and Park Avenue buildings were in marked contrast to the ostentatious display of wealth so prevalent among the earlier robber barons' palaces they replaced along the east side of Central Park during the first third of the twentieth century.

There was another reason Jackie was no naïf when it came to Manhattan real estate, especially the supreme addresses of choice designed by Candela. And that was because Jackie's grandfather, James T. Lee, was one of the most canny and prolific real estate developers in the city. Between the late 1920s and the early 1960s, Lee had built an unusual string of important Manhattan buildings, including 998 Fifth Avenue, an apartment house that remains one of New York's most prestigious residences, designed by McKim, Mead and White, and the handsome Shelton Hotel, which today is the Marriott East Side Hotel at 49th Street and Lexington Avenue. Lee was also instrumental in assembling land for One Chase Manhattan Plaza. Perhaps most notably, James T. Lee was the developer of Rosario Candela's sleek modernist masterpiece, 740 Park Avenue, the epitome of Jazz Age, Wall Street fortunes and, in 1929, the rise of the social power of Park Avenue. *740 Park, the Story of the World's Richest Apartment Building* was the subject of an entire book in 2005 by New York social historian Michael Gross.

James T. Lee's daughter, Janet, later to become Mrs. Hugh Auchincloss of Newport, married John V. Bouvier III. Their first child, named Jacqueline Lee (the middle name for her grandfather), was born in Southampton, Long Island. The couple also took the real estate developer's name for their second daughter, who became known as Lee Radziwill. Because of his free-spending, womanizing ways, and some stock-market reversals, John "Black Jack" Bouvier was forced to ask his hardworking father-in-law for financial help. The young family received a free apartment at 740 Park Avenue, which became Jackie's childhood home from 1932 to 1938, until her parents' separation and divorce.

Although Mrs. Kennedy Onassis once worked for Condé Nast Publications, 1040 Fifth is not to be confused with 1040 Park Avenue, a huge, red-brick apartment house on the northwest corner of 86th Street, in which stylish publisher Condé Nast's famous duplex penthouse made rooftop living chic back in 1925. His salons, decorated in the French manner by Elsie de Wolfe, were the scene of endless smart parties at which dazzling guest lists included people like Fred Astaire and Maxwell Parrish, politicians from Washington, and New York's most ravishing beauties. In *New York Streetscapes,* architecture historian Christopher Gray describes Condé Nast as "one of first New Yorkers to recognize that an open terrace is of only seasonal use. In 1926, he hired Deleno & Aldrich to design a greenhouse-like glass canopy to cover the terrace and had the ballroom extended to the edge of the building." The stock market crash of 1929 wiped Condé Nast out, and though he was left in only partial control of his high-style magazines such as *Vogue, Vanity Fair, Glamour,* and *Mademoiselle,* he held on to his extravagant apartment until his death. In 1941, he gave a party for Henry R. Luce, the founder and head of Time Inc., and his wife, Clare Boothe Luce. It was one of New York's all-time legendary evenings. In attendance were the French writer André Maurois, John D. Rockefeller, Mrs. Cornelius Vanderbilt and the Chinese ambassador to the United States, Dr. Hu Shih.

1040 Fifth Avenue was built a little later, in 1930, and soon became recognized as a gracefully refined entity in its own right. It contained generously proportioned apartments—nine- to fifteen-room suites typically, each with two or three wood-burning fireplaces, some with wood-paneled libraries, capacious dressing rooms, and glass-enclosed conservatories.

Among current co-op owners are several East Coast establishment families, as well as some socially prominent couples who were big business successes. There is William E. Flaherty, a former top honcho at Gulf & Western and retired chairman of Great Lakes Carbon with his tall, willowy wife Tina Santi Flaherty, the first woman elected vice president at three of America's largest companies: Colgate-Palmolive, GTE, and Gray Advertising. The dynamic couple, who live with their five large dogs in New York, Palm Beach, Pebble Beach, and Long Island, are involved in the ball and benefit circuits in all those locales. Then there is financier, environmentalist, and rare-book collector Gilbert Butler and his Hungarian-born wife Ildiko. They also divide their time between their 1040 duplex and homes in Maine, Sun Valley, the French countryside, and upstate New York. They have underwritten a comprehensive Metropolitan Museum exhibit of the British landscape paintings of Samuel Palmer, and Butler is involved in saving endangered marine life along the Carolinas and the Carolina coastline itself.

A very popular and good-looking family in the building is Count and Countess Loïc de Kertanguy and their three daughters. He is president of East Hampton's exclusive Maidstone Club and is one of those charming, beautifully mannered aristocrats from the provinces of *le fond de France*, who made his mark in New York importing French fabrics and marrying a beautiful socialite from St. Louis, the former Rebecca Dixon Williams. Also an exemplary couple of high achievement in the building is actress Candice Bergen and her husband, real estate tycoon Marshall Rose.

The Butlers, Flahertys, and Roses gave three of the famous Fifth Avenue dinner parties during the 150th anniversary celebration of Central Park in 2004. Attending them were such illustrious New Yorkers as Mayor Michael Bloomberg, Betsy Barlow Rogers, who founded the Central Park Conservancy, legendary choreographer Merce Cunningham, Atlantic Records midas Ahmet Ertegun and his wife Mica, Kaycee and ABC-TV evening news anchor Peter Jennings, actor Stanley Tucci, socialite Norma Dana, Diane von Furstenberg and Barry Diller, former General Electric head Jack Welch and his new wife and coauthor, Susan Wetlaufer, Priscilla Ratazzi and Chris Whittle, Anne Ford and Samuel P. Reed.

Jacqueline Kennedy Onassis's fifteen-room apartment, which occupied the entire fifteenth floor at 1040 Fifth Avenue, had four bedrooms, two dressing rooms, a staff room, a library, living room, dining room, conservatory, two terraces, three fireplaces, five-and-a-half bathrooms, and a wine room. It came into the former First Lady's possession, it is rumored, through the intercession of her friend Jayne Wrightsman, a highly schooled expert on French antique furniture, especially the Louis XV and Louis XVI periods Jackie herself so adored. The widow of Oklahoma oilman Charles Wrightsman, she had early in the 1950s befriended and become a pupil of the famous French decorator Boudin, of the Parisian house of Jansen. Because of her encyclopedic knowledge of antiques, Jayne Wrightsman had been influential in Jackie's redecorating of the White House. Jayne Wrightsman later donated a wing full of the rarest Boulle cabinets, ormolu clocks, and eighteenth-century marquetry pieces to what is today the Metropolitan Museum of Art's Wrightsman Collection.

The seller of Jackie's apartment at 1040 Fifth Avenue was Beverly Weicker, the divorced second wife of Lowell Weicker and stepmother of the future governor and senator from Connecticut, Lowell Weicker Jr. The Weickers were heirs to the Squibb pharmaceutical empire, flush with money from the discovery of insulin. Tall, good-looking, sportive, multilingual, and much-married, the three Weicker brothers, Lowell, Ted, and Fred, were followed by gossip columns on the New York–Long Island–Hobe Sound social circuit and were typical of the affluent, worldly, yet insistently low-key families who lived in the building. Beverly's ex-husband, Lowell Weicker Sr., had been president of Squibb and was among the early American power players in postwar Europe, stationed with NATO in Paris. For several years, he and Beverly lived in the splendid Château de Maule in the Normandy countryside, which was filled with the finest French antiques of the two Louis periods that both Jayne Wrightsman and Jackie Kennedy were mad about.

Jacqueline Kennedy Onassis has been the subject of numerous books and television documentaries since she was laid to rest in Arlington National

Cemetery, next to President Kennedy in May 1994. Her final illness came to light after she fell from a horse while fox hunting in Virginia during a weekend spent at her friends Paul and Bunny Mellon's Rokeby Farm. She was soon after told that she had incurable cancer. She decided not to pursue an aggressive medical treatment that would have slightly prolonged her life.

Six months later, over the objections of both family and doctors, she discharged herself from New York Hospital early on the afternoon of Wednesday, May 18. "She was determined to have a humane, merciful ending. Such a death required a great deal of preparation, as well as the cooperation of others," writes Edward Klein in *Farewell, Jackie.* Caroline helped her make the list of close friends and Kennedy family members who would be permitted to enter her bedroom chamber to say their last good-byes. Maurice Templesman, Jackie's longtime companion, arranged for round-the-clock nurses and a morphine drip with a PCA—a patient-controlled anesthetic button— that allowed Jackie to administer an extra dose of pain medication if she needed it.

She had hoped to have her funeral held at the Catholic Church of St. Thomas More, on East 89th Street, which was her parish. But that church could accommodate only three hundred and fifty people, less than half the number she planned to invite. She agreed to have the funeral service moved to the far larger St. Ignatius Loyola Church on Park Avenue and Eighty-fourth Street, where she had been baptized and confirmed and where a memorial service for Patricia Kennedy Lawford was recently held.

The Reverend Wallace Modrys, the pastor of St. Ignatius Loyola, would preside at the mass and give the homily. Ted Kennedy would deliver the eulogy. John would call Jessye Norman and ask her to sing hymns. She wanted readings by John, Caroline, Maurice Templesman, and two of Jackie's favorite friends, director Mike Nichols and writer Jane Stanton Hitchcock.

Flowers would be handled by her closest friend, whose taste she thought was flawless—Bunny Mellon. John Loring of Tiffany & Co., whose books she had edited, would oversee the proper wording and printing of the funeral invitations.

Jackie and Senator Ted Kennedy did not see eye to eye about the extent to which the funeral service should be public. Nonetheless, Jackie, who wanted everything private, realized that a lot of political figures would likely attend her funeral. She said that she wouldn't be surprised if Lady Bird Johnson, who was infirm and rarely seen in public, made the effort to come.

Another first lady, Hillary Rodham Clinton, would certainly want to be there, as would New York's senior senator, Daniel Patrick Moynihan, and two other senators who had known and loved Jack Kennedy, John Glenn of Ohio and Claiborne Pell of Rhode Island.

That same afternoon, May 18, according to Edward Klein in *Farewell Jackie,* Bunny Mellon arrived at Jackie's apartment. She was greeted at the door by Maurice Tempelsman, who was unshaven and looked as though he had not slept in days. He had absented himself from his diamond business to be near Jackie and take care of her.

Edward Klein describes her last hours: "Mrs. Mellon knocked softly on the bedroom door, then entered. The walls of Jackie's room were pale lime green. Jackie was propped up in a beautiful coral colored canopy bed. Books were everywhere. The only other person in the room was a nurse, who monitored the morphine drip."

Bunny Mellon sat next to Jackie and took her hand and whispered a few words to her. After a while, she got up, lit some candles, took the Gregorian chant CD that Jackie had selected out of its case and put it into a player. The Benedictine monks of Santo Domingo de Silos were heard singing "Alleluia, Beatus Vir Qui Suffert."

Singer and songwriter Carly Simon, one of Jackie's intimate pals, was asked to come over. By the time she arrived, thousands of people had already gathered on the street in front of 1040 Fifth Avenue. The police did not have enough time to set up barricades, and people crowded the sidewalk on both sides of Fifth Avenue. "Except for Maurice and John, and some other male members of the Kennedy family," Carly Simon later remembered, "only women were being allowed in the bedroom. She had a printed scarf over her head."

Throughout the night of May 18, Caroline, John, Maurice Tempelsman, and Bunny Mellon took turns at Jackie's bedside. They read passages aloud from Mrs. Kennedy Onassis's favorite poets: Robert Frost, Emily Dickinson, and Edna St. Vincent Millay. When she awoke in the morning, Jackie asked to have her priest, Monsignor Bardes, give her the last rites.

The next morning, May 20, John faced the media in front of 1040 Fifth Avenue. "Last night, at around ten-fifteen, my mother passed on," John began. "She was surrounded by her friends and family and her books and the people and things that she loved. And she did it in her own way, and on her own terms, and we all feel lucky for that, and now she's in God's hands."

The extensive obituary by Robert McFadden in the *New York Times* stated, "Although she was one of the world's most famous women ... she was a quintessentially private person."

As she lay dying, Jacqueline is said to have wanted her Fifth Avenue residence left untouched—perhaps preserved as a historic repository of Kennedy artifacts.

According to Edward Klein's book, *Farewell Jackie* (Penguin, 2004), several months after Jackie's death, John let Maurice Tempelsman know that he would like to have his mother's apartment to himself. Several families who live at 1040 remember encountering a slightly bewildered Maurice Templesman wandering in the lobby. He seemed to be at a loss as to where he would go next. However, neither John nor Caroline wanted to live permanently in Jackie's old apartment, and when they put it on the market, they created a sensation. Since Caroline and John did not have room for many of their mother's possessions, they sent them to Sotheby's for auction. Maurice was not in favor of the auction. "He didn't try to stop the auction," said one of Maurice's closest friends. "But he didn't like the idea. He told me, 'I don't want to see Jackie's possessions on public display. But the kids liked the idea. If it was up to me, I'd sell the stuff privately.'"

"I remember someone looking at the apartment, and [they] said, 'Oh, it's in such terrible shape,'" remarked the late interior designer Mark Hampton. "I thought to myself, 'They don't get it.' It was just in the shape she left it. It was immaculate and the floors were shiny, shiny. But it hadn't been painted in decades. That was what she loved. That's what a lot of people love. I think that has great charm, that look," he continued. "I admire it. And I think one of the critical aspects of her taste and her eye is the fact that her style didn't change. The rooms she decorated as a young woman in Georgetown and in their private rooms in the White House were very little different really in substance from the way some of the rooms at 1040 Fifth Avenue looked thirty years later. It was the same with her clothes, you know. You can see a picture of her all through those decades. She never looked out of style."

When Jackie Kennedy bought the apartment from Beverly Weicker in the 1960s, she paid only a little over $100,000 for it. Once the apartment came on the real estate market, it was swooped up by oilman, long-time bachelor turned new husband and father David Koch. He paid $9.5 million for it in 1995, which he thought was "an outrageous price," but he thinks that "by today's standards, it looks like a bargain."

David Koch is the executive vice president of Koch Industries, which became the nation's largest privately held company in the fall of 2005, when it acquired the paper maker Georgia-Pacific. He is No. 33 on *Forbes;* list of the world's richest people, with an estimated net worth of $12 billion. He and his wife, Julia, who hails from Arkansas, got a lot of media attention when they purchased Jackie's apartment. But alas, in mid-April 2006, the billionaire couple had put it on the market again with an asking price of $32 million.

Koch said that, after buying the apartment, he had numerous requests from the media to photograph or film Mrs. Onassis's former home, and that he always refused. "I thought I would have been dishonoring her memory to have done that, and I never let the press in there at all," he said. "I would hope anybody I sell it to would feel the same way."

Jackie's former apartment was in need of complete renovation, he claims, and he and Julia hired the interior designer Alberto Pinto to gut it, fix it up, and furnish it, a process that Koch estimated cost him another $5 to $10 million.

With their third child on the way, the Kochs decided Mrs. Onassis's former four-bedroom apartment would be too small for their expanding family. So they bought and renovated an apartment at 740 Park Avenue, which had belonged to the Japanese government and which was also coveted by the Russian entrepreneur Leonard Blavatnik. Koch paid $18 million in 2004 for his latest Manhattan home, not counting a few more millions for the interior architect Peter Marino's redesign.

On September 29, 2006, Paula Froelich of the *New York Post*'s Page Six reported the sale of Jacqueline Kennedy Onassis's former apartment to hedge fund manager Glenn Dubin. He agreed to pay David Koch $30 million. Koch said it was hard to leave Jackie's former Fifth Avenue apartment at the corner of 85th Street. Above all, he said, he will miss the view over the Temple of Dendur at the Metropolitan Museum of Art, the Central Park Reservoir—which will permanently and officially be renamed the Jacqueline Kennedy Onassis Reservoir—and everything beyond. "It's a glorious view," he said the day after the move. "I kind of had a tear in my eye when I walked."

Leighton Candler, a senior vice president of the Corcoran Group, when queried by real estate writer William Neuman of the *New York Times* as to whether the 2006 asking price of the apartment reflected a premium for its connection to Mrs. Onassis, answered, "It's the first thing that everyone notes about this apartment. But provenance isn't accidental. You have people who have the choice of the best apartments in New York. There's no accident Jacqueline Kennedy Onassis and David Koch both purchased this apartment."

· 16 ·

450 East 52nd Street

GARBO'S HIDEAWAY

$\mathcal{W}$HEN SHE LEFT Hollywood at the height of her celebrity, Greta Garbo, the mythic movie star for the ages, retreated to a seven-room apartment across from River House, in an elegant stone tower that predates its more famous neighbor and is known as the Campanile. Garbo's refuge, a slim Venetian-Gothic edifice rising at the rim of the East River, was one of the few celebrity havens on Manhattan's East Side.

Among the building's earliest occupants was the worldly, witty, legendary actor, playwright, and composer Noel Coward. Other early residents were H. J. Heinz, founder of the Pittsburgh ketchup fortune millionaires John Barry Ryan, Ralph Pulitzer, and Time Inc. founder Henry Luce, with his magazine editor and playwright wife Clare Boothe Luce. Alexander Woolcott was a longtime resident. In their 1984 book *Living It Up,* Thomas E. Norton and Jerry E. Patterson mention that Wollcott's third-floor apartment was the scene of his famous Sunday breakfasts for New York's literary crowd. His friends from the *New Yorker* made fun of the remoteness of his three-room digs on the third floor of the East River building and constantly complained about the difficulty of finding a taxi-

450 East 52nd Street

cab in the quiet area. But it was Dorothy Parker, a regular at the breakfast club, who gave the building the name that stuck: "Wit's End." Yet one more triumphant thespian of Britain, Rex Harrison of *My Fair Lady* fame, unwound from nightly performances across town playing the exacting Professor Henry Higgins opposite the young Julie Andrews. He was with the fourth of his six wives, the delightfully mischievous yet very proper English comedienne Kay Kendall, who died of leukemia at the height of her brief but effervescent career in 1959. Broadway musical superstar Mary Martin and her film editor and producer husband, Richard Halliday, kept a tremendously attractive apartment at the Campanile while she was performing in such blockbusters as *Peter Pan, South Pacific,* and *The Sound of Music.* Mary Martin's son from her first marriage, Larry Hagman, the star of two of the most popular TV shows of all time, *I Dream of Jeannie* and *Dallas,* frequently stayed at her light-filled, book-lined New York apartment, from which the Hallidays later moved to their coffee ranch in Brazil.

These suites had that rare country-in-the-city feeling, because each had its own private garden and because all the windows opened onto a view of the rapidly running East River, which is actually not a river but an estuary of Long Island Sound. Initially, the Mayfair Yacht Club, one of the swankiest speakeasies of the Prohibition Era, was part of the building, which was constructed in 1927.

Nowadays, this intimate, relatively small, brown brick and gray stone cooperative compound is a much cherished entity, partially because it contains only sixteen apartments. It boasts no fancy canopy, no sidewalk landscaping, but it has some fiercely protective doormen. Eye-pleasing balconies and bay windows grace the building's eastern façade.

Van Wart & Wein built it for Joseph G. Thomas, noting that, "It complimented the squat massing of Beekman Terrace with a soaring shaft that rose from a landing stage at the river's edge." Thus the name Campanile. Unlike most inward-facing Manhattan buildings, the Campanile turned a blank wall toward the throbbing midtown of the East 50s. It was completely oriented toward the East River, where its situation atop a bluff permitted the development of the prized riverfront garden apartments below the street, as well as a private boat landing at water level. Huge studios, light-splashed living rooms, handsome libraries, and three bedrooms are typical of the apartment units. But alas, the private yacht mooring, just as at River House, was eliminated by the construction of the Franklin D. Roosevelt Drive in the late 1930s.

These days no big-name show biz luminaries are known to hole up in the fourteen-story apartment house. More typical of present apartment owners is socialite Elizabeth Peabody. She is a true Eastern establishment blueblood. She is the daughter of one of New York's most prominent couples, Sam and Judy Peabody, who were among the early catalysts of Phoenix House, one of the city's first important rehabilitation centers for drug addicts. The family has also been active in the fight against AIDS.

Greta Garbo lived at the Campanile for forty years, from 1949 until she died on September 14, 1989. "I want to be alone," she had pleaded with the press when she retired from films. Though the media always recognized her on her many walks, they did not bother her and kept a distance. But in fact, Garbo was no hermit. In her East River garden apartment, where she was surrounded by paintings—Renoirs, Bonnards, and Rouaults, as well as works by Poliakoff and Atland—she entertained plenty of company. Her intimate friends and often daily visitors included health food guru Gaylord Hauser, photographer Cecil Beaton, and most especially millionaire George Schlee and his wife Valentina Schlee. The Schlees lived in the same building for thirty years, and it was rumored that Garbo and the couple had an ongoing ménage à trois. Garbo traveled a lot with all those friends, as well as with Aristotle Onassis and her two closest women friends, Cecile de Rothschild, a member of the baronial banking family, and Salka Viertel of Klosters, Switzerland. But after a trip to Venice alone with George Schlee, during which Schlee died of a heart attack, Valentina Schlee became Garbo's greatest enemy. Amazingly, the two women continued to live in the same building, but they never spoke to each other again.

Letters and correspondence between Garbo and poet, socialite, and notorious lesbian Mercedes De Acosta were unsealed on April 15, 2000, exactly ten years after her death (per De Acosta's instructions). The letters revealed no love affair between the two, as had been feverishly anticipated. The ultimate star of some of Hollywood's most romantic movies of the 1920s and 1930s, the enigmatic and elusive Swedish-born actress, who gained international fame in 1926 playing a temptress who comes to a bad end in *Flesh and the Devil*, eventually became an American citizen. She was voted by the *Guinness Book of World Records* to be the most beautiful woman who ever lived.

One of the screen's great sufferers, who often played disillusioned women of the world, offscreen Garbo fought recurring bouts of depression during her New York years through Eastern philosophy and a strict health food regimen.

Another reclusive Hollywood star lived for a while in the building. The introspective and brooding, psychologically complex Montgomery Clift, who, along with Marlon Brando typified a new breed of male movie actor in the 1950s. Clift would disappear from Hollywood for two- or three-year periods at a time and hide out in his Manhattan digs near the East River. Actually, the former stage actor was not as antisocial in New York as he was on the West Coast. He liked to party and was very much a part of the city's intellectual life. He had several intimate friends in New York, perhaps the closest of them being the first Mrs. Norman Mailer, Adele Mailer, and the vibrant nightclub singer Libby Holman, a sort of mother figure with whom he was often spotted around town. According to a friend who kept Clift company before he died at age forty-five, Clift's last words when asked if he would like to see one of his movies on TV, was a vehement, "Absolutely not. What do I have to do to prove I can act?"

The UN Plaza

· 17 ·

THE UN PLAZA

INSTANT INTERNATIONAL CACHET

*T*HE ACCUSER WAS Lily Cates, the estranged mother of actress Phoebe Cates, who is married to film star and acclaimed Shakespearean stage actor Kevin Kline. The Klines' young son and Lily Cates grandson, Owen Kline, was singled out in 2005 by *Time* magazine as one of the ten top film performers of the year, along with Philip Seymour Hoffman, Catherine Keener, Gong Li, and Viggo Mortensen. This was for his heartbreaking screen debut in the independent film *The Squid and the Whale,* as the younger of two distraught children caught in the messy divorce drama between a New York intellectual couple, played by Jeff Daniels and Laura Linney.

Lily Cates's ex-husband and Phoebe Cates's father was Joseph Cates, an early television pioneer, one of the creators of *The $64,000 Question.* After her divorce from Joseph Cates, Lily Cates—a flawless Asian-American beauty—had remarried, but now was the widow of Marshall Naify, who owned a chain of California movie theaters. Naify left an estate worth approximately $385 million; however, his widow inherited only $10 million of it.

Over the years, between her marriages, Lily Cates had developed a close, almost familial relationship with one of the most prominent international philanthropists of recent times, Alberto W. Vilar, whose Amerindo Technology Fund back in 1999 had soared from $24 million to $598 million in a single year. It was returning 249 percent to investors. As reported in the *New York Times, New York Post,* and *Wall Street Journal,* at its peak, Vilar's firm had about $8 billion in assets, which quickly launched him onto *Fortune* magazine's list of the wealthiest people. What he did with all that money is to make a big-time splash into the glamorous world of culture. He liked to say that he spent one hundred nights a year at the opera. So, above all, he lavished tens of millions of dollars on, as he expressed it, "the first love of my life, music."

He pledged $225 million to several major opera houses. Of this, he actually gave away at least half and always gave it with enormous ceremonial flourish. But he did all this with a much fiercer insistence on recognition than most big donors. Indeed, his name soon appeared on everyone's lips in the loftiest cultural and social circles. Suddenly there was the Vilar Grand Tier at the Metropolitan Opera, the Vilar Young Artist's Program at the Royal Opera House in Covent Garden in London, and the Vilar Center for the Arts in Avon, Colorado. He had also pledged millions to the Lyric Opera of Chicago, the Washington and Los Angeles operas, which both had Mr. Vilar's friend, the world-famous and much-beloved tenor Placido Domingo, as general director.

Alberto Vilar's love of the heady, operatic stage was echoed in his way of life. He particularly liked the lavish productions of director Franco Zeffirelli. And not unlike a Zeffirelli stage setting, his vast apartment at 860 United Nations Plaza was filled with art, richly ornamented with filigreed objects, and lined with mirrors. According to a report in the *New York Times,* he had combined four separate condominiums and eventually planned to make them into a private concert hall, where he had already on display a reproduction of the inner façade of the Mozarteum in Salzburg.

Vilar's financial success was turned to other generous gestures as well. He also was a consequential patron of medical research. For example, his $10-million gift established a professorship of neurological surgery and a spine regeneration program at Columbia University Medical Center.

But for this seeming financial savant and leader of legions of wealthy investors into mostly high-tech bets, the money that had once rolled in by the billions suddenly came to a dramatic stop. His first bubble burst in 2000.

Vilar and his clients stood by helplessly, watching his technology fund losing a steep 80 percent of its value. Three difficult years followed, during
which his philanthropic reputation also took a hit. There was no way he
could meet all his far-flung and grandiose cultural pledges. Then, suddenly,
salvation appeared. The technology fund roared back with the stock market, and Alberto Vilar again began taking steps toward a comeback into New
York's highest philanthropic circles.

But on May 26, 2005, a second bubble burst, and everything came crashing down. Returning from a speaking engagement at an investors' conference
in Las Vegas, Alberto Vilar was unexpectedly handcuffed by federal agents
at Newark airport. He was accused of stealing $5 million from a client and
using the money to make good on his charitable pledges. The case against
the art patron was filed in the Securities and Exchange Commission com-
plaint by a certain investor, identified only as "L. C."

Lily Cates, for whom Vilar back in the 1990s had increased a relatively
small investment to $18 million in value, had by 2005 become a disgrun-
tled investor. Their relationship of trust had completely eroded. To be sure,
grateful former beneficiaries of his beneficence, both in the world of opera
and in the prestigious halls of medical research, were pooling donations to
bail Alberto Vilar out of New York's Metropolitan House of Correction. The
financier, whose personal fortune in the mid-1990s was estimated at just
under $1 billion, was facing up to ten years in prison if convicted of con-
spiracy, securities fraud, investment advisor fraud, mail fraud, wire fraud,
and money laundering. After the initial charges, Vilar was released on $4
million bail, but restricted to his opulent duplexes near the United Nations.

Like other eminent international businessmen of considerable societal
circulation and clout, Alberto Vilar had chosen to make his huge impressive home in a Manhattan high rise that had instant worldwide recognition
as an important New York address.

The imposing dark-glass twin towers that ascend sleekly to thirty-eight
stories just north of the headquarters of the United Nations, on the corner
of First Avenue and East 48th Street, do not promise the exclusivity or dazzling Deco façades of New York's prestigious prewar buildings. Instead of the
palazzoesque bastions that had for decades set the standard along Fifth and
Park avenues, this 1960s complex followed Mies van der Rohe's dictum of
sharp, streamlined rectilinearity. It was more reminiscent of the great mid-
century modern glass office buildings such as Lever House, the Seagram

Building, and the former Union Carbide Building, all in nearby midtown on Park Avenue. Indeed, the somewhat brooding black glass colossus—two separate buildings sitting on a common six-story base that contains commercial space—is one of the most expensive and luxurious building ventures of its time. Its awe-inspiring, block-long driveway leading into a giant corporate-style lobby, with a breathtaking garden court, has social snob appeal. It is shared by residents of the co-op apartments with several floors of offices, belonging to blue-chip international companies plus the permanent mission, to the United Nations of Kenya, Panama, Monaco, Yemen, and Japan and the consulates of Finland, Angola, and Uzbekistan. The fact is that from the time 860 and 870 United Nations Plaza went up, to the present, they have consistently attracted a tantalizing list of rich and famous residents.

At home these days, behind the cool tinted-glass façades, in some of the warmly textured, opulently proportioned duplexes, many with wood-burning fireplaces, curving staircases, and their own elevators within the apartments, are some of America's most vital arbiters of taste and culture. One of these is S. I. Newhouse Jr., head of the Condé Nast publishing empire, who presides over such influential glossy magazines as *Vanity Fair*, the *New Yorker, Gourmet, Architectural Digest, GQ,* and *Vogue.* High on the list of the wealthiest men in the world, and one of New York's most astute collectors of modern art, he lives on the twenty-eighth floor of the 870 tower. He and his architecture-expert wife, Victoria, have combined two apartments for their gallery-like, minimally furnished rooms that allow their huge canvases by Barnett Newman and Rothko to dominate. Also at 870, right below the Newhouses, lives the former president of Cartier U.S.A., Ralph Destino. Handsome and gregarious, for many years he was a high-profile figure on Fifth Avenue's prestigious A-list of the world's most famous status merchants, as well as a much photographed participant in New York's glittering charity ball circuit. One of the building's most eminent longtime residents is George B. Munroe, the former C.E.O and chairman of Phelps Dodge Corporation, and his wife, the noted film and television title designer Elinor Bunim. Right after reciving his education from Dartmouth, Harvard Law School, and Oxford University, the Illinois-born Munroe, who was long associated with the prestigious New York firm Cravath, Swain & Moore, served as the youngest lawyer at the Nuremberg Trials. Dina Merrill, the beautiful, blonde society heiress and Hollywood star married to producer

Ted Hartley, is another luminary of the city's many civic-minded fund-raisers. The striking couple certainly contribute to the building's glamour quotient. They live in a high duplex in the 870 tower, considered the slightly more desirable of the two spires because it is closer to the dazzling views of the landmark skyscrapers of the mid-Manhattan metropolis. Also ensconced at 870 is the Guggenheim Museum's Asia department curator, Alexandra Munro, whose magistracy as to what is worthwhile on today's far-reaching global art scene is no small matter. Another UN Plaza apartment owner who wields terrific power over New York City's cultural pulse is Bruce Crawford of Omnicom Advertising. He was the chairman of Lincoln Center for the Performing Arts, one of the earth's most vibrantly throbbing confluence points of topnotch talent and cultivated audiences for grand opera, orchestral music, innovative theater, and classical dance.

What drew Thomas Armstrong III, director emeritus of the Whitney Museum of American Art, to this particular skyscraper? "My wife was determined to have light and a view. And I'm a gardener. Most things I have are related to nature." The couple had forsaken a traditional Park Avenue apartment for a smaller but sunnier perch on the twenty-third floor of 860 UN Plaza. All those glass walls cheerfully showcase their collection of mostly contemporary American art, such as a glazed earthenware wall sculpture by Betty Woodman, ceramics by Andrew Lord, and paintings by Andrew Masullo, Jan Matulka, and Andy Warhol. Four chromolithographs by John Frisk Allen depict the development of the Victorian lily, and an astonishing variety of shimmering colored glass pieces by Frederick Carder, the founder of Steuben Glass, catch the incoming rays among French, Chinese, and English antiques.

Generally, what these high-achieving occupants find so invaluable about their UN Plaza domiciles is the profusion of light streaming through their tall windows, the great views of the East River's boat traffic and of midtown Manhattan's signature skyscrapers. At night the fancifully lighted Art Deco towers of the Chrysler Building and the Empire State Building are almost palpable, so close are they. Then there is the uplifting view of the park and gardens of the United Nations nearby, not to mention the tree-lined charm of the surrounding townhouse-paved neighborhood of Beekman Place.

Virtually the minute it was completed in 1966, 860-870 United Nations Plaza was a fashionable address. Among the power elite who moved in that first year were the Fed's Alan Greenspan, talk-show legend Johnny Carson, and Robert Kennedy, soon to be New York Senator Robert Kennedy. Bathed in the lingering magic of the Camelot era, the former attorney general of President John F. Kennedy, originally from Massachusetts, was seeking to establish a New York State residency. The plan was to first run for the senate, then aim for the presidency, in a manner to be emulated decades later by another out-of-towner seeking the same office—Senator Hillary Rodham Clinton.

Yet one more former attorney general, William Rogers, was among the early apartment owners at the UN Plaza. He was soon to be followed by the son of President Eisenhower's secretary of state, Christian Herter Jr., a prominent international lawyer in his own right.

Possibly the most commanding presence among 870 UN Plaza apartment purchasers in the early days was a man whose economic and financial leadership would put America on the world stage. His name was Walter Wriston, and he was president, then chairman of Citicorp. He had guided the banking industry through many of the major crises of the postwar era, including Penn Central, Herstatt, First National, and later New York City's near brush with bankruptcy. During his long career in an era when it was difficult to find a public figure untainted by scandal or financial malfeasance, Wriston stood above the pack for personal integrity. While he became a very wealthy man as Citicorp chairman, there was absolutely no evidence that his business judgments, though they sometimes could be off the mark, were ever skewed by personal greed. He was among the most innovative financiers of his time. His decisions carried vast geopolitical implications for the massive information revolution taking place. He believed that human intelligence and intellectual resources were the late twentieth-century world's prime capital. He recognized early on the marriage possibilities of satellites, television, fax, cellular phones, and worldwide computer networks, and their world-shaking consequences—especially that their main result would be that national boundaries would become increasingly irrelevant. His peers considered Wriston "a giant of the banking industry," "a pioneer of the global economy," and yet "a very gentle man of the old school." After he retired, Wriston was awarded the Presidential Medal of Freedom at the Kennedy Center in the company of actress Doris Day, golfer Arnold Palmer, cosmetics mogul Estée Lauder, and National Geographic Society chairman Gilbert Grosvenor.

All these highly driven newsmakers lent the brand-new towers considerable heft. To top it all, America's all-time favorite television newscaster,

Walter Cronkite, and his popular wife, Millie, took up residence at apartment 25A of the 870 tower.

Next arrived a tsunami wave of chic: a handful of boldface men and women who seemed to be all over town, making all the columns, dining at the city's trendiest restaurants. Their comings and goings made the glass UN Plaza complex suddenly, fiendishly, à la mode.

Foremost among these celebrated characters was the best-selling author Truman Capote. He moved in at the summit of his fame and achievement, flush with money from his 1966 "nonfiction novel," *In Cold Blood*, a chilling account of the senseless and brutal murder of a Kansas family that is widely considered his finest work. He had just thrown a fabulous masked ball on November 28, 1966, at New York's Plaza Hotel ballroom, in honor of *Washington Post* publisher Katherine Graham, and the event had become not only the talk of the town but also the talk of the world. It has gone down in history as "Truman Capote's Black and White Ball" and was inspired by the Ascot scene in the film *My Fair Lady*. The guests' attire was restricted to black and white, plus masks and feathered fans for the ladies. The guest list included the most white-hot supernovas from the worlds of high society, politics, the arts, and literature. Those lucky enough to receive an invitation were considered in the eyes of the media "the Chosen." The ball became labeled "the Party of the Century." The "list to end all lists," put together by the "Tiny Terror," as the diminutive squeaky-voiced writer was known, was printed the day after the party in the *New York Times*. It included such social leaders as C. Z. Guest, Babe Paley, Gloria Guinness, Marella Agnelli— the tall, long-necked, best-dressed fashion stars of the time, whom Capote dubbed "my celestial flock of swans." The list was asparkle with the biggest names of the entertainment world: Richard Burton and Elizabeth Taylor, Frank Sinatra and Mia Farrow, Mr. and Mrs. Henry Fonda, Mr. and Mrs. Gregory Peck, Lauren Bacall, Candice Bergen, Merle Oberon, Claudette Colbert, Tallulah Bankhead. Then there were the world-renowned writers, playwrights, cartoonists, poets, and photographers: John Steinbeck, Edward Albee, John O'Hara, Lillian Hellman, Christopher Isherwood, Richard Avedon, Marianne Moore, Arthur Miller, Norman Mailer, Robert Lowell, Philip Roth. Other eminences of the day who came were Henry Ford II, presidential daughter Lynda Bird Johnson, Hollywood studio head Darryl F. Zanuck, *Vogue* editor-in-chief Diana Vreeland, and Pop artist Andy Warhol. Little noted, however, were those who were invited but did not attend.

These included, Greta Garbo, Jacqueline Kennedy, the Duke and Dutchess of Windsor, Clare Boothe Luce, Jack Lemmon, and Vivian Leigh. The ball was also called "the Last Gasp" of an elite culture founded on privacy, elegance, and breeding.

At about this time another widely known New York public personage also moved in to the UN Plaza and added a certain glitzy touch to the towers. He was television talk-show host and ladies' man David Susskind. But the most exuberant party-giver in the building was George Barry, chairman of Fabergé Cosmetics, an unrivaled bon vivant. The many evening gatherings at his thirty-second-floor duplex in honor of such friends as Cary Grant, Shirley Bassey, and Joe Namath were always full of music, fun, and plenty of pizzazz.

Gordon Parks, who captured the struggles and triumphs of black America as a photographer for *Life* magazine from 1948–1968 and then became Hollywood's first black director with *The Learning Tree* and the hit *Shaft*, was another elegant man of considerable stature to move into the twin towers as the 1960s gave way to the 1970s. Parks was best known for his gritty photo essays on the grinding effects of poverty in America and abroad, especially Brazil, and on the spirit of the civil rights movement. He covered everything from fashion for *Vogue* magazine to politics and sports for other publications, but he claimed, "Those special problems spawned by poverty and crime touched" him most. I dig into them with more enthusiasm. Working at them again revealed the superiority of the camera to explore the dilemmas they pose." From his tenth-floor UN Plaza apartment overlooking the East River, he also wrote fiction and composed music, two endeavors at which he turned out to be quite good. "Nothing came easy," he admitted. "I was just born with a need to explore every tool shop of my mind, and with long searching and hard work. I became devoted to my restlessness." The film *The Learning Tree* was based on Parks's 1963 autobiographical novel of the same name, inspired by his Kansas boyhood, where he was the youngest of fifteen children. In the story, the young hero grapples with fear and racism as well as first love and schoolboy triumphs. Parks also wrote the score for the movie, which in 1989 was among the first twenty-five American movies to be placed on the National Film Registry of the Library of Congress. The registry is intended to highlight films of particular cultural, historical, or aesthetic importance.

If New York had a favorite grande dame around the time the UN Plaza was luring the city's most successful people inside its towering glass walls, surely that was Mary Lasker. The beloved philanthropist was a champion of medical research and urban beautification, and was perpetually photographed at Manhattan's significant events. Remembered for her cyclamen-pink lipstick, beautiful smile, and trademark auburn bouffant hairdo, she was always perfectly put together with gloves, three strands of pearls, Van Cleef broaches and earrings, and her pastel-hued designer suits swathed in an amplitude of ranch mink. She seemed to be every place where scientific frontiers were pushed, where medical mavericks were furthering research on cancer, the heart, or eye disease. She also supported planting trees and flowers in the center of Park Avenue, providing fountains and lighting wherever it was appropriate. She was one of Lady Bird Johnson's closest New York friends, a volunteer lobbyist in Washington for medical causes, a grand Manhattan party hostess, and an art collector nonpareil with a fondness for Impressionist painters. Though she lived in a cream-colored Beekman town house, filled with flowering Monets and pastel Renoirs, it was her overflowing collection of Mirós that prompted her to take a second home at the UN Plaza and turn it into a sort of private gallery annex, where she loved to share her collection by entertaining visiting diplomats and dignitaries. Her presence in the building, plus the frequent arrivals at her apartment of such influential friends as the famed Texas heart surgeon Dr. Michael E. DeBakey or the ultimate New York power broker, former parks commissioner Robert Moses, certainly added to the cachet of the new residential towers. The Wisconsin-born widow of an early New York advertising maven, Albert Lasker, Mary Lasker was once described by Robert Moses as "the irresistible combination of Madison Avenue dreams—the blend of many essences in one beautiful package. Intelligence, vision, generosity, charm, kindness."

Over the years, the Lasker Foundation she and her husband established in 1942 has veritably helped shape medical history by recognizing and supporting promising clinical research, repeatedly singling out future Nobel Prize winners. They were early contributors to the study of cholesterol chemistry and its role in the clogging of coronary arteries. One of Mary Lasker's biggest personal successes was pushing for and getting funding for what ultimately became the National Institutes of Health. To the end of her life, she kept a busy pace on the board of trustees of the John F. Kennedy Center for the Performing Arts, the Museum of Modern Art, the Norton Simon Museum, New York University, and Braniff Airways. In 1989, a professorship was named for her at the Harvard School of Public Health. But her long-standing passion, for which she affectionately was called "Annie Appleseed," was furnishing tulips, daffodils, begonias, and chrysanthemums for various locations in New York. She was mainly instrumental for obtaining the lighted Christmas trees down Park Avenue during the holiday season and donated 300 Japanese cherry trees to the United Nations.

While the two towers have two addresses, they share a common co-op board. And although the scale of the complex is huge—there are 334 apartments, fifty-six of which are duplexes on the top eight floors—the UN Plaza is prized most for its outstanding services—several protective concierges, doormen, elevator men—and its quietness. So close to the river, so far from the unceasing hum of central Manhattan! The lower noise level here is in great contrast to Park Avenue, which despite its prestige is, after all, a four-lane highway.

Set on 2.3 acres of land, the building mostly has large eight-room apartments. There is a logical flow to their layouts. The longish living rooms lead into handsome libraries and spacious dining rooms. The duplexes on the top floors tend to have four bedrooms. The building sports a landscaped roof terrace and has an underground garage. Original prices for the apartments ranged from $27,600 to $166,000. Recent asking prices have skyrocketed to as much as $4.2 million with a maintenance of $6,776 a month, and the board expects purchasers to be worth about three times the price of the apartment they hope to buy.

Originally built on leased property owned by Alcoa, which was to run out in 2007 but was later renegotiated by Douglas Elliman, the towers represented a level of accommodation that was extremely rare in the postwar era. Despite its hulking mass and the absence of architectural ornamentation, the twin-towered structure was considered a handsome and pioneering residential addition to the UN complex. The project's design is by Wallace Harrison, who was very active in the original planning of the United Nations complex. It goes back to his original vision for a set of residential twin towers, in the tradition of New York City's elegant Central Park West twin towers such as the San Remo, the El Dorado, and the Majestic, built in the 1920s and 1930s. Harrison hoped such a high rise would boost the residential attractiveness of the area around the glass United Nations Secretariat building and eventually lead to other skyscraper development nearby. It took Harrison almost twenty years to realize his vision, which dated back to his original proposal of 1946. By mandate, the twin towers are slightly lower than the Secretariat's glass façade. Almost four decades later, with typical promotional fanfare, Donald Trump managed to erect a much taller apartment tower just across First Avenue from this complex and thus break through the skyline ceiling of the United Nations. He had hyped his Trump World tower by Costas Kondylis as "the tallest residential building in the world." Yet, despite this marketing ploy, the UN Plaza twin towers prevail as the neighborhood's most coveted place to live.

Other current residents include Dr. Mathilde Krim, a prominent crusader for AIDS research and the widow of Arthur Krim, head of Orion Pictures, one of the great art-film companies of the 1970s and 1980s and the original distributor of Woody Allen's films. Former Texas governor Ann Richards had an apartment here, as does former New York comissioner to the United Nations and international non-profit agency consultant Nadine Hack. Others on the roster of residents include Wamsutta textile tycoon Robert Bendheim and his St. Louis–born wife, Jane; former CBS chief Thomas G. Wyman; and U.S. Open champion and tennis-court tycoon Ham Richardson and his wife, Midge, a former Catholic nun who later became editor-in-chief of *Seventeen* magazine.

Part of the mythos of the UN Plaza towers is the oft-told saga of a valorous longtime resident named Brigitte Gerney. Like so many good-looking, personable European young women who flocked to New York City in the late 1950s and early 1960s, because of job opportunities, the vibrant postcollege social whirl, and perhaps the hope of meeting a husband, Brigitte Risch left her native Liechtenstein and almost immediately found all three. New York in those days was particularly hospitable to a clean-cut, enthusiastic blonde with a charming accent and warm Continental ways. Shortly after her arrival, she met and married a suave, ambitious part-Russian executive named Arkadi Gerney, who had a rising career in the steel industry. In no time at all, the attractive, sociable couple seemed to have attained everything people come to New York for. Arkadi was successful enough to buy into the brand-new all-glass apartment so admired by foreigners because of its meaningful nearness to the United Nations. The dream apartment was followed by a weekend house in the Hamptons and membership in all the right clubs. Above all, the couple were blessed with three nice children, who were gaining admittance to Manhattan's hard-to-get-into private schools.

Then a harrowing series of ill winds struck. First the couple lost a baby in a swimming pool accident. While the nanny ran into the house to answer the telephone, the child managed to wiggle out of a safety seat, crawl up to the pool, and fall in. A few years later on a family ski vacation, Brigitte and her young son, Arkadi, were on their way to the top of the mountain when the cable car whisking them up suddenly, inexplicably, broke off and crashed into the slopes. Luckily the young boy escaped unhurt, but Brigitte was hospitalized with a broken collarbone.

Yet, in this almost biblical tale of Job-like endurance tests, this was just the beginning of Brigitte Gerney's travails. A few years after the cable car trauma, at the apex of his business dealings, Brigitte's husband was diagnosed with cancer. Within a few months he was dead. Then, one sunny day in Manhattan, while this widow and mother of two was walking up Third Avenue between 64th and 65th streets, next to the construction site of a future skyscraper that would eventually hold the New York home of O. J. Simpson, she became the victim of the kind of occurrence feared by millions of New Yorkers who pass beneath scaffoldings where workmen are forever fixing and rebuilding this city. Suddenly, out of nowhere, a 35-ton crane came crashing down. She was thrown to the ground, pinned under its weight. While she remained conscious, she was in excruciating pain. Emergency medics were pretty sure both her legs were crushed. Careful consideration went into the way she should be moved because of fear of possible internal bleeding. She lay trapped on the sidewalk for hours. Her courageous words and remarkably smiling face amid the disaster made front-page news. The entire city followed her fate for days. Her plight elicited thousands of well-wishing letters. Even President Reagan called from the White House.

After several operations and years of intense physical therapy—helped, no doubt, by her can-do attitude and naturally upbeat personality—Brigitte Gerney eventually regained the use of her legs. In the course of her extensive medical treatment she met a noted New York orthopedic surgeon named Dr. Peter-Cyrus Rizzo III at St. Vincent's Hospital in Greenwich Village. Gradually, the two fell in love. They had just gotten engaged, when one night, Dr. Rizzo, working late in his office at St. Vincent's Hospital, was confronted by a man who, without warning, pulled out a gun and shot the seated doctor right between the eyes. As it turned out, the gunman was a retired fireman. He had sued the city, hoping to receive a sizable settlement for an on-the-job injury fighting a major fire several years earlier. Dr. Rizzo was chairman of a three-doctor panel reviewing fire department pension requests. The fireman had come straight from court in the early winter twilight. Angry about the negative judgment to the workers' compensation he had sought, he blamed Dr. Rizzo's medical report for the money denied him by the jury. The medical establishment was shocked by the death of the highly regarded physician, but Brigitte Gerney was heartbroken by the loss of the man she loved. Her concerned friends had a hard time reconciling the fact that so many bad things could happen to such a good person. But Brigitte Gerney went on, taking great solace from the achievements of her daughter, who became a recognized artist, and her son who got into Harvard Law School.

Yet there was even more tragedy waiting in the wings. When her daughter Nina married, she had moved to Baltimore. One day another horrific call came Brigitte's way. Her son-in-law, while taking a bike ride down a shady lane, was cut down by a car. His young life was instantly snuffed out. At the time of the accident, Brigitte's daughter was the mother of a three-year-old girl and five months pregnant with her second child.

How did Brigitte Gerney, friends and strangers still ask, manage to gather the strength of heart to repeatedly surmount all the adversity dealt her over all these years? She never seems to have asked, "Why me?" She is a devout Roman Catholic. She has the support of a big Central European family. And she basically has a sunny personality. After each ordeal she retreated for a while. Then she somehow recharged her batteries and reached out to her many friends—circles and overlapping circles of friends that a sweet and outgoing woman can make over time in a big and varied city like New York, even if she arrives as a foreigner. For when it comes to unjust injury and suffering, New Yorkers can really rally.

One Sutton Place South

· 18 ·

ONE SUTTON PLACE SOUTH

HIGH SOCIETY BASTION

ONE OF THE original "cloud palaces" when it went up in 1926, One Sutton Place South was an opulent pioneer of a new lifestyle for Manhattanites. "It showed the rich how to live on the waterfront; its porte-cochere led to a private garden on the banks of the East River where a yacht landing facilitated the weekend trip to the country," claims Elizabeth Hawes, author of *New York, New York: How the Apartment House Transformed the City (1869–1930)*. Architect Rosario Candela, she maintains, "was literally building the leading edge."

Still one of the most prestigious addresses in New York, though the neighborhood around it is aging a bit, this grand and glorious building at the southeast corner where East 57th Street abuts the East River, has a resplendent nighttime view of the necklace of lights that is the Queensborough Bridge and the millions of multicolored, luminous objects moving across the immense borough of Queens, out toward the two busy airports and the highways of Long Island.

Right below the side of the building and its exquisite exclusive garden, steps lead down to a tiny waterside park, open to the general public. This is one of the city's most romantic spots, immortalized in Woody Allen's black-and-white valentine to New York, the 1979 film *Manhattan,* in the scene where the lovers cuddle on a bench silhouetted against night falling on the bridge.

The building's architectural highlight is, indeed, its fully recessed porte-cochere entrance, where arriving guests stepping out of taxis and limousines on the gracefully curved driveway are met by a flurry of courteous, uniformed doormen, porters, elevator men, concierges, and others who fuss and greet. The regal lobby, with its golden sunburst mirrors and innately luxurious articulation of space, both dazzles and intimidates. It also kindles a momentary touch of envy in most mortals who enter it.

In their 1984 book *Living It Up,* Thomas E. Norton and Jerry E. Patterson attribute the buildings and streets called "Sutton" to the real estate acumen of Effington Sutton, member of a New York shipping family who, with James Stokes, purchased the land at the east end of 57th Street back in 1875. Initially, at Sutton's direction, several brownstones were built there. But because of the rapid industrialization taking place nearby at the same time, the brownstones lost their appeal for the rich almost immediately after they were built. It was not until the 1920s, when a clutch of New York society women became passionately interested in that part of Manhattan where the land slopes down to the East River, that renovating brownstones or building new houses on Sutton Place was really "in" again.

The group of society ladies was headed by Mrs. William K. Vanderbilt and included Anne Morgan, the daughter of J. P. Morgan; Elizabeth Marbury, who was the literary agent of Oscar Wilde; and New York's favorite decorator in those days, Elsie de Wolfe, who, after her marriage to a titled Englishman, would be known as Lady Mendl. The others in the group had names that carried the glow of Old New York: Griswold, Olin, and Olcott. It was they who really made Sutton Place a fashionable address.

One Sutton Place South was originally built to be something of a family compound for the four children of Henry Phipps and their circle of friends. The Phippses made their fortune during the Gilded Age, along with Andrew Carnegie and J. P. Morgan.

John S. Phipps, the president of Henry Phipps's estate, commissioned architects Rosario Candela and the firm of Cross & Cross to create the thirteen-story structure in 1925, and to top it all with an exceptional additional penthouse. The elegant enclave originally housed thirty-three apartments, had a garden spreading out to the river, an indoor tennis court under the garden, and a private yacht landing below that. The penthouse for many years belonged to Amy Phipps, Henry Phipps's daughter, and her husband Frederick Guest, a cousin of Winston Churchill and thus related to the Dukes of Marlborough. Their son was the illustrious sportsman and dashing polo player, Winston Guest.

For a couple of years after Amy Guest's death, the Winston Guests lived in the spectacular 6,400-foot penthouse, wrapped by a lush, landscaped terrace, and flinging open eight French doors to the breeze coming off the East River. They referred to it simply as "the roof house."

Amy Phipps's daughter-in-law, Winston's wife, was, of course, the famous C. Z. Guest, who for decades, starting with the 1950s, embodied the fashionable, privileged American woman.

Mrs. Winston Guest, a statuesque Boston-born blonde christened Lucy Cochrane, made her mark as a debutante, briefly became a showgirl, and most of her adult life was recognized as an outstanding horsewoman and exemplary society pacesetter. She was much photographed and admired for her clean-cut, unadorned taste in clothes—mostly custom-made by impeccable New York couturier Mainbocher—and for her flair in party-giving and expertise in gardening. *Town & Country* and *Life* magazine photographer Slim Aarons, who famously and lovingly photographed her beside the serene, Grecian temple pool at her mother-in-law's oceanfront estate, Villa Artemis in Palm Beach, called C. Z. "the queen of high society in the second half of the twentieth centry. She is an icon of patrician style that will not come this way again."

Slim Aarons was not the only one enamored of C. Z.'s cool, ice-blond looks and polished insouciance. She was also frequently photographed by Horst, Louise Dahl-Wolfe, and Cecil Beaton. In most of these photographs she wears pristine white bathing suits, simple white T-shirts, and shorts— always in a coltish, long-legged pose and usually barefoot, with minimal makeup over her perfect, moderate suntan. If not in white, she was mostly in beige or black—sleek, neat, uncluttered sheath dresses, only a string of pearls, a cashmere sweater tossed or tied with elegant abandon over the shoulder. It was C. Z. Guest who first popularized those timeless all-American favorites, the classic sweater set and the little black dress.

C. Z. often voiced the opinion that the two-winged roof house at One Sutton Place South with its pair of ballroom-sized elliptical parlors and skylit towers was "the most magnificent apartment in New York City, but impractical for a young family." She found it difficult that she and her husband lived on one side and their son, Alexander, and the nanny lived on the other side of the penthouse, each side separately orbiting its own enormous parlor with clusters of bedrooms, libraries, and sitting rooms, connected only in the center through the foyer, several huge halls, including a long, substantial dining room, pantry, kitchen, service halls and maids' rooms. C. Z., whose favorite words were "comfortable" and "cozy" divided these huge rooms into congenial conversational groupings of furniture, yet the decor was nothing if not grand: seventeenth-century Aubusson rugs, antique pink Queen Anne boisserie on the walls, the finest eighteenth-century English furniture, and the extensive porcelain collection that had once belonged to the banker J. P. Morgan.

Winston and C. Z. Guest's daughter, Cornelia Guest, was twenty years later named "Deb of the Decade" and was briefly linked romantically to Hollywood's Sylvester Stallone.

Around 1941, some of the apartments at One Sutton Place were subdivided and the roster of residents broadened to include others besides Phippses, Guests, and their other cousins, the Bradley Martins—who were early supporters of animal preservation, especially tuned into the plight of the diminishing population of rhinos in East Africa—and their families' nearest and dearest friends. Among these were the J. Thornton Wilsons, whose palatial Newport cottage was a major pulse point of that blueblooded resort's summer social life, and whose Far Hills, New Jersey, horse-country estate was even bigger than that of tobacco heiress Doris Duke. Today, perhaps the most socially prominent couple in the building are Virgil and Betty Sherrill. Betty for years presided over New York's most prestigious debutante party, the Infirmary Ball, and was the final arbiter of which pedigreed young woman was qualified to be included on the sought-after list of those making their bows in Society. She is the daughter of a New Orleans architect and heads one of Manhattan's top interior decorating firms, McMillen Inc. Among her many famous clients—whom she calls "my fair ladies"— have been Mrs. Richard Rodgers, Mrs. Henry Ford, and Mrs. William Paley—all known for their discriminating taste and beautifully decorated homes. Both she and her investment banker husband—with whom she divides the year among New York, Southampton, and Hobe Sound—have served as presidents of the relatively strict co-op board at One Sutton Place South. So for the last forty years, the couple has pretty much had the last word on who gets in and who is kept out of the coveted riverside edifice.

Other recent apartment owners in the building have included Brownlee Currey of Nashville and his Swedish-born wife, Agneta, with their three equestrian daughters; former Bear Sterns and Co. chairman, the late Paul Hallingby—one of the best-looking men in New York—and his fifth and sixth wives, the Estonian-born Mai Ercklentz Hallingby Harrison, and Jo Davis Hallingby, a crackerjack lawyer in her own right—frequent society and gossip column items in recent years; well-known plastic surgeon Dr. Peter Linden, married to the former Faith Golding, who was the first wife of the much remarried chairman of Revlon, Ronald Perelman; former U.S. senator from Connecticut Abe Ribicoff and his wife Casey; President Kennedy's sister Patricia Kennedy Lawford; and retired Wall Street tycoon George Gould, who served as undersecretary of the treasury under President George H. W. Bush. And although One Sutton Place South has a reputation as a society perch rather than a celebrity building, it has had its share of famous denizens with household names. Among them were fashion designers Bill Blass and Carolyne Roehm, and the movie star Sigourney Weaver, who lives there with her husband and daughter.

In the 1960s, the fabulous penthouse apartment of Amy Phipps and C. Z. Guest was bought by Janet Annenberg Hooker, one of the distinguished philanthropic daughters of Moses L. Annenberg, an immigrant from East Prussia who, starting with a newspaper distribution service for the Hearst Corporation and soon moving on to his own racing guides, racing wire services, and the *Daily Racing Form*—which associated him with Chicago mobsters—launched the highly profitable communications empire that, under his more famous son, Walter Annenberg—later U.S. ambassador to the United Kingdom—came to include *TV Guide* and *Seventeen* magazine. A considerable amount—hundreds of millions—of the family's multibillion dollar fortune from Triangle Publications, which in 1988 was sold to Rupert Murdoch, have been funneled into good works through the Annenberg Foundation. Most notable of these is the Annenberg School of Communication at the University of Pennsylvania, the Philadelphia Zoo, and the National Institute of School Reform at Brown University. Janet Annenberg Hooker lived at One Sutton Place South for thirty-five years and entertained on a grand scale. Perhaps her most famous party in the "roof house" was the eightieth birthday extravaganza she gave for Elmer Bobst, the august chairman of Warner-Lambert Pharmaceuticals. It was attended by eighty guests, among them President Richard Nixon.

Soon after Mrs. Hooker died in 1997, a good-looking overnight multi-millionaire from Houston, Texas, who made his fortune through a Colorado-based cell-phone company, appeared as an avid suitor for her unique piece of real estate. His name was J. Shelby Bryan, and at that time he was still married and not openly linked to the also very-much-married editor of *Vogue* magazine, Anna Wintour. Both couples soon after divorced their respective spouses. It was rumored that one of the powerful members on the co-op board, a staunch Republican, wanted to keep the Texan from C. Z.'s sublime roof house because of a huge fund-raiser Bryan and then wife Katherine had given, amid much publicity, for President Bill Clinton. Others say politics had nothing to do with it. Because of this board member's unmatched societal circulation, she knew everything about everyone, and had caught an early whiff of the gossip surrounding the secret affair between Bryan and the glamorous editor, herself a major wielder of power in New York's influential fashion industry, one who can make or break the careers of designers, cosmetic products launchers, photographers, and models. "What I believe in most," this very social member of the co-op board is fond of saying, "is families. Mothers and fathers. Husbands and wives. Children and grandchildren. That's what I value. Couples who stay together. I don't much like single people living with each other."

Janet Annenberg Hooker's apartment—where the current maintenance costs $13,500 a month—was most recently bought by Lisa Perry, who removed the Phipps family's original coffered ceilings and eight-foot French doors to create seamless white walls for her eye-popping collection of op and pop art. Her Lichtensteins, Rauschenbergs, Bridget Rileys, Vassarelys, Oldenbergs, and Tom Wesselmans are paired with streamlined 1960s furniture by Aero Saarinen, sixties-style Courreges minidresses that hang on the wall, and rock-music memorabilia such as a Lucite guitar that belonged to the Rolling Stones.

Just as C. Z. Guest was photographed for a *Life* magazine cover when her mother-in-law, Amy Phipps, owned the apartment in 1957, so Lisa Perry was snapped for a major twelve-page spread in *Vogue* in 2003. Was it Anna Wintour's revenge? Perry, a perky brunette with a short geometric haircut, sported a personal style quite different from C. Z. Guest's. Dressed in bright splices of leather, she was pictured sinking confidently into a minimalist sofa strewn with a jumble of pillows, all graphically printed with whirring black-and-white optical-illusion motifs.

· 19 ·

---

19 East 72nd Street

THE STING OF THE CO-OP BOARD

*E*XCLUSION AND AIRS of superiority do not belong to any one New York luxury building. East Side or West Side, tales of humiliating rejections abound. There are plenty of impossible, snooty co-op boards all around town, ready and willing to test the nerves, will, and stamina of potential buyers who have not failed so much as a pop quiz in their achievement-filled lives. But of all the classic white-glove apartment houses of impeccable design and intrinsic worth, the one invariably named "the hardest building to get into in all Manhattan" is 19 East 72nd Street.

This quintessential upper-class New York building is most famous for its somewhat messy turning down of former President Richard M. Nixon. But whispers of its tyrannical board, petty internecine politics, and applicants disheartened in the face of arrogance and hubris have only grown louder in recent years.

Located at Madison Avenue and 72nd Street, catty-corner from the landmark Rhinelander Mansion (better known as Ralph Lauren's many-splendored flagship store), this sleek, subtly modernist, seventeen-story, forty-unit structure of peerless 1930s limestone perfection was Rosario Candela's last

19 East 72nd Street

major project. Its spiffy hunter-green awning juts out from an unusually whimsical door frame of white marble relief panels, populated with storks, deer, turtles, cupids, and other creatures of nature and myth. These mostly zoological motifs by C. Paul Jennewein—whose other bas-relief works grace several of the Rockefeller Center skyscrapers—are also carved into the handsome wood entrance doors that are watched over by a gloved, uniformed doorman, and right behind him a concierge. Inside the austerely elegant black-and-white marble lobby, a lovely formally landscaped garden court with a bronze sculpture of a fawn is visible through a broad expanse of glass. And again, lizards, snails, and rather frightening big fish eating little fish, etched in bronze relief, cover the inside panels of the impressive sets of elevators located to the far right and far left of the long wide lobby leading to the building's two "end pavilions." Upstairs to the west, all the apartments are eleven-room duplexes. Somewhat smaller but still opulent, varied suites—a few of them duplexes—characterize the upper floors of the Madison Avenue side of the building.

Richard Meier, one of America's foremost architects, creator of the Getty Museum and winner of the 1984 Pritzker Prize, lives in one of the penthouses. A fourteenth- and fifteenth-floor duplex belongs to financier Frank Richardson and his wife, Judge Kimba Wood, one of President Clinton's three savvy, sidelined women nominees for attorney general, who was tripped up by "Nannygate" for the job that finally went to Janet Reno. One of New York's Old Guard grande dames, Mrs. Flavia Hackett, who takes a daily constitutional wearing little veiled hats, beautifully tailored suits, and white gloves, and whose son, Montague H. Hackett Jr., is president of the Southampton Bathing Corporation, probably the most sought-after beach club on the East Coast, has been a longtime resident. A recent purchaser of an eleventh-floor duplex is real estate scion Scott Resnick, and one of the spacious twelfth-floor apartments is owned by Campbell Soup heiress Charlotte C. Weber. Current U. S. ambassador to Jamaica, Brenda Johnson, and her husband, J. Howard Johnson, have had a home in the building for years. Another of the penthouses belongs to real estate tycoon K. P. Thomas Elghanayan, whose ex-wife, Sharon, dates New Jersey Governor John Corzine. Jon Wurzburger, a Wall Street mogul whose private plane whisks him to a spate of health-related charities he is involved with in several cities, has one of the choice apartments on the sixteenth floor. Not long ago, he and his wife, Riva, had to hire a twenty-story crane to lift a spectacular greenhouse to their penthouse terrace. And in July 2006, Donald L. Bryant Jr., a St. Louis businessman, astute collector of works by Jackson Pollock, Willem de Kooning, Jasper Johns, and Robert Rauschenberg, who is a trustee of the Museum of Modern Art and founder of the Bryant Family Vineyard in Napa Valley—which makes a Cabernet Sauvignon that has become a cult wine, selling for hundreds of dollars a bottle—after raising a family in the Midwest, bought a three-bedroom duplex at 19 East 72nd Street.

For many years, one of the penthouses was the New York home of Charlie Chaplin's beautiful widow, Lady Oona O'Neill Chaplin, who was the daughter of the great playwright and Nobel Prize winner Eugene O'Neill.

The late Joseph Cullman, chairman of the Philip Morris tobacco company, former chairman of Newport's Tennis Hall of Fame, and a pioneer of women's tennis through establishing the Virginia Slims Circuit, was—with his popular wife, Joan, a theatrical agent—a penthouse resident until their deaths in 2004. Their neighbors have included Minot Milliken, of the textile company Deering Milliken; author and *Harper's* magazine editor-in-chief Lewis Lapham; major art collector and gallery owner Jeffery H. Loria, who was a personal friend of Pablo Picasso and is the owner of the Florida Marlins; Dr. Chin Wing Chu and his wife, Gloria Rada Chu; Hamm beer heiress Alexandra Hamm Ryan; artist Senen Ubina; and Vanderbilt descendent Virginia Burke, whose father, Earl E. T. Smith, was mayor of Palm Beach and one of the last American ambassadors to Cuba.

Past and present apartment owners include such prominent Social Register and philanthropically active couples as Robin and Jane Maynard, Walker and Nicolette Bingham, Anthony and Cettie Ames, Stephen and Evelyn Owen, and the now divorced Dixon and Pauline Boardman.

In *The Upper East Side Book,* Carter Horsely praises the building's "undulating base that is perhaps the most attractive in the city as its sinuous curves ripple and soften the building's mass." Then, he adds, "There are many, although not enough, limestone-clad buildings in the city. Such facades, in fact, probably are the easiest clue that an apartment is truly 'luxury.'"

In their scholarly work, *New York, 1930: Architecture and Urbanism between the Two World Wars,* Robert A. M. Stern, Gregory Gilmartin, and Thomas Mellins also devote considerable attention to Candela's last luxury apartment statement, designed in collaboration with Mott B. Schmidt, who was supposedly brought in to rein in Candela's high-flying creativity at a time when the Great Depression had cut down on many architectural commissions in the city.

Candela's building, with its metal balcony rails, its bands of cyma moldings probably inspired by Joseph Hoffman's Austrian Pavilion at the 1925 Paris Exposition des Arts Decoratifs, replaced McKim, Mead & White's fabled Tiffany family mansion, which had stood at the important street's northwest corner since 1882.

Amazingly, the Tiffany home, which in its time inadvertently pioneered the idea of more than one well-to-do family sharing a grand house was torn down without much notice by the public. When it first went up, it excited constant attention on the part of New Yorkers. The huge six-story brick fortress on a rough-hewn stone base, with steeply pitched gables, an amazing array of chimneys, a side tower of bay windows, and a large stone-paved arch under a grilled front entrance was believed to be a collaboration between the mutual admiration society of Stanford White and Louis Comfort Tiffany, at that time America's leading decorator as well as the famous creator of the multicolored glass lamps and windows treasured to this day. The imposing residence, filled with somewhat theatrical exotica from Pompeii, Arabia, India, and Japan, had a huge ballroom, dramatic staircase, charming breakfast room, and Louis Tiffany's studio. It housed the families of the founder of America's most prestigious jewelry emporium, Charles L. Tiffany, as well as that of Charles's married daughter, and his son, Louis Tiffany, and his family.

According to the *New York Times's* Streetscapes columnist Christopher Gray, when John Thomas Smith, the general counsel to General Motors, paid $2.25 million cash for the Tiffany house site after the death of Louis Comfort Tiffany in 1933, 19 East 72nd Street was notably the first luxury apartment to go up since New York's building boom during the Roaring Twenties. Rosario Candela, who had had a torrent of twenty-seven sumptuous co-op commissions in 1929 alone, by 1936 had only a trickle of them. At his office's peak, there had been fifty draftsmen designing the most luxurious accommodations in New York, "then . . . practically nothing." Smith, who took the biggest and best apartment at the top for himself, according to one of his grandchildren in a 1996 interview, said that the owner was slightly afraid Candela might become "too extreme, too Art Deco-y."

"A 1937 account in *The Real Estate Record & Guide* indicated the kind of tenant for whom the building had been designed," Gray reports, "Air conditioning was not offered because it is expected most of the tenants will live in their country or shore places in hot weather."

In Manhattan, where life is uniquely both anonymous and intimate, no apartment is an island unto itself. In this vertical arrangement, people literally live on top of one another. Even in the finest apartment houses, you can occasionally hear your neighbors taking a shower, playing the guitar, and sometimes raising their voices in an argument. From practically every apartment in the city, you can see into the apartment and private life of someone else, and someone can see into yours.

Unlike most other cities, where the condominium mode of apartment ownership is the norm, in Manhattan, where each building is considered a sort of community unto itself, the issue of control looms large. In these closely quartered communal homes, the notion of the right people—like-minded souls—allowed to join the little group are of paramount concern. And so the cooperative apartment has long been the most favored plan of apartment ownership. Yet whether co-op or condo, you're not just buying a place to call home, you're joining a sort of political regime. If you subscribe to the Three Musketeers school of thinking—"all for one, one for all"—and are prepared to link your fortune and fate with those of your fellow apartment mates, then co-op living is for you, according to Sylvia Shapiro, author of *The New York Co-Op Bible*. But if you're "cut from the Marlboro Man mold—determined to go your own way, free from the ties that bind to communal ownerkind"—then condo country is the way for you.

In a condo, you actually buy the space you call home. You own the cubic feet enclosed within its walls outright and pay common carrying charges based upon its size. In addition to owning your own unit, you also get an undivided proportionate interest, together with your fellow dwellers, who are owners in the common areas you all traverse: lobbies, corridors, basements, sundeck. As proof of ownership, you receive a deed—"the better for the taxing authorities to find you out," quips Sylvia Shapiro. But, "you are your own residential lord and master. You can save some shrink bills and rest assured that your residential sanity will remain intact." In a co-op arrangement, Shapiro maintains, "you have a more schizophrenic status." You are both a tenant and also sort of partial owner and, collectively with the other people who live in the building, the landlord. What you are buying, in the legal sense, is not a home or a piece of property, but shares in a corporation. The co-op corporation owns the building and usually the land it sits on and it issues stock. While each owner has exclusive occupancy of his or her apartment, each also owns a portion of the whole entity, represented by shares of stock. These shares are sold in blocks proportional to the size, desirability, and perceived value of each apartment. A duplex penthouse with a terrace, for example, will command more shares than a darker, similarly sized apartment on a lower floor. Yet, it's not the number of shares that really count, but the percentage of the total of the building's shares your apartment represents. So depending on your proportion of shares—your own block of interest in the corporation—you're given, through the election of directors and the exercise of your vote, varying degrees of power in how the property is to be managed.

One reason the cooperative method has been so popular in New York is its great tax advantage to the building. Because only stock changes hands during a purchase, the holding corporation pays no capital gains taxes, no matter how much the property accrues in value. Furthermore, since buying stock in a private company is a private transaction, there is no public listing of sales or prices. Meanwhile, the prices of New York condominiums and town houses are recorded deeds, available to the media, or anyone for that matter, through city records. Still, co-op prices, especially the stratospheric recent figures, manage to leak out, sometimes through the real estate broker's computer listing, sometimes simply through indiscreet word of mouth. This will change. In July 2006, Governor George Pataki signed a bill into law allowing the city to make the price of co-op apartment sales public for the first time.

Manhattan co-op boards have been likened alternately to ferocious watchdogs and Soviet-style dictatorships, because of the secrecy with which they operate and because of the vehemence with which they guard the tenor and tone of their buildings.

In his 2006 stage satire *The Right Kind of People,* actor-playwright Charles Grodin drew a scathing portrait of the pettiness of the rich defending their real estate. He allowed a glimpse into just how silly, snobbish, and outright scary seemingly rational people can be when it comes to running a fancy, coveted building and deciding who may live there. Grodin, who, before moving to Connecticut, for six years served on the board of a Fifth Avenue co-op, demonstrates through a series of increasingly rancorous meetings that there is a bit of a bigot lurking in everyone. "Do we want a divorced woman?" might be the kind of debate Grodin reveals. "Do we want somebody on the elevator coming to date this divorced woman, do we want teenage children, what height and weight limit should we set for the dogs?"

The board of directors has the legal authority to run the co-op without the interference of the shareholders. What this usually amounts to is running it like a private club. They set the rules, decide the amount of monthly maintenance fees, which is basically co-op language for rent. Each shareholder is expected to live by the rules outlined in the codex of policies and enforced by the board of directors. It covers almost every situation imaginable from installing a new sink, putting up wallpaper, disposing of garbage, or drunken misbehavior in the lobby. But most importantly, board members decide who else will be allowed to buy into the building—that is, allowed to enter the gates and be a fellow proprietor of an apartment. The co-op board may legally reject an applicant for almost any reason, aside from outright discrimination. What's more, the board is not bound to state the basis for rejection. Of course, in most buildings, people are blackballed all the time for reasons of age, gender, race, and religion. But these days it's nearly impossible to prove a civil rights violation, because boards operate with complete autonomy and total secrecy.

The clandestine process of getting a deal approved by a co-op board can be among the most mystifying and exasperating experiences of anyone trying to get into an A-plus Manhattan apartment house.

One prerequisite of admission is set in cement: you have to be able to pull your weight financially. In a building like 19 East 72nd Street, where most apartments are in the $10-million range with roughly $8,000 monthly maintenance, you also need to have the liquid assets to deal with whatever may come along.

Here's the standard acquisition procedure. A potential customer makes an offer through the buyer's broker and negotiates with the seller's broker. If the offer is accepted, the seller's attorney draws up a contract. The contract then is negotiated and signed, first by the buyer, who puts up 10 percent of the purchase price. Next the seller signs the contract. At this point, the buyer has to submit a "board package" with the help of his or her broker. Usually, you have ten business days to complete this and hand it in to the managing agent. The board package consists of the contract, the purchase application, about five personal references, two or three business references, financial information of the potential buyer's net worth (with all of it backed up by bankers and financial institutions), a lead paint disclosure form, and usually an agreement to sign a paper relating to the work rules in the building. Some buildings only let you do heavy, noisy renovation work from Memorial Day to Labor Day. If you are not finished with the heavy work, you will have to wait until the following Memorial Day to continue. These are generally called "Summer Rules." Painting, paperhanging, and carpet installation are usually permissible all year.

The board package has to include one original copy and usually ten more copies for the other board members. These get circulated from the building's managing agent and, after studying them, the board decides whether to give the applicant an interview. Usually, if the applicant appears to have the right profile for the co-op, he or she will be invited for an interview. By the time someone is invited for a board interview, chances are high that he or she will be accepted.

Certain circumstances can cause rejection. The applicant must be dressed conservatively: no cleavage and very little jewelry for women. Wearing a flashy fur coat is discouraged by brokers. No T-shirt and Bermudas for the men, on even the hottest New York days. Business attire is the correct way to respect the occasion.

What exactly do these scrupulously protected enclaves want to know about you? How much should you tell? What are the unspoken rules of behavior at a co-op board interview? What is it like to meet with these sometimes highly intimidating, sometimes snippy, sometimes greatly self-important people? Who gets in and who gets turned down?

Talking too much or saying the wrong thing can mean trouble. Boasting about a gun collection does not go over well with a group of New Yorkers. One buyer, who signed the contract, told the agent just before the interview, "I know how to get out of this if I want to." He proceeded to tell the board that he had a rock band and that the band would be coming to the apartment every night to practice. He was obviously rejected. The real estate broker was stunned.

There are, of course, clashes between applicants and board members. Agents specializing in exclusive Manhattan listings have priceless stories of strange happenings at interviews. For example, one customer took an apartment with his girlfriend. Because the girlfriend broke up with him, at the last minute he changed the co-op board package to take the apartment with his wife. A nasty and irrational seller of a glorious Fifth Avenue apartment could be dealt with only in the morning before he hit the bottle. One wealthy couple who bought a pricey apartment was astonished to find out that their attorney had absconded to the Cayman Islands with the huge 10 percent money attached to the contract.

It is the managing agent who will receive the decision from the board. Sometimes, it will happen right away and sometimes it will take a long time. It varies from building to building. Sometimes a board requests additional information before it makes a decision. If you don't find out right away whether you got into the building, don't be presumptuous and try to come with an architect or decorator. And above all, don't let it get to you. It isn't always personal. One man didn't get into the building of his dreams because the head of the board had the same last name and didn't want the mail mixed up. One extremely qualified couple did not get accepted into a great Fifth Avenue building because the husband was having an affair with a woman in the penthouse, and someone on the board knew about it. Some buildings have an unspoken quota on, say, how many Jewish families they want in their building. Another Park Avenue building turned down a young couple with all the right credentials because they were Catholic and "will probably have lots of children." And, finally, there's the jealousy factor. Sometimes longtime residents, who seem so strict, so rigid, so forbidding bought their apartments twenty-some years ago. If their net worth were to be put on the table, there is no way they could afford to buy an apartment in the building today. They simply can't control their envy, and they camouflage their anger toward an applicant who is obviously very successful, very rich, and in an entirely different financial stratum than they could ever hope to be.

While the board package is basically an assets and liabilities statement, many purchasers of co-ops, particularly foreigners, find it an insultingly intrusive scrutiny of the life of the applicant. Many people resent having to endure a group of total strangers inspecting their financial *curriculum vitae*—and often prying into personal aspects of their lives to see if they're worthy of living under the same roof with the already chosen. First of all, the expense of gathering the financial statements, copying them, and assembling the copies demanded by the board can be quite costly. At this echelon, it can involve financial advisors, accountants, and sometimes lawyers. Then there are the letters of recommendation. In this time-pressed epoch of cell phones and instant messages, formal handwritten letters attesting to character, propriety, and probity seem quaint and antiquated.

Joan Sacks, an associate broker at Stribling, who sits on the board of her own Sutton Place apartment building, was quoted in the *New York Times:* "Many people believe falsely the letters will never be considered because who would give a bad one? But the quality of the letters will speak of the kinds of people the applicant knows, their ability to write well, and most importantly, the ability to provide a sense, at a personal level, what the applicant and his family are like."

Real estate agents are adamant that, depending on the building and the candidate, the quality of the letter writing can make the difference between acceptance and rejection. Unfortunately, they feel many people misunderstand the ritual and take it lightly, as if it were a joke, sometimes faking letters and often bungling them—sometimes to comic effect. For example, one board package submitted a note on behalf of an aspiring couple, which to the horror of the agent read, "Both applicants are of the highest moral turpitude."

Basically, the letters should describe through specific anecdotal illustrations that the candidates have a solid base in society in terms of relationships; that they are convivial, get along with their neighbors, and accommodate themselves to others' needs. Of course, this is New York, and who is writing can make all the difference. Then, too, the right names depend on the personality of the building. Also, engraved stationery counts. And with especially clubby building boards, it helps to figure out who they are and try to have someone write who personally knows them.

Yet in the end, the meticulous picking and choosing of neighbors is one of the rewards of co-op ownership. So is the comforting notion that, if anything in the building goes wrong and needs significant investment, fellow members of the club will share the pain.

But overly strict boards that too often, and sometimes gleefully, torpedo the applications of other high-and-mighty can ultimately have an adverse effect on an otherwise praiseworthy building. A reputation for exclusivity, if overdone, can produce negative reactions in sensitive people shopping for a new apartment. They don't like to be rejected. Real estate brokers know this and hesitate to expose potential purchasers to all-too-possible turndowns.

Also, for every rejected applicant, there is a current shareholder who wants, and sometimes desperately needs, to leave and cash out. When too many potential buyers—already prescreened by a tactful, all-knowing realtor—are turned away, the seller feels that he is held hostage by the fussy co-op board.

That's exactly how a former resident felt, who, after more than thirty years in the building, bought another irresistible home but found that he could not move out, because for two years the board refused to approve a purchaser for his 19 East 72nd Street apartment. Candidate after qualified candidate was refused entry through the hallowed gates. He began to wonder whether it was a personal vendetta on the part of the chairman of the board, with whom he had had several skirmishes.

Three decades before, when this former resident himself had bought into the building, he recalled his entrance was a breeze. "In those days, we were lucky enough to have Minot Milliken as the chairman of the board. He was a benign despot. Ran every detail related to the building. One of the unique features of the building is its beautiful basement. All the pipes are color-coded. Everything is perfectly engineered. There are extensive storage cages. Everyone has a laundry cage, and there is a private wine cellar. Minot may have been an old tyrant, but he was a gentleman, always quite fair," he recalls. "What is now an agonizing co-op board procedure seemed much simpler back then. A friend of mine on the board told Minot we were OK. We talked with him for two minutes. If he decided you were right for the building, you were in. The building was always very particular. But Minot was smart and he did not want 19 East 72nd Street to have a reputation for being a 'restricted' building. He looked at individuals instead of thinking in stereotypes."

The chairman of the board can be absolutely critical to the image of a building and the happiness of those who live there. In the superexpensive buildings, New York apartment owners tend to be extremely busy with their own competitive careers. They do not have the inclination, let alone the time, to get involved in the details of the building management. They are only too willing to let two or three, or perhaps just one, board member run the show. A slate of directors is nominated by the board each year and usually voted upon as a whole. The election is rarely contested. The board elects a chairman. Once a chairman is in office, the apathy of the tenant-shareholders tends to lengthen his regime. A misplaced sense of politeness is his strongest supporter. "We're just one big happy family," one chairman tells his annual meeting. "Let's keep it that way." He makes dissent sound antisocial, if not out-and-out subversive.

Being chairman of a co-op is, in truth, a pretty terrible job. It can be very time-consuming, and, of course, it is not salaried. The chairman can get phone calls in the middle of the night from a tenant concerned about a stopped drain. Few tenants really want to be chairman despite the high-sounding title, the cachet, and the very real power. That is not to deny that some very able, dedicated people serve in this capacity and do a very good job for their neighbors. On the other hand, it is not surprising to find the post filled with someone who's been a quasi-failure in the business world but still wants to run something. He is often not the brightest bulb on the Christmas tree; *that* fellow would be out making money.

There is one very simple mechanism that can help: a system of rotation on the board. Term limitation, if you will. The bylaws of the building can provide that a board member, including the chairman, may serve three years, or perhaps six, and then become ineligible for reelection for the next year or so. Most of the better New York co-ops now have some form of term limits. The building at 19 East 72nd is a notable exception. Two individuals have each served as directors for more than twenty years, and one or the other has been chairman for most of that time.

While the chairman pretty much runs the show when it comes to managing the day-to-day affairs of the building, that doesn't mean the constituents have been stripped bare of power. Under New York State law, shareholders in a co-op have the power to make decisions on fundamental and extraordinary matters of co-op governance. Shareholders have the right to elect their directors and remove their directors. They have the power to oust officers and effectuate change.

A few years ago, another blueblooded Manhattan building, just down the block from 19 East 72nd Street, became totally fed up with the autocratic head of the co-op board. Residents—who included several historically prominent families, an important art collector and ambassador, a major backer of Lincoln Center, and a famous hotelier—were upset enough to band together and get rid of him. They elected a new president who was more of a team player.

There are ways to redress an imbalance, or fight the power you're up against and swing the pendulum back the other way. Most of the time, a vote on a board election is just a vote, but if the co-op has written into its bylaws what is called "cumulative voting," that is another story. In theory, co-ops are set up to be run democratically, despite what often appears to be arbitrary selectivism in choosing new members. Cumulative voting allows minority shareholders to maneuver to have their views represented on the board despite the difficulty of getting on the official building slate at election time.

Cumulative voting works this way: If you have 100 shares and there are 10 seats on the board, you can cast 100 votes for each of the 10 candidates. Or you can cumulate and cast all your 1,000 votes for the one candidate whom the board has not nominated, or spread your votes among any combination of candidates. Needless to say, this mechanism is not favored by boards of directors in power.

Most votes in co-op elections are cast by proxy. The board routinely solicits proxies from all the shareholders, who give their voting rights to certain named powers in the building. The proxy cards are presented at the annual meeting, and persons in the audience who have not given proxies are permitted to vote in person. The votes are counted by "inspectors of the election" appointed by the chairman. They are usually employees of the building management firm that is paid by the board. The tabulation is complicated, and management can easily defeat cumulative voting by cheating. Sadly, cheating is not unknown in the co-op world.

Some years ago, at 19 East 72nd Street, suspicion arose when the inspectors returned from the counting room after a very long hiatus in the election meeting, and the results they announced struck tenants as strange. It is, however, very difficult and expensive to go to court and overturn a building election. This rarely happens. Also, by the time a court could act, the year would be almost over. Shareholder apathy tends to prevail.

When people live under one roof, over the years, love-hate relationships develop. All sorts of small irritants accumulate from petty bureaucratic micromanaging or long-festering resentments of, say, a tacky, ill-spoken wife of a board member. But when they are finally aroused, most New Yorkers feel pretty passionate about their particular foothold on Manhattan Island and will go to great lengths, when it's truly threatened, to defend their basic rights.

In the divisive summer of 1990, the chairman of 19 East 72nd Street decided to eliminate cumulative voting. One of the lawyers in the building—and this is why some buildings are reluctant to have lawyers move in—remembered from law school an ancient principle: If you are going to change the voting rules, you have to buy out the shareholders who will not consent to your change. These are $10-million apartments. This news surprised the special meeting of the stockholders called for the purpose. It also surprised the building's attorney, a noted real estate specialist who was present for the occasion. The proposal was withdrawn.

Then there was the episode about the building's windows. Someone on the board came up with the idea that everyone should have new double-hung windows whether they wanted them or not. It turned out that there were residents who were proud of their 1930s windows put in by Candela's architectural team. What's more, some apartments had upward of thirty-five windows, and the cost of the change would have been significant. Then came the fatal memo: "The Landmarks Preservation Commission requires you to put in these new windows." Again, it was met with residents' comeuppance. One irate owner wrote his own letter to all the tenants: "The Landmarks Preservation Commission never says 'you *must* do this.' It only lets you know what you *cannot* do. Call them up and check." And that was the end of that.

A few years later, two physical fitness buffs on the board had the brain-storm of building a gym in the basement. "All the Good Buildings have them," the letter insisted. But this time, all sorts of heretofore silent voices were heard from. Turned out, if there was a sacrosanct place in the structure that everybody in the building had a soft spot for, it was their perfect color-coded basement. "We will not give up our laundry cages!" the corps d'elite replied. Even the two elderly grande dames, who speak every day on the phone, Mrs. Flavia Hackett and Mrs. Maynard Womer, piped up: "We don't see ourselves going to the gym." But it took one of the building's avid historians to pull out his treasured, browning, frayed, 130-year-old copy of the Viele Map, the bible of Manhattan's underground waterways. Made by Colonel Egbert L. Viele, the Zelig-like civil engineer who pops up often in nineteenth-century New York history, it illuminates what the island looked like before it was filled in, paved over, dug up, and forested with skyscrap-ers. Colonel Viele fought in the Civil War and lost out to Frederick Law Olmsted in the competition to design Central Park, but he served as the chief engineer for what would later become the subway system. His map is still indispensable to the city's structural engineers. It is as current as the foundations poured across Manhattan today.

The Viele Map did it.

Unbeknownst to most residents of 19 East 72nd Street, their building sat right next to the Bloomingdale River, a slightly zigzagging underground stream coming all the way from across Central Park and the American

Museum of Natural History and flowing pretty much along Madison Avenue in the lower seventies. It was the breeding ground for trillions of water bugs that apparently commuted regularly to parts of their basement. What's more, the city building code would require an extra stairway from the lobby down to the basement gym. The cost of building the proposed athletic facility would start at $300,000—requiring an assessment of at least $10,000 per apartment whether the owner used the gym or not. In view of all this, the board was wise enough to turn down the proposal.

Quite a lot happens in the life span of an apartment house, and many deeply discomforting events test the judgment of the co-op board. Often, these matters are known only to the board members, and the tenants as a whole have only a vague idea of them. During some dramatic occurrences, however, people tend to take sides.

There was a brief space of time when fellow residents found they had a flasher among them. What's more, he turned out to be a prominent New Yorker. He would fondle himself in the window, right across the street from two preteen girls, whose hysterically upset mother was, of all things, a psychiatrist. Then there was the mysterious fire and simultaneous robbery in Oona O'Neill Chaplin's apartment. Many years later, there was a second and truly serious fire caused by a computer malfunction in a library lined with hundreds of precious books, after which the upstairs neighbor sued the already devastated owners of the burned-out suite as well as the board of the building. And then, of course, there is the perpetual nuisance of the smelly hot-dog vendor on the corner, who just won't go away.

But of all the excitement that took place in and around the building's premises, none matched the headline-making furor with which the building turned down Richard Milhous Nixon in 1979.

True, five years after Watergate, the former president of the United States, who had quietly retreated to his Casa Pacifica in San Clemente, was still one of the most hated men in America. He was looking for a place to live in New York City, which he felt would be the ideal spot—now that some time had elapsed—to return to public life gradually, as an elder statesman. The late Minot Milliken, then the chairman of the co-op board at 19 East 72nd Street, had been a minor fund-raiser for the Republicans. When approached by the Nixons, he simply promised Nixon an apartment in the building.

There was a lot of chatting at the time in every corner of the complex. Residents would later have a little taste of what it's like to have a highly protected world figure on their street when the newly elected pope, John Paul II, visited a house the Vatican keeps in New York across from their apartment building. There were concrete barriers put up all over the block. Sharpshooters were posted on the roof. There were Secret Service in front of the building. Residents coming and going to 19 East 72nd Street had to be vetted by police and carry IDs to show they actually lived where they lived.

Many residents were taken by surprise when, in July 1979, the *New York Times* reported that Nixon and his wife, Patricia, had been approved by the twelve-member co-op board at 19 East 72nd Street to buy a nine-room penthouse in the building for $1 million.

As admired, beloved, and endowed with power and strength as the captain of the ship that Minot Milliken was, there was instant mutiny among the rest of the residents in the apartment house. Jane Maynard, an elegant sportswoman, known to be a political person and not a shrinking violet when it came to exercising her women's rights, picked up the campaign to reverse the decision. She was quoted in the press: "He is very controversial." She explained that Nixon was in constant danger of endless assassins who would like to have a crack at him. The Secret Service would have to check everyone, and everyone's visitors to the building, to intercept a possible tragic incident. Jane Maynard, whose cousin, Moorehead Kennedy, had been a hostage in Iran, would exclaim, "Can you imagine what would happen if the Shah of Iran visited Nixon in the building?"

Hurt and humiliated by the brouhaha, the Nixons withdrew their offer. Their deposit was promptly returned, which is more than what happened to the ex-president when he tried to buy a nearby Fifth Avenue condo. There, he lost the nearly $100,000 he had put down.

10 Gracie Square

· 20 ·

---

10 GRACIE SQUARE

SHOCK AND DRAMA

$\mathcal{E}$VER SINCE THE days of Fiorello LaGuardia, the first mayor of New York to take up residence in Gracie Mansion, well-connected, well-known Manhattanites like orchestra leader André Kostelanetz, power broker Robert Moses, movie actors Anthony Quinn and Patricia Neal, Yale University's Benno Schmidt, Columbia University's Osborn Elliot, as well as civically distinguished figures like Constantine Sidamon-Eristoff, have flocked to live in its delightful surroundings. Especially agreeable, and more tranquil than most corners of Manhattan, is the easternmost block of East 84th Street, called Gracie Square.

Facing a lovely landscaped sprawl bound by a sinuous esplanade overlooking Hell Gate's churning waters, and near the charming Queen Anne row houses of the Henderson Place historic district, since the 1980s Gracie Square has become particularly attractive to families with children. This is because of its proximity to two of the Upper East Side's top private schools, Brearley and Chapin. Of the handful of handsome high rises on the block, without question the most sought-after are the terraced duplex apartments fronting the East River at 10 Gracie Square. Yet this apartment house, one of the few in the city to have a gated through-the-building driveway entrance, which is closely watched not by lobby doormen but by guards standing in a glass booth at each end, was the site of two of the most horrific happenings to take place in such a pedigreed building. One involved murder; the other, suicide. So in spite of the high desirability of the fifteen-story cooperative and its impressive roster of owners, some believe that 10 Gracie Square is jinxed.

In 1982, detectives from the 19th Precinct arrested Frances Schreuder, a Lily Tomlin look-alike, twice-divorced mother of three, in her apartment at 10 Gracie Square. She was a direct descendent of Massachusetts pilgrim William Bradford, a member of the prestigious Huguenot Society, and on the board of directors of the New York City Ballet. On their first attempt to arrest her, police were denied access to the building. The men guarding the entrance in the glass booths refused to let "New York's Finest" in without a search warrant. Frances Schreuder was charged with the murder of her father, a Utah auto parts multimillionaire who had been shot to death, surprised from the back with a gun to his head, four years earlier in 1978. She was accused of conspiring with her seventeen-year-old son, a product of the finest schools in New York and one of the finest East Coast boarding schools. During the trial, the son, Marc, eventually turned on his mother, testifying that she had coaxed him to kill his grandfather. Frances had been a big spender and couldn't wait for her inheritance. The story was told in two books: *At Mother's Request,* by Jonathan Coleman, and *Nutcracker,* by Shana Alexander. Both books were turned into television movies, with Lee Remick playing Frances Schreuder in one of them. Both mother and son were found guilty by the jury. Frances Schreuder was given a life sentence, but she died in prison in 2002. Her son received a sentence of five-years-to-life.

The most tragic incident in the building was the 1988 suicide of Gloria Vanderbilt's son and CNN television newscaster Anderson Cooper's brother, twenty-three-year-old Carter Vanderbilt Cooper. The brothers, who were close, were the sons of the writer and editor Wyatt Cooper, Gloria Vanderbilt's fourth husband.

In Anderson Cooper's 2006 book, *Dispatches from the Edge,* he describes the wrenching effects the suicide had on him and especially on his mother, who was standing nearby when it happened. Shortly after graduating from Princeton, Carter threw himself off the fourteenth-floor balcony of the famous heiress's penthouse duplex.

Gloria Vanderbilt had been accepted into the prestigious riverside building after being denied entry into the exclusive River House, reportedly
because of the close company she kept with cabaret singer Bobby Short.

"After hearing about all her problems with River House, thirty blocks
down the East River," recalls one tenant at 10 Gracie Square, "Al Gordon, the
president of the co-op board, called her and said, 'Come live up here!'" Gloria Vanderbilt knew 10 Gracie Square well. It was where her aunt, Gertrude
Vanderbilt Whitney, founder of the Whitney Museum, had lived for many
years, as had her cousin, Flora Whitney Miller. So she sold her apartment at
447 East 57th Street and moved in. But after the catastrophe, she wanted to
leave the place. In 1990, she sold the Gracie Square penthouse to Jean Stein,
one of the daughters of Music Corporation of America magnate Jules Stein
and mother of Katrina van den Heuvel, the editor and frequent television
commentator. Jean Stein is a producer who lived most of her life on Central
Park West and cowrote with George Plimpton a best-selling book on Andy
Warhol's self-destructive underground film starlet, Edie Sedgewick.

The building, despite its exclusive aura, is proud of never having had a
quota system, unlike some of the other buildings in the area, including Gracie Terrace on the next block.

A longtime resident of the building was Madame Chiang Kai-shek, one
of the most famous women of the twentieth century. Madame Chiang Kai-
shek lived to be 105. In order to prevent bedsores she spent her last days
sleeping in a hammock in her New York apartment, until her death in
2003. Though during her girlhood she lived in Macon, Georgia, and spoke
English with a Southern accent all her life, the Wellesley-educated daughter of a Shanghai businessman and Methodist minister, did not move to New
York City until 1975, after the death of her husband, Generalissimo Chiang Kai-shek, who, along with Mao Zedong and Sun-Yat-sen, was the most
important political leader in China's recent history. He fought for Sun Yat
sen's United Revolutionary League to overthrow China's imperial dynasty,
but by the 1920s he split with the Communists led by Mao. After the
death of Sun Yat sen, who was married to Madame Chiang Kai shek's sister,
Chiang seized control of the government. Still engaged in a civil war with
the Communists, the general led his army against the Japanese invaders in
Manchuria in 1937.

Madame Chiang Kai-shek, who was introduced to America at age ten and
to her husband at age twenty, became an important goodwill ambassador for

her war-torn country during World War II, serving as translator for her husband, going on an international tour, and in 1943 becoming the first Chinese national—and the second woman ever—to address a joint session of the U.S. House and Senate to drum up support for China's fight against Japan. Chiang did get the support of the Allied Powers and became supreme commander of the China theater during the war. But by 1949, when Communist forces gained control of China's major cities, the couple fled the mainland, declaring Taipei, Taiwan, to be the temporary capital of China. Mrs. Chiang continued to play a prominent role in international affairs, writing several books, and she pursued her passion for aeronautics. In later years, she owned the Central American airline TACA and she was quoted as saying, "Of all the inventions that have helped unify China, perhaps the airplane is the most outstanding. Its ability to annihilate distance has been in direct proportion to its achievements in assisting to annihilate suspicion and misunderstanding."

There have always been a number of highly placed foreign dignitaries among the residents of 10 Gracie Square. The consuls general of Turkey and Norway have spacious homes there today. John Fairchild, the sassy, erudite founder and publisher of *Women's Wear Daily* and *W* magazine, sold his splendid fourth-floor apartment to peripatetic social star and real estate manager Beth Rudin de Woody in 1987 for around $3.5 million. Hazel-eyed society beauty Amanda Burden owned the maisonette apartment before she married Time Warner head Steve Ross. Kenneth D. Brody, who left Goldman Sachs to work for President Clinton as president of the Export-Import Bank of the United States, sold his apartment in the building for $4 million in the 1990s, when he moved to Washington, D.C. And it was while she was living at 10 Gracie Square that Brooke Marshall was proposed to by Vincent Astor, whose millions she so generously lavished on the New York Public Library.

Others in the complex are Richard S. Braddock, chairman of MidOcean Partners and his wife Susan, who leads the Metropolitan Opera Guild; Lehman Brothers investment banker Alan Washkowitz and his wife, Barbara, who is a caterer; Hillary Cushing Block, who was a vice president of Sotheby's; Eugenie C. Havemeyer, who runs an arts service and is a member of the wealthy sugar family; investor Richard Cashin, a former Olympian; Yvonne Quinn, a crackerjack lawyer with Sullivan & Cromwell; financier Richard Salomon; and Philip Geier, chairman and CEO of the Interpublic Group.

Writer of society novels Jane Stanton Hitchcock and her mother, Joan Stanton, each have their own apartment at 10 Gracie Square. They are the daughter and widow of Frank Stanton, who was president of CBS from 1946 to 1971. One of the most admired broadcast executives during the early, critical growth period of television, Stanton's opinions were routinely sought, his speeches repeatedly quoted. He applied his doctoral research at Ohio State, into the psychology of how people perceive various stimuli, to analyze and measure the audio and visual effectiveness of information transmission. He is credited with devising the audience-appeal measuring system nicknamed "Little Annie," which had had an accuracy rate of 85 percent. But perhaps his most important contributions were his efforts in the area of how network news handled political issues. He was instrumental in bringing about the 1960 Kennedy-Nixon presidential debates. He was a staunch campaigner for making broadcast journalism's access and protection rights equal to those of the printed press.

Stanton's biggest battle with government occurred during the 1971 controversy over the CBS News documentary about the promotion of militarism, *The Selling of the Pentagon*. But long before Watergate and Vietnam, CBS was responsible for the earliest television exploration of the negative side of Washington. This took place on *See It Now*, the news program hosted by Edward R. Murrow, which brought about the downfall of Senator Joseph McCarthy and was the subject of George Clooney's Academy Award–nominated 2005 movie *Good Night, and Good Luck.*

10 Gracie Square does not have a big status lobby à la Park Avenue, but, three elevator banks off the drive-through, with separate, town house–style entrances to the two brick towers and the one limestone tower of the complex. Seven years after it was constructed in 1930, the complex went into foreclosure and almost went bankrupt. The building had another crisis in 1992, when part of it was pretty much deconstructed and virtually put together again, because after 60 years the river had rusted the steel supports of the building's stone exterior. With scores of stone blocks removed from the building's eclectic facade, which strangely but attractively combined elements of neo-Greek and modern classicism, during the renovation an unnerving discovery was made. In this super-luxury building, the steel shelf angles that supported the stone on every floor had never been rustproofed. The original design had been a collaboration between two architectural firms, and whether the failure to protect the steel-framed building

against corrosion was from ignorance or duplicity remains a conundrum. In any case, it was corrected during the $175,000 restoration by architect Darius Trobay. And previously, like other grand apartments on the banks of the East River—One Sutton Place South and River House—owners of the co-op had to sacrifice a private yacht club, about a quarter-mile downstream, when the Franklin D. Roosevelt Drive was built. Although that docking pleasure has long been forgotten, the building still has some curious lower floors, which once served as part of the access to the water and as recreational facilities related to the club. Some of these rooms below street level were originally also used to house servants. For a long time, about two dozen of Madame Chiang Kai-shek's staff lived there. One co-op owner describes the lower three floors now as "subterranean," something resembling "the bowels of a ship, as if the building itself were a yacht on the river."

· 21 ·

POWER TOWERS

THE PRIVATE HOTEL RESIDENCES
AT THE CARLYLE, THE PIERRE,
THE SHERRY-NETHERLAND,
AND THE WALDORF-ASTORIA TOWERS

$\mathcal{T}$HE COLLECTIVE MOJO of moguls, movie stars, politicians, and potentates who are living it up sky-high—literally and figuratively—in the
fabled tower apartments of New York's grand and legendary hotel establishments is unrivaled in the world. When notoriety is to be avoided at any
price, the cost of these secret cocoons in the clouds, where an impeccably
trained staff provides a high degree of privacy as well as silky smooth,
twenty-four-hour service, well, the sky's the limit.

These supreme skyscraper suites, in beautiful buildings with names that
are synonymous with the best of everything, are run like cooperatives.
Except that their monthly maintenance fees tend to be higher, because
they make available at all times the kind of attentive and enthusiastic cater-
ing to residents' wishes that habitués of grand hotels love. These apartments are never advertised anywhere. Nor are they officially ever "on the
market." Not in so many words that is. And the select real estate brokers who
have kid-glove relationships with their rich and famous owners are not
always at liberty to show them to interested buyers. When they do show
them, they can't talk about the price. At least, not exactly. These brokers often

The Carlyle

The Pierre

The Sherry-Netherland

The Waldorf Towers

do not take credit openly for their multimillion-dollar sales, to protect the privacy of both the seller and the purchaser of the opulent piece of real estate. Their clients have no desire to end up in the newspapers. Publicity is to be avoided at all cost. And normally, when these apartments are sold again, no one other than the same discreet real estate agent, who has carefully nurtured a personal dialogue with both buyer and seller is called upon. These select brokers to the world's superelite stay select because their lips are sealed. They go to infinite lengths to ensure their clients' anonymity. Their clients come from around the world. These people do not want to be taken advantage of but are willing to pay anything for the best—best location, best space, and best service. Brokers approach these precious hotel suites, which are often encrusted with their own rich histories, as if they were the crown jewels.

Perhaps the most whispered about of these hidden tower gems is the penthouse apartment at the sleek, 426-foot-high art deco Hotel Carlyle on Madison Avenue and East 77th Street, known as the "JFK Suite." It has long been rumored that President John F. Kennedy, who during the 1960s frequently stayed at the Carlyle, entertained Marilyn Monroe there. Later in that decade, another charismatic leader with an eye for the ladies, Detroit auto tycoon Henry Ford II, was one of its celebrated residents. In the 1990s, multimillionaire buyout king Henry Kravis moved in after he split with his second wife, fashion designer Carolyne Roehm.

The eight-room penthouse—which has three bedrooms, three-and-a-half baths, and splendid, large terraces with awesome views of Central Park and, at night, the illuminated metropolis beyond—is, in the words of one broker, "the kind of apartment that seems always for sale. But is not really on the market, because it is just about impossible to show, since the people who live in such apartments demand the utmost privacy." Another topnotch broker explains that this particular penthouse suite in the Carlyle has been passed down over the years from one powerful man to another and used as a bachelor pad—even though some of the occupants were married. The real estate agent also quipped that another reason it may have changed hands so often is its outlandish price. Consensus among brokers of these fabled hotel apartments is that the monthly maintenance fees at the Carlyle are "outrageously high," "moderately high at the Sherry-Netherland," and "fairly reasonable at the Pierre."

Built in 1930–1931 as an apartment hotel by the Calvin Morris Corporation, with Bien & Prince as its architects, the graceful green and gold, thirty-eight-floor Carlyle tower is still incredibly chic. It dominates the skyline of the Upper East Side in a neighborhood of lovely five-story brownstones and exquisite Madison Avenue boutiques, jammed with the world's status-label clothes, jewels, and art objects. Transient guests—often couples in the limelight whose romance has captured the frenzied public interest—in March 2006, included Tom Cruise and Katie Holmes, on a shopping spree a month before the birth of baby Suri. In years past, there were Ryan O'Neal with Farrah Fawcett, or Warren Beatty and Annette Benning, staying for a short time. The couples used the hotel entrance on East 76th Street. There in the Carlyle lobby, surely one of the most attractive public spaces in the city, they are treated discretely, but like royalty.

Long before President Kennedy, what had originally put the Carlyle on the international map was that President Harry S. Truman, beginning in 1948, stayed there whenever he came to New York. His favorite little browsing walks in the area became front-page headlines in newspapers around the world. Soon after that, the Rockefeller Brothers bought the building, but leased it back to the original owners, City Investing Company. Later, the building was bought by a perfectionist realtor, Peter Sharp, who in 1970 turned the 50 East 77th Street apartments, with their elegant sunken living rooms, into co-ops. Among the earliest apartment owners (besides Henry Ford II) were Walter Chrysler's daughter, Mrs. Edgar Garbish, and her colonel husband, who loved the late-night scene at Bemelmans Bar and listening to Bobby Short at the Café Carlyle. They were followed by Diane von Furstenberg; Sid Bass after he left Ann Bass and before he married Mercedes Kellogg; gregarious man-about-town Bill Murray; duty-free multimillionaire Tony Polaro; and Michael Fuchs, founder of HBO television.

Of all New York City's extremely expensive top-notch hotel residences, the green-and-copper roof of the Pierre is most often cited as the ultimate power address. Sumner Redstone, chairman and CEO of Viacom and CBS Media Conglomerate, which are the parent companies of CBS, Paramount Pictures, MTV Networks, UPN, Comedy Central, Nickelodeon, Showtime, the 185 radio stations of Infinity Broadcasting, Simon & Schuster book publishing, outdoor advertising, and theme parks had his New York home at the Pierre. So does financier and philanthropist Lionel Pincus, former head of Warburg Associates who for years had squired Princess Firyal of Jordan to all of New York's noteworthy charity events. Pincus's fabulous duplex overlooking Central Park reached a new peak in 2000 when he bought it at a record price of $6,000 per square foot.

But few real estate purchases in recent history made more of a splash than the 1988 acquisition of the forty-first, forty-second, and forty-third-floor triplex at the Pierre Hotel, bought for a reported $12 million by Lady Fairfax of Australia. It is an unbelievably extravagant apartment. The triplex looks out on all the great skyscrapers of midtown Manhattan, Wollman skating rink in Central Park, the Hudson River in the distance, and the orange hills of New Jersey each evening as the sun dips into the darkness on the horizon. Lady Fairfax unveiled her lavishly decorated domain at the top of the tower with a Christmas Season dinner she gave for Prince Edward of England in 1993. The centerpiece of the colossal apartment, the grand staircase to what was once a ballroom used by the hotel guests, elicited "oohs and ahs" from even her most sophisticated guests.

When the real estate agent first took her to see the place, the space was all boarded up, but Lady Fairfax knew exactly what she wanted to do with it and what she wanted it to look like. She climbed up on a table and pulled down the boards that were blocking twenty-three-foot windows that reached up to the ceiling. Outside it were four magical balconies, one on each corner. The rest of the apartment consisted of several large and small sitting rooms, a grand drawing room for entertaining, a lovely library, a duplex of private quarters with three bedrooms, and several rooms that served as "the corporate apartment."

Lady Fairfax, whose decorating style was once described as a sort of "Franglais," constantly collected, and she spent four years finding such knockout pieces as a Rodin nude for the foyer, two Rothschild chests, and several Picassos and Chagalls. She had a fireplace behind the bathtub in the opulent master suite, all sorts of reading nooks all over the place, and an atmospheric French country kitchen. The bedrooms were carpeted in white shag rugs, and each of the many kitchenettes, otherwise empty, boasted an orange juicer. Though Lady Fairfax never had a tenant, she repeatedly received offers from someone to rent the place for $50,000 a month.

Over the years, other major art collectors had homes at the Pierre. One was Janice Levin. Another was Pierre Berge, the business brain behind Yves Saint-Laurent's fashion empire. And still another was Baron Heinrich Thyssen-Bornemisza, the German industrialist, one of the richest men in the world and perhaps the greatest art collector of the twentieth century. His priceless treasures spanning the centuries from Giotto to Lucien Freud are now housed in Madrid's famed Thyssen-Bornemisza Museum across from the Prado.

And young, attractive, socially prominent couples, like investment banker Christopher Birch and his fashion designer wife Tory, continue to move into the Pierre's uppermost floors. One of the great international hotels, this graceful green-and-copper roofed tower was built in 1928 by Anthony Campagna and designed by Schultze & Weaver. Chris Birch sits on the Pierre's co-op board.

Almost next door at 781 Fifth Avenue on the northeast corner of East 59th Street, the Sherry-Netherland has its devotees. Willowy blond interior designer Joanne de Guardiola, who chairs half-a-dozen charity benefits every year, and her financier husband, Roberto, bought five apartments—almost an entire floor—after they sold their East 64th Street townhouse for $30 million in 2005. Diana Ross keeps an apartment in the building, and recently, cell phone tycoon George Lindemann and his wife, Freya, settled in. Steel magnate Wilbur Ross and his new bride, the former Hillary Geary, who writes a society column for *Quest* magazine, ensconced themselves in a splendid Mario Buatta–decorated tower suite. They had bid fiercely but lost out to Rupert Murdoch for the $44-million Laurance Rockefeller penthouse at 834 Fifth Avenue in 2004.

Completed in 1927 to the designs of Schultze & Weaver and the firm of Ely Jacques Kahn, this forty-story high-rise chateau, with its Gothic green-gabled roof, was named after Louis Sherry, a renowned New York restaurateur of the *fin de siècle*, whose firm first managed the hotel, and the New Netherland Hotel, which once stood at the site and was built in 1890. In 1970, the Sherry-Netherland became a co-op. Max Fisher, a well-known Detroit businessman, Palm Beach figure, and advisor to several U.S. presidents, and his wife, Marjorie, had a modern-art-filled apartment for years and entertained friends from all over in the famous private club Doubles, located in the Sherry-Netherland's basement.

One triplex has quite a history of its own. Once upon a time, it had belonged to Jack Warner, head of the great Hollywood movie studio Warner Bros. It was later bought by Mercedes-Benz heir and jet-setter Mick Flick, a famous German playboy. Flick's former lower floor was converted into one huge U-shaped living space, with windows that go from floor to ceiling. At this altitude at the Sherry-Netherland, the outside of the building is ringed by gargoyles, which rivetingly jut out beside the windows. A spiral staircase was designed to afford the maximum pleasure every step of the way. Another great apartment close by belonged to photographer and costume designer Cecil Beaton, who conceived the famous black-and-white outfits for the Ascot scene of *My Fair Lady*.

Cole Porter, Herbert Hoover, General Douglas MacArthur, Adlai Stevenson, the Duke and Duchess of Windsor, Frank Sinatra—they all maintained permanent apartments in the Waldorf Towers, the high-security, twin-towered summation of all that was grand and unequaled in the world about New York's five-star hotels after World War II.

In the minds of many people, fantasies partially spun by newspapers and Hollywood movies, the Waldorf was one mythic, enormous block of luxurious exclusivity, splashy fun, and black-tie formality. The residential tower suites of the Waldorf have their own private elevators, completely separate from the enormous hotel, which opened in 1931. With forty-seven stories, the art deco knockout on Park Avenue and 50th Street was called "the tallest and most beautiful hotel in the world." Architects Schultze and Weaver included such amenities as a private rail siding under the hotel, for immensely wealthy clients who in those days had their own private railroad cars. The name comes from the old Waldorf-Astoria Hotel, which was on Fifth Avenue and 34th Street but was demolished to make room for the Empire State Building. It was named after the Astor family mansion, which first stood on that site, and the town in Germany where the Astors came from.

The Waldorf's Presidential Suite, 35A in the towers, was inaugurated in 1954 by President Eisenhower. The four-bedroom suite, which is not reserved for just heads of state and may be booked by lesser mortals for thousands of dollars a night, has sheltered Britain's Queen Elizabeth, France's Charles de Gaulle, Japan's Emperor Hirohito, Jordan's King Hussein, Spain's Juan Carlos, the Sultan of Brunei, Russia's President Putin, and frequently, President and Mrs. Ronald Reagan.

In addition to the Presidential Suite, there is Suite 42A, the only American ambassadorial residence not owned by the U.S. government. George H. W. Bush lived in this Waldorf Tower suite when he was ambassador to the United Nations. And Madeleine Albright lived there for six years.

Despite their lavishness and aura of permanence, the Tower apartments are not co-ops but rentals. The Waldorf, estimated to be worth over $1.6 billion, is owned today by Hilton Hotels. When it was sold to the Hilton chain in 1949, the purchase was made by Conrad Hilton personally. The parents of tabloid princess Paris Hilton, Kathy and Rick Hilton, have their New York home in the Waldorf Towers. Patricia Duff, the third ex-wife of Revlon chairman Ron Perelman, occupies a fabulous apartment on the thirty-first floor, and Patricia Kluge, the ex-wife of Metro Media magnate John Kluge, has a handsome New York pied-à-terre on thirty-second. The widow of General MacArthur, a tiny woman who was regularly photographed at charity balls by the *New York Times,* lived in a tower apartment until 1989. Millionaires Lee Iacocca, Nelson Peltz, and W. R. Grace had spacious apartments in the Waldorf Towers, but even these were eclipsed by the Tower suite of Consolidated Foods chairman Nathan Cummings, which contained paintings by Degas, Gaughin, Monet, and Van Gogh. But it was tire-retread heiress Mrs. Donald Rinn, who passed away in the summer of 2006, who was known to pay the highest rent in the history of Manhattan: a walloping $60,000 a month!

The residential suites are elegantly homey but spacious. Most are comprised of a foyer, a living room, a boudoir, and three or four bedrooms and baths. The living rooms and dining rooms have open fireplaces. Many have Louis XV marble mantles. Most rooms have beautiful molding and the finest eighteenth-century Adam Brothers–style woodwork. When the interiors of these Tower apartments were done, the world's most famous decorators and designers were imported from Paris and London to consult on how to make them the sanctums of privilege they remain to this day.

"There's never a dull moment at the Waldorf Towers," laughs Andrea Stark, who with her children and Stark Carpet multimillionaire husband had lived there for years. "Whenever President Clinton or President George W. Bush came to town, Secret Service men swarmed the place. The security is phenomenal. They know how to have a perfect lockdown. When Colin Powell declared war on Iraq, we had to evacuate. When Putin stayed on our floor, we all had to go through the kind of X-ray screening that happens at airport security. That was a bit of a nightmare but it's balanced by all the fun—the little vignettes you glimpse of Michael Jackson with his daughter, or Elizabeth Taylor being fussed over as she makes endless requests of the staff, or dogs running through the halls trying to 'sniff out' this or that. You never know what to expect."

173 and 176 Perry Street

· 22 ·

173 AND 176 PERRY STREET
165 CHARLES STREET

CONDO COOL

*A*ND NOW THE incomparable urban island is turning into a crystal canyon. Let the light in! Raise the glass high! Forward-looking towers of slick minimalism and architectural bravado are breaking ground all over Manhattan. The high end of downtown has become a virtual laboratory of condo cool. But all over town—on the Upper West Side and on East End Avenue, in Chelsea and at Gramercy Park—new gleaming high-rise apartments continue their dizzying upward soar. And the phenomenon is sending up cheers from trendsters, scenesters, celebrities, and a new generation of solid young rich.

The almost manic pace of luxury residential development all over New York has persisted to defy skeptics. The escalation of co-op and condominium prices, on the other hand, has leveled a bit at this writing. Rare, new residential skyscrapers, many designed by star architects and often featuring the hip live-in/work-in concept of lofts, in what are arguably the currently most sought-after neighborhoods—TriBeCa, SoHo, the West Village, the Meatpacking District, the Flatiron District, the East Village, and even the Wall Street area—have finally gone live. About to lift off for the high

165 Charles Street

life are the Lower East Side, what is increasingly called Madison Square North—already the site of some of New York's most exciting restaurants—and the so-called High Line, the long dormant former elevated railroad strip along the far Lower West Side.

Many of these ultramodern towers—with their sometimes undulating glass façades, curtain walls of horizontal bands of glass set at irregular angles, or alternating patterned glass scrims—create a novel sense of visual rhythm and give the kind of striking abstract illusion artistic New Yorkers and Hollywood celebrities seem to like.

Most of today's hot movie, music, and fashion personalities who have New York homes choose to live downtown. With the exception of Oscar-nominated star couples Heath Ledger and Michelle Williams, and Paul Bettany and Jennifer Connelly, who own properties in Brooklyn, these stellar talents, for the most part, prefer to live in remodeled lofts, cozy brownstones, and glassy new condominium towers scattered around Greenwich Village, SoHo, TriBeCa, and Chelsea. These denizens include Sarah Jessica Parker and Matthew Broderick, Kate Winslet and her director husband Sam Mendes, Iman and David Bowie, Susan Sarandon and Tim Robbins, Julianne Moore and her director husband Bart Freundlich, Heidi Klum and Seal, Meryl Streep, Kevin Spacey, Liv Tyler, Kate Hudson, Matt Damon, Jon Stewart, Norah Jones, Philip Seymour Hoffman, Edie Falco, James Gandolfini, Edward Norton, Jeffrey Wright, Harvey Keitel, Parker Posey, Famke Janssen, Molly Ringwald, Stephen Dorff, Wes Anderson, Chris Noth, Chloë Sevigny, Stone Phillips, Debbie Harry, Zac Posen, Alan Cumming, Iggy Pop, Blythe Danner, Brian de Palma, Tatum O'Neal, Claire Danes, Billy Crudup, Macaulay Culkin, Sophia Coppola, Billy Crystal, and Nathan Lane. A cluster of illuminated names grace the grand old prewar co-op buildings on lower Fifth Avenue just above Washington Square. This is where Julia Roberts, Jessica Lange and Sam Shepard, Drew Barrymore, Rufus Wainwright, Uma Thurman, Holly Hunter, John Leguizamo, and Winona Ryder own homes.

Pitched to celebrities, young Wall Street tycoons, and high-profile media types, much of the new downtown real estate is marketed these days with as much fanfare as a Hollywood blockbuster.

In truth, so much hype and hullabaloo in the last decade have swirled around the emerging glassy condos transforming the city that the hip, innovative architects, designers, and developers behind them are perpetually in the limelight and have become media stars themselves. Take André Bal-azs and Ian Schrager. These two entrepreneurs have not stopped polishing downtown to its current sheen. Their New York hotels "became blueprints for modern luxury living," according to *New York* magazine, "and both are expanding in every direction. Balazs is building two new hotels on the High Line," where, the magazine insists, "all roads in New York architecture lead, the greenest … one-and-a-half elevated miles of concrete planks, mini meadows and sundecks. The park won't open until summer 2008, but it has already had a stunning impact on the adjacent blocks, where a forest of 27 new residential towers, hotels, offices and museums is rising."

While Balazs's dazzling new 40 Mercer condos, with their huge retractable panes of glass designed by Jean Nouvel, are earning kudos, he is also behind 158 Mercer, to be the tallest apartment building in SoHo. Meanwhile, Schrager and partner Aby Rosen have completed 50 Gramercy North, the glass condominium building, with access to the newly renovated Gramercy Park Hotel's amenities and floor-to-ceiling windows looking onto the lush, green calm of Gramercy Park. Schrager and Rosen are also developers of one of the most ambitious projects, the smashing condo-minium complex 40 Bond Street by the Pritzker Prize–winning Swiss duo, Jacques Herzog and Pierre de Meuron, whose avant-garde prism reinterprets downtown's loft vernacular.

Unprecedented numbers of big name architects from all over the world are currently working on what amounts to "sculptures for living" all over Manhattan.

Fresh off the drawing board is Santiago Calatrava's 80 South Street Tower. Inspired by the prize-winning Spanish architect's own works of sculpture, and based on his formidable understanding of structural engi-neering, the slender, soaring tower will be Calatrava's first residential proj-ect in America. Its breathtakingly unconventional form is expected to make the building another symbol of downtown Manhattan's resolute resur-gence after 9/11. The airy, translucent tower—stacking essentially twelve four-story cubic glass town houses into the sky—has already generated international interest and is promoted by the builder, Sciame Develop-ment, Inc., as "an opportunity to live in a work of art."

There's Philip Johnson's Urban Glass House, a forty-condominium unit in SoHo at 328 Spring Street, based on the late architect's original design, an offspring of the oft-photographed fishbowl that was his home in New

Canaan, Connecticut, and completed by the team of Alan Ritchie, SLGE Architects, and Annabelle Seldorf. Enrique Norten's fantastic, glassy, loft condo complex, ascending between and above, filling in and linking two nineteenth-century buildings at One York Street, promises to become the latest TriBeCa icon. At 210 Lafayette Street, where SoHo meets Little Italy, architect Richard Gluckman, responsible for the spacious serenity inside the Gagosian and Mary Boone galleries, is creating a beautiful eleven-story loft apartment that wraps its curvy façade into an ethereal yet steely ribbon pattern. One unit has already been bought by Marcy Klein, fashion designer Calvin Klein's daughter.

Coming soon: French architect Philip Starck's dramatic downtown high-rise at 15 Broad Street; Dutch architect Winka Dubbeldam's wonderously inventive 497 Greenwich Street; and a huge condo complex at 101 Warren Street, designed by the Time Warner Center's David Childs of Skidmore, Owings & Merrill in TriBeCa. Then there's the winner of the MOMA-PS 1 competition of 2001, a young architect's first multidwelling residential project: Lindy Roy's High Line 519. It has distinctive space-age scrims on its cooler-than-cool glass-curtain wall. Luxurious projects up and downtown by Cesar Pelli, Peter Marino, Costas Condylis and Yale University architecture dean Robert A. M. Stern are attracting buyers from all over. Stern's extraordinary block-long complex, developed by Arthur and William Zeckendorf, is selling fast. Film star Denzel Washington and financier Sandy Weill are among those reported to have bought spacious penthouses, and hedge fund manager Daniel S. Loeb is reportedly in contract for another super-sized penthouse for $45 million, which would eclipse Rupert Murdoch's Fifth Avenue penthouse record of $44 million.

While many of the recently created glass towers are veering into new architectural territory, conversions of marvelous old downtown buildings into luxury condos also seem to have captured the imagination and pocketbooks of many New Yorkers, who are being lured from the Upper East Side to the cobbled, sometimes desolate ancient streets of lower Manhattan. Among these is the Cipriani Club Residence at 55 Wall Street, a former hotel, which will have thirty-seven furnished condos and is being developed by Steven C. Witkoff and Guiseppe Cipriani of the Venetian hotel and restaurant clan. The condos, which come with a two-year membership in the Cipriani Club, located in the building and including a spa, screening room, and free breakfasts, have already attracted some hip, young, top-of-the-

246 •   High Rise Low Down

world purchasers such as Claudio Reyna, the captain of the United States World Cup soccer team, nicknamed "Captain America." He and his wife, Danielle, hunted on and off for an apartment for four years before contracting at the Cipriani to pay $1.4 million for a one-thousand-square-foot, one-bedroom apartment. The Hubert, a regutted and remodeled candy factory where Rupert Murdoch lived for years, has enticed the likes of Frederick M. Poses, the chief executive of American Standard Companies, to trade in his prewar Carnegie Hill apartment and pay $12 million for a duplex penthouse with fabulous views and plenty of space, including five bedrooms. In the same fifteen-story co-op building, fashion designer Elie Tahari is said to have paid somewhere between $25 and $27 million, the biggest price elicited so far downtown, for the Murdoch triplex penthouse in 2006.

20 Pine Street, a 1920s office building way down in the canyons of Manhattan's financial district—an austere structure that may turn out to be the perfect canvas for Armani/Casa, the design firm noted for its use of earth tones, exotic woods, and their love of lavish, large, ultramodern rooftop swimming pools—is currently being converted into a 409-apartment condominium complex.

When the curtain rose on the first two big-name, architect-powered downtown projects of the twenty-first century, expectations were understandably high. The verdict is still out on Charles Gwathmey's wavy, blue-green glass tower on Astor Place at 445 Lafayette Street. Celebrities like actress Scarlett Johannson, Gwyneth Paltrow, and supermodel Amber Valetta were reported to have checked out apartments and, within days of the opening, eleven of its thirty-nine apartments were said to have been poised to go into contract. But critics have been tough on the greenish blue glass shell and the funky shape of some of the rooms inside, resulting from the curvy drama of the exterior. Preservationists have scorned it as "too aggressive for the neighborhood." Then there is the land lease aspect to the building, which tends to scare off buyers. The land under the building belongs to Cooper Union, and instead of selling it to the developers, Related, the company behind the new Time Warner Center, the school chose to lease it for ninety-nine years. That meant Astor Place had to become a co-op. And the downtown buyer these days tends to be a condo buyer.

The glass condo boom has made sophisticated buyers choosier. Besides being well designed and innovative aesthetically, the old truism of luxury real estate, "location, location, location," still holds.

Which of these upstart downtown "starchitect" creations will have the staying power of 960 Fifth Avenue and 778 Park Avenue, or the Beresford, River House, and the Dakota? A sure bet, among Manhattan's top-market real estate agents that were surveyed seem to be the three glass towers of world-renowned architect Richard Meier, on the far west side of Greenwich Village. Looking out over bustling West Street to the Hudson River beyond, these three condos, actually the Pritzker Prize winner's first ground-up structures in New York, were almost instantly swooped up by celebrities and architecture connoisseurs, who knew what Meier's design was all about: light and air. And, of course, the views: three of the eight-foot walls are made entirely of glass in most of the rooms and offer panoramas to the north, west, and south. To the north, you see the Empire State Building. To the south, you see the Statue of Liberty. You almost feel as if you were in a boat floating on top of the sparkling water, which is exactly what the architect intended.

First among celebrities to fall for Meier's crisp-edged lines was fashion designer Calvin Klein. From the start, he had his eye on the penthouse, so before the construction even reached that height, he took the white-haired, bespectacled architect, best-known for the Getty Museum in Los Angeles and the Atheneum in New Harmony, Indiana, up with him in a helicopter to hover precisely at the spot where the planned 4,000-square-foot penthouse of the south tower—176 Perry Street—was to be. This was in 2000. "Klein was ecstatic and paid $8 million for the top two floors," according to a report by Vicky Ward in *Vanity Fair* magazine. He later bought another floor just below the other two, for $6 million more, to create a triplex. Klein then brought in the minimalist British architect John Pawson, who did Klein's Madison Avenue flagship store, to construct the custom interior. The result has been described to be "like a film set." And Klein is said to have lavished $20 million in total on the sleek, streamlined digs.

Another early condo owner at 173 Perry—the north tower—was the intense, blue-eyed, independent movie director and actor Vincent Gallo, best known for *Buffalo 66* and *Brown Bunny*. An architecture buff, he called it "the most beautiful building I've ever seen in New York." Other buyers were Paul Sinclaire, a former executive of Club Monaco and partner in the investment conglomerate JM and A; internationally acclaimed chef Jean-Georges Vongerichten, who today runs the highly successful restaurant Perry Street on the ground floor of the south tower; and Bill Joy, the cofounder and chief scientist of Sun Microsystems, who paid $15 million for an eighth, ninth, and tenth floor triplex, the largest apartment in the Perry Street buildings.

Next, in moved two high-profile movie stars from Australia, both at the zenith of their careers. Nicole Kidman bought the apartment under Calvin Klein, but has since sold it. And Hugh Jackman, who at the time was in the Broadway show *The Boy from Oz,* was subletting the sixth floor apartment for $35,000 a month from director of commercials Bob Giraldi.

For a while, Martha Stewart owned the top two floors of the north tower, but sold it the year she famously went to prison. Also owning in the building are the British-born head of Universal Television Group, Michael Jackson, filmmaker Gavin McFarland; and Michigan real estate tycoon C. Michael Kojaian.

The third Meier tower—165 Charles Street—went up a little later, built by another developer. It is larger than the Perry Street building and has the added luxury of even higher ceilings and a fifty-foot swimming pool with a waterfall. Another sleek, gleaming architectural triumph, it replaced a six-story red brick building owned by a socialist publishing company called the Pathfinder Press. Having initially refused to sell to the developers of the Perry Street project, but watching the real estate boom along the Lower West Side Manhattan waterfront, and hearing the prices people paid for Perry Street apartments, in a very unsocialist gesture Pathfinder Press maneuvered for and collected a cool $20 million for their old brick headquarters.

The newest towers command among the highest prices in the city, starting at $5 million and going up. Among those who are owners in the building are Hollywood hottie Natalie Portman, star of Mike Nichols's *Closer* and *V for Vendetta,* and Martha Stewart's daughter, Alexis Stewart, who was featured on her mother's 2005 version of *The Apprentice* TV show and is an entrepreneur in her own right. The $20-million duplex penthouse, where the price works out to $4,581 a square foot, belongs to the latest girl-about-town, Canadian-born Louise T. Blouin MacBain, a publisher of art magazines, who moved to New York from London, where she was named England's sixteenth wealthiest woman, sandwiched "between pop and pomp": Madonna at number eighteen and Queen Elizabeth at number fifteen. MacBain comments, "The space is magical, because it's all in glass and with a view that is extraordinary. Close to the stars. And the sun. And the clouds."

Will there be enough buyers for these adventurous condos of New York's twenty-first-century building binge? Will downtown become the Fifth

Avenue of the future? There are some who believe so. For decades, New York's graceful, exquisitely constructed prewar bastions of privilege have lorded it over the cookie-cutter, cost-conscious, low-ceilinged apartment houses that went up in the 1950s, 1960s, 1970s, and 1980s. The bold new "couture condos" are creating an entirely new category of real estate. A younger-than-ever moneyed class has outgrown the self-validation that getting into a big-name, palatial prewar co-op has always held for a successful New Yorker. They do not want to expose themselves to the scrutiny of a stuffy, zealous co-op board. They have embraced a modern design ethos—plug-and-play amenities, time-saving hot-stuff kitchens, and instead of a traditional, elegant Park Avenue cocoon, transparent rooms where the kinetic energy of the skyscraper city is invited to intrude with its excitement. They think it's cool, like discovering and buying new art, to live in an imaginatively showy, vividly singular, New Guard architect-fashioned, crystalline high-rise.

Acknowledgments

The authors would like to express their deepest gratitude to the legion of remarkably knowledgeable and contagiously enthusiastic individuals without whose generosity and guidance this volume could not have been realized.

The first thank you is reserved for John Calicchio. Without his encouragement, patience, inspired input, and unflagging support, this book could not have come about. Our heartfelt thanks to Hal David, who had faith in us and was confident in our abilities, expectant that our work would be a success, and helped us keep our spirits up while we completed this project.

A big thank you to Ethel LeFrak for all her support, knowledge, and insights, Allison Koffman and Jennifer Diggins for their love and enthusiastic help, and Roberta Amon for her constant encouragement and sisterly friendship.

The authors received invaluable help from several of New York City's top real estate brokers. Foremost among them was A. Laurance Kaiser IV of Key Ventures, whose encyclopedic knowledge of Manhattan's luxury residential real estate is exceeded only by his astute social observations. He is a living, breathing repository of the history and lore of Fifth and Park Avenues. We have been fortunate to benefit from the professional insights of such top-tier Manhattan realtors as Kirk Henckels, Executive Vice President of Stribling Private Brokerage; Linda Stein; Allison Koffman, Roberta Golubook, and Lois Nassar of Sotheby's International Real Estate; and Elizabeth Savage who works with Edward Lee Cave.

Some of the most prominent builders and developers who gave us their trust and time are William L. Mack of Apollo Real Estate Advisors, Stephen M. Ross of Related, Bruce Warwick, and Beth Rudin de Woody. We were greatly aided by the personal graciousness of the following: Alana Frumkes, Juliana Terian, Joan and Charles Lazarus, Julia Haubner, Norma Dauphin, Barbara Cates, David Patrick Columbia, Edgar Lansbury, Dr. Peter Neubauer, Pilar Molyneux, Warren Kallbacher, David Paler, Michael Martin, Richard Kagan, Stanley Bard, and Harold Holzer, Abraham Lincoln historian and author of *Lincoln at Cooper Union*.

Because the buildings in this book are home to some of the most powerful people in the world as well as successful men and women whose names and faces regularly appear in the media, dozens of our sources spoke to us on the condition of anonymity. On the whole, co-op boards and directors were very protective of their buildings and of their neighbors, and thus, declined to be interviewed. Others spoke proudly of the unique beauty of their particular apartment houses, pointed out special architectural features and shared with us their family histories.

Some of our biggest help in writing this book came from the city's sterling institutions, all treasure houses of extraordinary information: the New York Public Library, New York Historical Society, Landmarks Preservation Commission, Museum of the City of New York, and New York's Housing Authority. Several authors before us have been immersed in the subject of New York's architectural history and the sociological implications of elite apartment living. We are particularly indebted to three of them: Elizabeth Hawes, Andrew Alpern, and Christopher Gray of the office of Metropolitan History. Our book was also greatly enhanced by the ever-expanding real estate sections of New York–area newspapers and the relatively recent trend across America of magazines and gossip columns avidly reporting on the home-purchasing patterns of the rich and famous.

We would like to express our thanks to Jeff Samuels for his independent research on the Dakota; to Heather Smith and Kim Carollo, students at Columbia University, for their initial research on the architecture and design of some of the buildings featured in the book; and to Valerie Livingston for later research on entertainment-world figures and contemporary cultural and social history.

We would like to say an especially big thank you to Kenneth N. Brown for his indefatigable processing of the vast amount of factual details and for his computer expertise in preparation of the manuscript. The book would have been impossible to achieve without his consistent, creative, and reliable work on the project. We would like to thank our agents, Marianne Strong and Lord Colin Campbell of the Marianne Strong Literary Agency, for their belief in the concept of the book and their steady good advice. And finally, we would like to express our enjoyment of working with the Barricade Books staff: Carole Stuart, our always positive editor and publisher, who shepherded our book through its various challenges; designer Pauline Neuwirth; copy editor Alexis Greene; and the grace under pressure of Barricade production chief Ivy McFadden.

Denise LeFrak Calicchio

Denise began working professionally in real estate in 1986. Born into a prominent real estate family, her formative years were filled with blue prints, floor plans, and contracts. Denise was employed in the family business for several years and graduated Syracuse University with honors before pursuing the Manhattan world of real estate on her own.

As a specialist in Manhattan real estate at Sotheby's since 1991, Denise has represented exclusive New York properties and has built an excellent reputation as a broker who knows how to close a deal.

As a trustee of Marymount College, Denise was active in setting and maintaining high standards of post-secondary education. She has served on various committees and boards including the New York Philharmonic, Development Committee of ABT Lincoln Center, Member of the Women's Bank Advisory Board, Secretary of the Board of Directors for Tenant Committee, Executive Member of the Guggenheim Art and Museum Committee, the Executive Board of the Albert Einstein College of Medicine, and the Photography Committee of the Guggenheim Museum. Denise was a member of the board of the Cancer Research and Treatment Fund, raising money for Cancer Research. She travels extensively with the Guggenheim Museum and her museum involvements also include serving as co-chairman of the Patrons' Circle.

The LeFrak Family foundation funded a new theatre for the Museum of Natural History, which was dedicated in May 2002.

Denise and her husband live in New York.

Eunice David

Eunice David was appointed by the Los Angeles County Board of Supervisors to the Los Angeles County Music and Performing Arts Commission, a 15-member Commission, which apportions County funds to various arts organizations, such as the Los Angeles Philharmonic, Center Theatre Group, and the Music Center Opera, as well as a wide variety of other performing arts groups throughout Los Angeles County.

She was involved in urban planning, as Director of Zoning for the City of Valencia, from its inception through the development of the new, now flourishing city.

Mrs. David and her husband, the Academy-Award-winning songwriter Hal David, annually produce the highly acclaimed show "The Writer, The Singer, The Song," featuring songwriters telling stories about their songs and showcasing the artists who made those songs popular.

Eunice chaired the Distinguished Artist Award Gala for the Los Angeles Music Center (the west-coast equivalent of the Kennedy Center Honors) and sits on the boards of the prestigious Blue Ribbon Organization in Los Angeles as well as the Board of Directors of the Los Angeles Music Center. She is the author of numerous travel journals, which incorporate her passion for writing, travel, and photography.

Eunice currently serves on the California Arts Council.

She and her husband live in Los Angeles and New York.

Kathryn Livingston

Kathryn Livingston is a New York–based writer and editor who served as a creative consultant on several documentary films. She is the author of five books: *Bedlinens, Eclectic Interiors: Room by Room, Victorian Interiors: Room by Room*; a biography, *Yesterday is Gone*; and *In the Spirit of Aspen*. Her articles on personalities, lifestyle, food, health, architecture, and travel have appeared in Condé Nast *Traveler, Gourmet, Town & Country, House & Garden, Connoisseur*, and *Travel & Leisure*.

She was a staff writer at *Harper's Bazaar* before becoming executive editor of *Town & Country* magazine, and a stint at Time Inc. followed. She returned to the company after its merger into Time Warner, and served as part of the company's development team for 140 television segments on Women's Health issues for a weekly program titled *Your Mind & Body*, which was shown on CBS.

Born in Budapest, raised in Cleveland, she brought up her two children in Manhattan and continues to be enthralled with New York.

Trevor Augustus Brown

Trevor Augustus Brown was born in Kingston, Jamaica, but a lifetime of living in New York City has infused his photographs with an intensity and vigor common to the "Big Apple". He has done advertising for some of America's and the world's most famous brands. His editorial work has appeared in magazines from *Town & Country* to *Playboy*, and has his photographs on book jackets have won him many awards. His hobbies are speed skating and freestyle Frisbee.

BIBLIOGRAPHY

BOOKS:

Alexander, Shana. *Nutcracker—Money, Madness, Murder: A Family Album.* Garden City, New York: Doubleday & Company, 1985.

Alpern, Andrew. *Luxury Apartment Houses of Manhattan.* New York: Dover, 1992.

———. *The New York Apartment Houses of Rosario Candela and James Carpenter.* New York: Acanthus Press, 2001.

———. *New York's Fabulous Luxury Apartments.* New York: Dover, 1975.

Bartlett, Apple Parish and Susan Bartlett Crater. *Sister: The Life of Legendary American Interior Decorator Mrs. Henry Parish II.* New York: St. Martin's Press, 2000.

Bender, Marilyn. *The Beautiful People.* New York: Coward-McCann, 1967.

Biddle, Flora Miller. *The Whitney Women and the Museum They Made.* New York: Arcade, 1999.

Birmingham, Stephen. *Life at the Dakota.* New York: Random House, 1979.

———. *"Our Crowd."* New York: Harper & Row, 1967.

Blackhall, Susan. *Ghosts of New York.* San Diego, California: Thunder Bay Press, 2005.

Brandt, Clare. *An American Aristocracy: The Livingstons.* Garden City, New York: Doubleday, 1986.

Coit, Margaret. *Mr. Baruch.* Boston: Houghton Mifflin, 1957.

Coleman, Jonathan. *At Mother's Request.* New York: Atheneum, 1985.

Collier, Peter and David Horowitz. *The Rockefellers: An American Dynasty.* New York: Holt, Rhinehart and Winston, 1976.

Cooper, Anderson. *Dispatches from the Edge.* New York: Harper Collins, 2006.

Davis, Deborah. *Party of the Century: The Fabulous Story of Truman Capote and His Black-and-White Ball.* Hoboken: Wiley, 2006.

Davis, John H. *The Bouviers.* New York: Farrar, Straus & Giroux, 1969.

Edinger, Claudio, *Chelsea Hotel.* New York: Abbeville Press, 1983.

Ehrlich, Judith Ramsey and Barry J. Rehnfeld. *The New Crowd: The Changing of the Jewish Guard on Wall Street.* Boston: Little, Brown, 1989.

Farrow, Mia. *A Memoir: What Falls Away.* New York: Nan A. Talese/Doubleday, 1996.

Flaherty, Tina Santi. *What Jackie Taught Us.* New York: Perigee, 2004.

Gaines, Steven. *The Sky's the Limit: Passion and Property in Manhattan.* New York: Little, Brown and Company, 2005.

Gray, Christopher. *New York Streetscapes: Tales of Manhattan's Significant Buildings and Landmarks.* New York: Harry H. Abrams, 2004.

Gregory, Jamee. *New York Apartments/ Private Views.* New York: Rizzoli 2004.

Gross, Michael. *740 Park: The Story of the World's Richest Apartment Building.* New York: Broadway Books, 2005.

Hawes, Elizabeth. *New York, New York: How the Apartment House Transformed the Life of the City.* New York: Alfred A. Knopf, 1993.

Klein, Edward. *Farewell, Jackie.* New York: Penguin Books, 2004.

Konolige, Kit and Frederica Konolige. *The Power of their Glory/America's Ruling Class: The Episcopalians.* New York: Wyden Books, 1978.

LaGuardia, Robert. *Monty, A Biography of Montgomery Clift.* New York: Arbor House, 1984.

Mason, Christopher. *The Art of the Steal.* New York: G. P. Putnam's Sons, 2004.

Newman, Peter C. *Bronfman Dynasty: The Rothschilds of the New World.* Toronto: McClelland and Steward, 1978.

Norton, Thomas E. and Jerry E. Patterson. *Living it Up, a Guide to the Named Apartment Houses of New York.* New York: Atheneum, 1984.

Parish, Sister, Albert Hadley and Christopher Petkanas. *Parish Hadley: Sixty Years of American Design.* Boston: Little, Brown and Company, 1995.

Rodengen, Jeffrey L. *The Legend of Cornelius Vanderbilt Whitney.* Ft. Lauderdale, Florida: Write Stuff, 1998.

Rosenberg, Pierre. *Wrightsman Collection and Her Donation to the Museum.* Metropolitan Museum of Art, New York and Yale University Press, 2005.

Ruttenbaum, Steven. *Mansions in the Clouds: The Skyscraper Palazzi of Emery Roth.* New York: Balsam Press, 1986.

Shapiro, Sylvia. *The New York Co-Op Bible.* New York: Thomas Dunne Books, 2005.

Stern, Richard A. M., Gregory Gill Martin, and M. Thomas Mellins. *New York 1930's: Architecture and Urbanism between the Two World Wars.* New York: Rizzoli, 1987.

Trager, James. *Park Avenue: Street of Dreams.* New York: Atheneum, 1990.

Wecter, Dixon. *The Saga of American Society: A Record of Social Aspiration 1607–1937.* New York: Charles Scribner's Sons, 1937.

White, Norval and Elliot Willensky. *AIA Guide to New York City: The Classic Guide to New York's Architecture.* New York: Crown, 2000.

PERIODICALS:

Newspapers

Andreatta, David. "Lennon's Final Days." *New York Post,* 12/7/05.

Anderson, Polly. "Gordon Parks, 93, Photographer Filmmaker." *New York Post* Obituary 2005.

Ash, Agnes. "Romancing the Stones." *Palm Beach Daily News,* 8/13/86.

Atlas, Riva. "A Fight Brews over Proceeds of Metromedia." *New York Times*, 12/9/05.

Baldwin, Johanna. "She Loved Him, Yeah, Yeah, Yeah." *New York Times*, 12/4/05.

Barbanel, Josh. "Are There Enough Buyers to Go Around?" *New York Times*, Real Estate Section, 7/9/06.

Bloomberg News and Post Wire Services. "Opera Man's Cons." *New York Post*, 11/12/05.

Bruni, Frank. "Sushi at Masa: It's a Zen Thing." *New York Times*, 9/1/04.

Calderone, Michael. "Quick Lerner: Billionaire Trades Up to 740 Park." *New York Observer*.

———. "While the Bubble Balloons — Tales of Real Estate Mania." *New York Observer*, 5/05.

———. "Gotham-ist Jason Binn Snaps Up Tribeca Condo for $1M, Jane Pauley Sells on C.P.W. for $13M; Lincoln Slept Here!" *New York Observer*, Manhattan Transfers, 10/10/05.

———. "Lily Safra's Apartment Being Flipped by Investor for $6M Profit." *New York Observer*, Manhattan Transfers.

———. "Forward, March!" *New York Observer*, 3/27/06.

Carter, Bill. "Mark Goodson, Game-Show Inventor, Dies at 77." *New York Times*, 12/19/92.

Chamberlain, Lisa. "A Year in the Life." *New York Times*, 6/4/06.

Drape, Joe. "In Horse Racing, an Odd Couple Seek the Reins." *New York Times*, 3/8/05.

Dunlap, David. "Amid All the Signs, Confusing a Circle for a Square." *New York Times*, 6/24/04.

Dunning, Jennifer. "Under the Exotic Flair, Always Miss Dunham." *New York Times* 5/23/06.

Efrati, Amir. "The Home Front." *Wall Street Journal*, 12/23/05.

Eichenwald, Kurt and Wakin, Daniel. "The Double Up and Downs of a Philanthropist." *New York Times*, 5/30/05.

Fabricant, Florence. "Gray Kunz: Out of the Fire into the Frying Pan." *New York Times*, 9/1/04.

Fox, Margalit. "Pierre A. Rinfred, 82 Dies; Lost to Cuomo in '90 Race." *New York Times*, 6/06.

Friedwald, Will. "From Club to Concert Hall." *New York Sun*, 10/18/04.

Giglio, Anthony. "Kunz's Return." *New York Sun*, 10/27/04.

Gilmore, Mikai. "Why This Band Plays On." *New York Times*, 8/24/05.

Gray, Christopher. "Bohemian and Ornate, It Began as a Co-op in 1884." *New York Times*, 2/15/98.

———. "When Automobiles Replaced the Yacht." *New York Times*, 2/27/05.

———. "A 1927 Building of Full-floor Duplexes and a Triplex." *New York Times*, 7/2/2000.

————. "Quality Developer with a Legacy of Fine Buildings." *New York Times,* 3/12/95.

Halbfinger, David. "Investor Seeks Bidding Edge for Landmark on 42nd Street." *New York Times,* 6/17/97.

Halbfinger, David M. and Allison Hope Weiner. "Pellicano Case Moves beyond Hollywood." *New York Times,* 6/25/05.

Hamilton, William. "From the Dakota to the Danube." *New York Times,* 2/23/06.

Heller, Billy, and Michael Kane, Lindsay Powers, and Philip Reccha. "It Was 25 Years Ago Today." *New York Post,* 12/8/05.

Henson, Meg. "Creative Thinking." *New York Times,* 12/23/03.

Horowitz, Jason. "Ms. MacBain Presents." *New York Observer,* 2005.

Huxtable, Ada Louise. "David Childs and Mustafa K. Abadah." *Wall Street Journal,* 1/7/04.

Johnson, Richard. "New Charge Hits Met Donor." *New York Post,* Page Six, 6/2/05.

————. "Horse King Un-steedy in Grave." *New York Post,* Page Six, 10/7/05.

————. "Re Steven Cohen." *New York Post,* Page Six, 9/29/04.

————. "Dakota Bars Chapman Movie." *New York Post,* 12/12/05.

Kane, Michael. "The Hotel in Chelsea That Art Calls Home." *New York Times,* 10/4/94.

Keil, Braden. "How Realty Market Is Truly Hot: Ex-Model, 19, a Power Player." *New York Post,* 5/24/04.

————. "A Piece of Eight." *New York Post,* 11/13/04.

Konolige, Kit. "The Posh Parties that Keep Society Whirling." *New York Post.* 7/9/85.

Krebs, Albin. "David K. E. Bruce, Diplomat, Dies." *New York Times,* 12/6/77.

Marino, Vivian. "Good Neighbors Make Good Profits." *New York Times,* 2/27/05.

Maslin, Janet. "One Building as Microcosm of Life on a Silver Platter." *New York Times,* 10/17/05.

McMullen, Troy. "The Home Front: Condos with a Name." *Wall Street Journal,* 3/31/06.

Michaelis, David. "The Notorious Need Not Apply at River House." *East Side Express,* 12/22/83.

Miller, Stephen. "Andrea Bronfman Killed by a Car as She Walks Her Dog on 65th Street." *New York Sun,* 1/24/06.

————. "Pierre Rinfret, 82, Quixotic Gubernatorial Candidate in 1990." *New York Sun,* 6/29/06.

Moules, Jonathan. "Towering Technology: Jonathan Moules Says Time Warner Center Combines Views, Luxury — and Great Gadgetry." *Financial Times,* 10/4/03.

Moerk, Christian. "Ciao, Edie; Warhol Girl Gets 15 More Minutes." *New York Times.* 2/19/06.

Muschamp, Herbert. "The Secret History." *New York Times*, 1/8/06.

———. "Shopping Centers: Glamorous Glass Gives 10 Columbus Circle a Look of Crystallized Noir." *New York Times*, 2/4/04.

Newman, William. "Who's Who and What They Paid." *New York Times*, Real Estate, 11/21/04.

———. "The Allure of Downtown Continues to Attract Uptown." *New York Times*, 12/26/04.

———. "Hedge Fund Moguls Collect Art and Now Real Estate." *New York Times*, 5/1/05.

———. "Drawing Up a Deal." *New York Times*, 2005.

———. "Big Deal." *New York Times*, 12/15/05.

———. "Balazs Goes Way Downtown." *New York Times*, 12/18/05.

———. "Moving Uptown on Park." *New York Times*, 2/12/06.

———. "The Bargain Hunting Billionaire." *New York Times*, 3/12/06.

———. "A Rich Man Spurned." *New York Times*, 3/12/06.

———. "A Condo with a Door to the Park." *New York Times*, 3/26/06.

———. "Big Deal: Well, It's Not 39,000 Square Feet." *New York Times*, 4/9/06.

———. "Big Deal: Liquid Funds for a Penthouse." *New York Times*, 4/23/06.

———. "A New Place for Their Rackets." *New York Times*, 6/12/05.

———. "A Private Gallery Is Born." *New York Times*, 7/30/06.

———. "Like Mother, Like Daughter." *New York Times*, 8/13/06.

O'Brien, Timothy. "The Man with the Golden Slingshot." *New York Times*, 6/5/05.

Ouroussoff, Nicolai. "Engaging the City's Intimate Connection to Jazz." *New York Times*, 10/21/04.

Pace, Eric. "Mary W. Lasker, Philanthropist for Medical Research, Dies at 93." *New York Times*, 2/23/94.

Palmer, Brian. "(Photos) What Menu." *New York Times*, 3/17/04.

Peyser, Andrea. "Strawberry Fields Forever—and Young Fans Prove the Point." *New York Post*, 12/9/05.

Ramsby, Lauren. "Great Views—But If You Have to Ask, You Can't Afford It." *New York Observer*, 12/13/93.

———. "Low Turnover and High Living: Candela's 778 Park." *New York Observer*, 1/21/94.

———. "Behind the Bronze Door at 820 Fifth; 18-Room Apartments." *New York Observer*, 3/14/94.

———. "The Private World of River House: Keep Off the Grass!" *New York Observer*, 4/11/94.

———. "10 Gracie Square: Cachet with a Soupçon of Scandal." *New York Observer*, 6/13/94.

Ratliff, Ben. "The Making of a Jazz Statesman." *New York Times*, 10/18/04.

Reccha, Philip, with Powers, Lindsay, Huhn, Mary, Heller, Billy, and Kane, Michael. "City Apple of Lennon's Eye." *New York Post*, 12/8/05.

Reisman, Paul. "Pirro Fatigue." *Journal News*, 12/11/05.

Rogers, Teri Karush. "Peeking behind the Gilded Walls." *New York Times*, 10/9/05.

———. "Indulging the Quirks of the Stars." *New York Times*, 2005.

———. "Is Prewar Losing Its Status to the New Glass Towers?" *New York Times*, 3/19/06.

Romero, Simon. "Coup? Not His Style, but Power? Oh, Yes." *New York Times*, 4/28/02.

St. John, Warren. "Mr. Mover, Meet Ms. Shaker." *New York Times*, 8/28/05.

Scott, A. O. "Lennon as Superior to Nixon." *New York Times*, 9/15/06.

Siklos, Richard and Geraldine Fabrikant. "An Empire Shaken." *New York Times*, 8/2/05.

Slesin, Suzanne. "All That Curvy Glass: Is it Worth It?" *New York Times*, 2006.

Stewart, Sara. "Dirty Doings in the City's Swanky Digs." *New York Post*, 4/17/05.

Strauss, Robert. "Wait 'Till You See His Vacation Pictures." *New York Times*, New Jersey Edition. 12/23/05.

Thomas Jr., Landon. "The Making of a Wise Man." *New York Times*, Business, 11/28/04.

Vogel, Carol. "Prosperity Sets Tone at London Auctions." *New York Times*, 6/26/06.

Wakin, Daniel. "Heiress Is Identified as Victim in Case Against Arts Patron." *New York Times*, 2005.

Weisberg, Lori. "A Place in the Clouds." *San Diego Union Tribune*, 8/15/04.

Yazigi, Monique P. "Big, Beautiful Numbers: 820,834,960." *New York Times*, November 23, 1997.

PERIODICALS:

Magazines

Andersen, Kurt. "Surrender the Pink." *New York*, 6/26/06.

Andrews, Suzanne. "Hostage to Fortune." *Vanity Fair*, 12/04.

Aronson, Steven M.L. "Portraits in Limestone." *Town and Country*, 11/93.

Brewster, Aariel, with contributors Katie Charles, Nick Hofstadter, Yael Kohen, Kai Ma, Rebecca Milzoff, Lauren Schuker, Bee Shaffer, Matthew Stevenson, Davis Thompson, and Rachel Wolff. "Star Map: Where to Find the City's Famous People. Not That You'd Ever Look." *New York*, 8/13/06.

Clarke, Gerald. "The View from the Top." *Architectural Digest*, 2006.

Dunne, Dominick. "Fatal Charm: The Social Web of Claus von Bülow." *Vanity Fair*.

Esterhazy, Louise J. "Go West, Louise: The Countess Ventures to the West Village for a Night Out, but the Traffic and the Women—Both Loud—Are Less Appetizing." *W,* May 2006.

Fishman, Steve. "In the Precarious Hedge-fund Bubble, It's Either Clean Up-or Flame Out." *New York,* 11/22/04.

Gill, Brendon. "Historic Houses: The Breakers." *Architectural Digest,* 4/95.

Gray, Christopher. "603 Park Avenue." *Avenue.*

Gross, Michael. "Edifice Complex." *Bergdorf Goodman Magazine,* Spring 2006.

Heilemann, John: Architecture & Design. "The Influentials/2006 Santiago Calvatra, Richard Meier, Robert A. M. Stern, Andre Balazs and Ian Schrager." *New York,* 5/15/06.

———. "It's Rupert's World." *New York,* 5/15/06.

Mahler, Jonathan. "What Rupert Wrought." *New York,* 4/11/05.

———. "Love and War in the House of Murdock." *New York,* 9/19/05.

Mason, Alice. "At The Top, Alice's Five Favorite Co-ops." *W,* 1/1993.

Norwich, William. "Saratoga's Queen Reigns in Splendor and Rain." *Uptown/Downtown.*

Parfit, Michael. "35 Who Made a Difference: Maya Lin." *Smithsonian,* 11/03.

Platz, David. "Quote." *Avenue and Slate,* 5/06.

Reginato, James. "The Real Central Park West." *W,* 9/95.

Rich, Motoko. "Make an Offer." *New York Times,* 10/13/05.

Robledo, S. Jhoanna. "What Went Wrong at Astor Place." *New York,* 6/26/06.

Richardson, John. "A Family and a Fortune." *Vanity Fair* Postcript.

———. "Jeremy Does Claus." *Vanity Fair,* 11/1990.

Seal, Mark. "Driven by Dynasty." *Vanity Fair,* 2/2006.

Scaggs, Austin. "Q & A." *Rolling Stone,* 5/4/06.

Singer, Sally. "Sienna Miller." *Vogue,* January 2006.

Slocum, Bill. "Warwick's Circle." *Greenwich Magazine,* May 2003.

Treshiowski, Alex, Hope Hamashige, Jeffrey Slonim, Nina Burleigh, and Nicole Weisensel Egan. "The Battle for Brooke." *People,* 8/14/06.

Vuillamy, Ed. "The Georgian Suite Haute Cuisine in a Sidestreet Hideaway." *Avenue,* May 1981.

———. "Murdock's $44M City Unit." *New York,* 12/19/04.

———. "Man of Steel." *Avenue,* 1/05.

———. "Love and War in the House of Murdock." *New York,* 9/19/05.

Ward, Vicky. "Faulty Towers." *Vanity Fair,* June 2004.

Witchel, Alex. "William Ivey Long Keeps His Clothes On." *New York Times Magazine,* 1/29/06.

INTERNET:

Antrim, Taylor. *Launch Pad.* www.forbes.com/business/fyi2006/0313/104.html

Bittar, Christine. *Nuskin's Tillotson Scores Direct Hit,* www.findarticles.com/p/aracticles/mi mOBDW/is 24 40/ai 5496054

Cuozzo, Steve. *Inside Towers for Our Time; A Beaut is Born at Columbus Circle,* Global.factiva.com/en/arch/display.asp. 11/6/03

Cuozzo, Steve. *Time Warner Center Hopes for Magic Mix,* Global.factiva.com/en/arch/display.asp 11/18/03

Fermino, Jennifer andRobinson, Ed. *Towering Triumph — Time Warner Center a Hit,* Global.factiva.com/en/arch/display.asp 2/5/04

Goldberger, Paul. *The Sculptor,* www.newyorker.com/critics/skyline/articles/05103 1crsk skyline

Goldberger, Paul, *Green Monster,* www.newyorker/printables/critics/050502crsk skyline

Gregor, Alison. *Celebrity Architects: Behind the Curtain Wall,* www.therealdeal.net/issues/january 2005/1105451472.php

Keil, Braden. *$45M AOL-Time Warner 2 Fl. Condo Sets Record,* Global.factiva.com/en/arch/display.asp 7/10/03

Keil, Braden. *A $45 Million View; Inside Park Tower's Priciest Perch,* Global.factiva.com/en/arch/display.asp 7/13/03

Keil, Braden. *King of the Castle — 45M AOL Pad's Mystery Buyer Unmasked,* Global.factiva.com/en/arch/display.asp 7/15/03

Keil, Braden. *An Amazing Fete,* Global.factiva.co/en/arch/display.asp 8/17/03

Keil, Braden and Becker, Anne. *Apts. Are High-Riser$,* Global.factiva.com/en/arch/display.asp 1/15/04

Keil, Braden. *Calif. Chef will Close Laundry, Move Here,* Global.factiva.com/en/arch/display.asp 7/30/04

McGee, Celia. *For Elevated Tastes,* Global.factiva.com/en/arch/display.asp: 10/24/03

MightyMap.com

Plotz, David. *Overrated Father, Misunderstood Son.* www.slate.com/id/1862/ 4/26/1998

Sherman, Gabriel. *Rock Hudson Penthouse, The Beresford,* Internet 4/26/04

St. Bernard's School, www.stbernards.org 2/20/06

www.thecityreview.com/ues/parkave/par/740.htm

www.eddiecantor.com/bio.html

www.atu2.com/band/bono

www.thestahlman.com

www.tennesseenclyopedia.net

www.smallbusiness/businessencyclopedia

www.nyc.architecture.com

www.cmgworldwide.com/stars

www.sony.classical.com/artists

www.brainyencyclopedia.com

www.brni.org/pages/blanchetterockefeller.html

www.thecityreview.com/ues/parkave/park820 htm

www.hotelchelsea.com

www.swinginchicks.com/jackiekennedy.htm

www.usatoday.com/time/life/special/jackie/ljack 015.htm

www.time/com/time2003/jfk/story.html

www.britannica.com

www.newyorksocialdiary.com/partypictures 1/11/05

www.famoustexans.com

http://seattlepi.newsource.com/books

www.celebritywonder.com

www.answers.com

www.encyclopedia.com/html/c/capote t.asp

www.lapetitezine.or/davidTrinidad.htm

www.thecity review.com//sutton/ump860.html

www.medaloffreedom.com/walterwriston.htm

www.businessweek.com/chapter/zweigch.htm

www.cityrealty.com/neighborhoods

www.nypost.com

www.clown.ministry.com/index oona o'neil chaplin biography dedicated wife

www.frommers.com/destinations/newyorkcity/S27609.html

www.museum.tv/archives: *Frank Stanton's TV Career*

www.infoplease.com/biography

www.nytheatre-wire.com/jt03053t.htm

www.gizmag.com/g03766

www.triplemint.com/triplemint/ndw york/index.html

www.pritzkerprize.com/meier.htm

www.kondylis.com/resume.html

Slate.msm.com 4/26/98

www.en.wikipidea.org

Taylor, Robert. *For Incomparable Rex Harrison, Talent and Ego Went Hand in Hand,* http://seatlepi.newsource.com/books

www.vivendiuniversal: *Divestitures; as fast as Acquisitions?Case ref: CYG-002*

Forbes Richest People List www.forbes.com

Paul Nitze's Legacy for New World, www.state's news service.com 4/15/04

onlinedirectoryassistance: whitepages.com

INDEX